About the Writers

Irving Hexham is professor of religious studies at the University of Calgary, Alberta, Canada. He obtained his Ph.D. in history from the University of Bristol and is the author of seven books, including two written with his wife, Karla Poewe.

David Bershad is professor of art history at both the University of Calgary and St. Mary's in Calgary, Alberta. He received his Ph.D. at UCLA. David has written numerous articles on the people and places in Italy and has received many honors and awards.

Carolina Mangone is pursuing her masters in art history. She is active in both the art community and the Italian-Canadian community. Carolina studied in Rome and has traveled extensively in Italy and throughout Europe.

http://www.christian-travelers-guides.com

Visit our Web site for even more information. You'll find:

- Links to many of the cities and sites listed in our guidebooks
- Information about Christian hotels and bed and breakfasts
- Lists of English-speaking churches so you can plan where to worship
- Information about evangelical organizations in each country
- Diagrams comparing different architectural styles
- Examples of Christian art
- Brief essays on topics of interest to Christian scholars and travelers
- Readings from key historical texts
- Suggested readings for daily devotions as you travel around Europe

Plan your next trip with
http://www.christian-travelers-guides.com

"In an era that often overlooks the significance of the past as such, and certainly the Christian past, Professor Hexham's well-crafted guides for heritage tourists truly fill a gap. Don't leave home without one!"

J. I. Packer
professor, Regent College, Vancouver
author of *Knowing God*

"Using vacations to discover the riches of the Christian tradition is a great idea that's long overdue."

Bruce Waltke,
professor, Regent College, Reformed Theological Seminary
and a member of the *NIV* translation team

"At last! A guidebook which treats churches as windows onto the living faith of Christianity and not just as museums or graveyards. These books bring church history alive."

David V. Day
principal, St. John's College, University of Durham
and frequent broadcaster on the BBC

"Excellent...we can all learn from these books."

Terry Muck
professor, former editor-in-chief of *Christianity Today*

THE
CHRISTIAN
TRAVELERS GUIDE TO
ITALY

IRVING HEXHAM, GENERAL EDITOR
written by DAVID BERSHAD AND CAROLINA MANGONE

ZONDERVAN™

GRAND RAPIDS, MICHIGAN 49530 USA

WWW.ZONDERVAN.COM

ZONDERVAN™

This series of books is an unintended consequence of serious academic research financed by both the University of Calgary and the Social Sciences and Humanities Research Council of Canada. Both institutions need to be thanked for the support they gave to the original academic research that allowed some of the authors to visit many of the places discussed in these books.

The Christian Travelers Guide to Italy
Copyright © 2001 by David Bershad and Carolina Mangone

Requests for information should be addressed to:
Zondervan, *Grand Rapids, Michigan 49530*

Library of Congress Cataloging-in-Publication Data
Bershad, David.
    The Christian travelers guide to Italy / Irving Hexham, general editor; David Bershad and Carolina Magone.
        p.   cm.
   ISBN: 0-310-22573-6
    1. Italy—Guidebooks. 2. Christians—Italy—Guidebooks. I. Magone, Carolina. II. Hexham, Irving. III. Title
DG416.B369 2001
914.504'93—dc21   00-046289
                                                     CIP

Interior design by Todd Sprague

Printed in the United States of America

Contents

Preface 7

Part I: Italian History

Christianity in Italy 11
An Overview of Italian History 13

Part 2: Italian Literature, Music, Art, and Architecture

Italian Literature 16
Italian Music 19
Italian Art 19
Architecture Styles 22
How to Enjoy Your Visit to an Italian Church 28

Part 3: Christian Heritage Sites in Italy

Top 10 Christian Sites in Italy 33
Key to the Texts 34

Abazia Di Fossanova
(Abbey of Fossanova) 36
Arezzo 37
Assisi .42
Bari 47
Camaldoli 49
Certosa Di Pavia 50
Chiusi 51
Città Di Castello 52
Cortona 53
Empoli 56

Firenze (Florence) 57
Foligno 79
Gubbio 81
Loreto 84
Lucca 85
Massafra 90
Milano (Milan) 91
Monreale 98
Monte Cassino 99
Monte Oliveto Maggiore 100
Montepulciano 101

Napoli (Naples) 103
Orvieto 114
Padova (Padua) 116
Palermo 121
Perugia 126
Pienza 129
Pisa 131
Pistoia 139
Prato 143
Ravello 146
Ravenna 147
Roma (Rome) 151
San Galgano 181

San Gimignano 181
Sansepolcro 184
Sant'Antimo 185
Siena 186
Spoleto 191
Subiaco 195
Todi 196
Torcello 198
Torino (Turin) 199
Urbino 202
Venezia (Venice) 205
Volterra 220

Map of Key Christian Heritage Sites in Italy 35
Glossary of Religious Terms 225

PREFACE

Remember how the LORD your God led you.

Deuteronomy 8:2

The task of history . . . is to establish the truth of this world.

Karl Marx (1955:42)

Memories of paintings, sculptures, museums, churches last a lifetime.

Edith Schaeffer—*The Tapestry*

Our series of books is designed to awaken an awareness of Europe's Christian heritage among evangelical Christians, although we hope all Christians and others who are simply interested in Christianity will also find them helpful. Anyone visiting a large bookstore will quickly discover that it is possible to buy travel guides with titles like Pagan Europe, Occult France, Magical Britain, and The Traveler's Guide to Jewish Germany, alongside more traditional travel guides which attempt to take in everything worth seeing. Yet even books like the Frommer's, Fodor's, and Rough guides, although they mention Christian places and events, tend to underplay the Christian contribution to Western Civilization through neglect or a negative tone. Therefore, our guides have been written to correct what we see as a major oversight in existing works.

Our series is concerned with people and events of historical significance through their association with particular places. Thus we attempt to locate the development of ideas which have changed the world through their relationship with people and places. Consequently, we suggest visits to particular places, because by visiting them you can gain a better understanding of the times when important events took place.

The central theme of these books is the contribution of Christianity to Europe and the world. But not everyone discussed in these books was Christian. Indeed, many of the people we mention were strongly anti-Christian. Such people are included because it is impossible to understand our own times without appreciating the destructive forces that have attempted to replace Christianity by secularism and neopagan religions.

HISTORY AND MEMORY

Christianity is rooted in history. The New Testament begins with a genealogical table that most modern readers find almost incomprehensible (Matthew 1:1–17). The purpose of this genealogy is to locate the birth of Jesus in space and time according to the standards of Jewish history. The appeal to "the first eyewitnesses," in the prologue to the gospel of Luke, is also clearly intended to engage the skepticism of Greco-Roman readers by providing specific historical data against which ancient readers could weigh the writer's claims (Luke 3:1–2). The Gospels contain many references to historical data and specific geographic locations. So important is historical truth that its denial becomes a mark of heresy for New Testament authors (1 Corinthians 15:1–8; 1 John 4:1–3).

Clearly, the Bible is steeped in history and the remembrance of history. Both the Old and New Testaments constantly reminded their readers about particular historical events (cf. Deuteronomy 4:9–14; Acts 7). Thus, parents are commanded to teach their children the significance of history (Deuteronomy 6:4–25) both by retelling the story and through commemorations which enact the central acts of salvation (Exodus 13:3–16; 1 Corinthians 11:23–26). Further, an appeal is frequently made to visible memorials that remind people of God's wonderful deeds (Acts 2:29–36). We also find both Jews and early Christians visiting historic sites as acts of devotion (Luke 2:21–41; Acts 21:17–27).

The importance of history, and the way in which we remember past events, is recognized by many influential opponents of Christianity. Karl Marx, for example, argued that the ability to control history, or rather the interpretation of history, was an essential step in the abolition of religion. Almost a century later, Adolf Hitler made a similar appeal to history and historical necessity. Both Marx and Hitler, following in the footsteps of Enlightenment skeptics like Tom Paine, sought to establish the truth of their revolutions by denying the validity of Christian history.

Our books are, we hope, a small contribution to the reestablishment of a sense of history and cultural pride among Christians. Following the biblical model, we believe that visiting places and seeing where great events took place help people remember and understand the present as well as the past (Joshua 4:1–7). It is our hope that these books will bring history alive, and with a sense of history a growing awareness of the realities of faith in our world. As Francis Schaeffer loved to point out, there is a flow to history because Christian faith is rooted in space and time. To forget our history is the first step to the abandonment of our faith, the triumph of secularism, the ascendancy of New Age spirituality, and the rebirth of paganism.

SEEKING SPIRITUAL ROOTS

The great truth of the New Testament is that Christians are children of God by adoption. Today many people have forgotten that the New Testament preaches the revolutionary doctrine that our relationship to God is not through physical descent, but by adoption (Romans 8:23; Galatians 4:5; Ephesians 1:5).

The implications of this doctrine are profound. All Christians are united by bonds of faith and love, not physical relationships (Ephesians 2). Thus, Christianity is not a tribal religion rooted in local communities bound by kinship bonds. Rather, it is a world faith that unites all believers.

Repeatedly, both the Old and New Testaments point to examples of faith which we are encouraged to follow and remember (Joshua 4; Luke 11:29–32; Acts 7; Hebrews 12). Remembering acts of courage and obedience to God strengthens our own faith. This fact was long recognized by the leaders of the church. Throughout history, Christians have told and retold stories of courage and faith. Yet today these stories are all but forgotten. Lives of the saints which were once standard texts for every educated person and pious believer are now rarely read, and books like *Foxe's Book of Martyrs* (1554) are left unopened.

Today, Christians are quickly forgetting their rich spiritual heritage as Christian biographies are replaced in popular culture by secular gossip. Popular magazines, radio, and television are full of "lives." But they are the lives of pop singers, film stars, television personalities, and secular politicians. Instead of teaching spiritual lessons, they repeat trivia and revel in scandal. Something has been lost. And it is this something that can be recaptured by Christians who begin to search for their spiritual roots.

Visiting Italy to learn about great acts of faith can be a rewarding experience, and it is something all Christians, regardless of race or nationality, can find profitable. This spiritual quest helps us see our own lives in perspective and understand our times against a much greater backdrop than tonight's television news. That is the quest this book encourages you to begin.

9

PART I

ITALIAN HISTORY

CHRISTIANITY IN ITALY

Christianity spread to Italy following the death and resurrection of Jesus as a sect within Judaism. Large Jewish communities in Italy provided a fertile base for Christian preachers who soon began to make converts among native Italians. Other converts visiting Rome as traders or soldiers assisted in the spread of this new religion, which soon provoked bitter opposition. Persecution quickly followed, and according to tradition Rome was the site of St. Peter's death and the imprisonment of St. Paul, who many believe eventually died in Spain.

After three centuries of intermittent and often very violent persecution, Emperor Constantine recognized Christianity as the official religion of the Roman Empire in A.D. 324. Shortly afterwards he abandoned the old capital of Rome for his new, and more easily defended, capital of Constantinople, modern Istanbul. Thus in A.D. 395 the de facto split between the Eastern and Western Roman Empires became a reality with two emperors, one in the East based in Constantinople, and the other in the West based in Rome.

Within a short time the Western Empire was devastated—as Constantine's decision to move his headquarters to the East suggests he anticipated—by a series of barbarian invasions. The eternal city, Rome, which had stood unchallenged for a thousand years, was sacked in 410 by the Visigoths, leading St. Augustine to write his classic *The City of God*. In 476, the last ruler of the Western Roman Empire, Romulus Augustus, was deposed by barbarian Lombards and Goths who sacked the city.

In Milan, Bishop Ambrose, through whom St. Augustine was converted, played a key role in stabilizing Western Christianity in this time of turmoil and invasion. Converting pagan barbarians and warding off the theological threat of Arianism was the major task facing orthodoxy during this period. Benedict of Nursia responded to the chaos of the times by establishing western monasticism as a major social force that preserved learning and the Christian tradition throughout Western Europe. At the same time the bishop of Rome asserted the authority of the papacy as a bulwark against growing chaos. Under the able leadership of popes like Gregory the Great, the foundations were laid for centuries of mission activity that led to the final conversion of all European pagans by the 12th century. Richard Fletcher tells this sometimes exciting story in his book *The Barbarian Conversion: From Paganism to Christianity.*

In the year 800 the pope crowned Charlemagne, Charles the Great, as Holy Roman Emperor, thus laying the foundation for the 9th-century revival of learning in Western Europe. Muslim invaders entered Italy in the 9th century, and the city of Palermo fell to the Arabs in 831. Fifty years later, in 881, the Sicilian Arabs plundered much of southern Italy and penetrated as far north as Monte Cassino, which was sacked. Norman knights saved Italian Christianity by driving back the Muslim invaders and reconquering Sicily between 1060 and 1091. At the same time, Jerusalem fell to Turkish Muslim armies, and Christian pilgrimage to the Holy City was interrupted with many pilgrims being sold into slavery. Consequently, in 1095 the pope declared the First Crusade (1095–99) to free the Holy Land from alien rule. During this period too the final break between Eastern and Western Christianity occurred when the pope excommunicated the patriarch of Constantinople and other Eastern Orthodox bishops in 1054.

During the 12th century a Frenchman, Peter Waldo (1190–1206), began a reform movement which quickly took root in Italy as the Waldenes. This movement foreshadowed the work of John Wycliffe (1330–84), John Huss (1370–1415), Girolamo Savonarola (1452–86), and Martin Luther (1483–1546) in preparing the way for the Reformation of the 16th century. This period also saw numerous disputes between rival popes and constant political turmoil throughout Italy, which was divided into numerous small states and princedoms. At the same time there was a growing renaissance of art and literature throughout Italy based on deep Christian convictions, including the great Italian writer, perhaps of all time, Dante Alighieri (1265–1321). Art and architecture flourished, and by the end of the 16th century, Italian Christianity dominated the arts and sciences.

All of this creativity was shattered by the Reformation, which saw the lavish productions of Italian artists as an affront to God because they were funded by contributions collected through the sale of indulgences and other practices which were decidedly non-evangelical. After the Reformation, a weakened papacy and Roman Catholic Church continued to dominate Italian life. Although art and architecture continued to flourish in a lavish Christian Baroque style, the power of the Catholic Church was on the wane.

The 19th century saw a low point in the fortunes of Italian Christianity with a reactionary church hierarchy, external political enemies, and the rise of a virulent secularism linked to political nationalism. Only in the late 20th century under the able rule of Pope John the 23rd (1881–1963), who presided over the Second Vatican Council (1962–65), was profound theological change initiated in Roman Catholicism. His equally able and perhaps far more politically astute successor, Pope John Paul II (b. 1920), has reestablished respect for the power and prestige of the papacy throughout the world.

AN OVERVIEW OF ITALIAN HISTORY

Italian history can be traced back to lake settlements around 70,000 B.C. Around 2000 B.C. the peninsula was invaded by various tribal groups known as the *Italic*. Later, around 900 B.C., the Etruscans, a North African people of Middle-Eastern decent probably related to the Phoenicians, colonized central Italy. Greek colonists arrived in Southern Italy in the 8th century.

Sometime in the 8th century, tradition says in 753 B.C., a settlement was founded on the banks of the Tiber river which became the city of Rome. According to legend it was either founded by the twin brothers Romulus and Remus or by the refugee Trojan Aeneas, who fled to Italy after the destruction of Troy by a coalition of Greek armies. Rome was conquered by the Etruscans, but in 509 B.C., a virtuous Roman virgin, Lucretia, committed suicide in full view of gathered townsfolk after being raped by the Etruscan king Tarquinius Superus. This outrage and her brave act of defiance against an unpopular conqueror ignited a popular revolt, and the Etruscans and their kings were expelled from Rome, which became a citizen's republic.

The subsequent history of Rome was a long struggle against Etruscan dominance and foreign invaders like the armies of the Etruscan ally Carthage. The Punic Wars were fought from 264–146 B.C., and included Hannibal's great feat of bringing an army including elephants across the Alps. The Romans defeated and utterly destroyed Carthage, razing it to the ground and then sowing it with sea salt to make the area infertile.

Slowly, as a result of an increasing need to defend its borders, the city-state of Rome extended its power across Northern Europe, Northern Africa, and the Mediterranean. During this period many of the basic concepts of Roman law, which became the basis for the legal systems of all European nations, were created. An efficient system of imperial administration was established, stretching from Northern Scotland to the Rhine and Danube to the Middle East, including Egypt and Northern Africa.

As the republican empire reached its height, it was racked by civil wars as rival generals sought increased power. Eventually Julius Caesar (100–44 B.C.) was proclaimed emperor only to be assassinated by republican rivals on March 15, 44 B.C. His death led to a long and bitter civil war that saw his nephew and heir, Octavian (63 B.C.–A.D. 14), become the emperor Augustus, who became the absolute ruler of the Roman empire. His reign, from 27 B.C. to A.D. 14, is seen as the golden age of Rome. His death was followed by a series of palace intrigues and assassinations aided by incest and debauchery that provided the novelist Robert Graves with the basis for his popular novels and TV series, *I Claudius.* Despite the apparent chaos of the times, Imperial Rome continued to dominate Western Europe for another 400 years. In the East its successor empire, Byzantium, based in the imperial city of Constantinople (modern Istanbul), maintained the Roman imperial tradition in a Christianized form for another 1500 years. It was destroyed by Muslim armies led by Sultan Mohammed II (d. 1481), who stormed Constantinople in 1453 and killed the last Eastern Roman emperor, Constantine XI.

In the West Rome itself was sacked in 410 and again in 476 when the Western Empire was dissolved. The fortunes of both Rome and Italy for the next 500 years were, to say the least, chaotic. Only in the 13th century did the fortunes of Italy's city-states like Florence, Vienna, and Rome slowly begin to revive. By the 14th century, however, a major revitalization movement affecting large sections of Italian society was underway. Known as the Renaissance, it was further stimulated by refugees from the Muslim invasion of Byzantium. Art and architecture, music and literature, philosophy and science, all flourished in an outpouring of creativity which spread throughout Western Europe, creating one of the major turning points of European intellectual history.

The 16th and 17th centuries saw foreign domination from Austria and Spain, both of which occupied parts of Italy and tried to control the rest. Italy was invaded by Napoleon Bonaparte (1769–1821) in 1798, who united Italy for the first time since the 5th century under the rule of his brother Jerome (1768–1844), whom he made king of Naples in 1806. Napoleon's defeat led to a new division of Italy which was dominated by Austria in 1815. But the Napoleonic period had sown the seeds for the secular nationalist movement. The power of the papacy declined after the unification of the country in 1870 and the establishment of a kingdom under Victor Emmanuel II (Vittorio Emanuele) (1820–78). He was succeeded by his son, Victor Emmanuel III (1869–1947), who ruled Italy until he was deposed in 1946 and Italy became a republic.

During World War I, Italy was on the side of the Allies, England and

France, who were latter joined by America. In 1922 Benito Mussolini (1883–1945), a former Communist agitator turned Fascist, proclaimed himself dictator after a dramatic march on Rome by his followers, the Blackshirts. The king reluctantly accepted this development and attempted to rule as a constitutional monarch. Mussolini quickly reached an agreement with the Vatican to establish the Vatican State as an independent city-state through the Lateran Treaty of 1929. He reformed much of Italian society and began a series of imperial adventures in Ethiopia, Libya, and Albania. When Germany seemed bent on winning World War II, Mussolini entered the war on the German side only to see his achievements crumble as the Germans were slowly driven back from Russia and then the rest of Europe. He was eventually captured by partisans on April 28, 1945, and executed near Lake Como.

A new, if somewhat unstable, democratic state was established in 1948 with a republican constitution. Although many outside observers, particularly in England and America, scorn the multi-party Italian system which is prone to crisis, Italy is one of the few democratic states where Communists and right-wing parties have shared power with the ruling party without such power-sharing leading to a dictatorship. This is surely a rare achievement, as is the increasing economic prosperity of what was once one of the poorest countries in Europe. Today Italy is a proud, independent nation with a rich past that plays an important role in the European community.

PART 2

ITALIAN LITERATURE, MUSIC, ART, AND ARCHITECTURE

ITALIAN LITERATURE

Italy's rich literary heritage begins in the Roman classical period. The language of choice for the Roman Empire's authors was classical Latin, and Latin was the preferred mode of communication for philosophers, historians, orators, poets, and eventually, priests. The language of politics and faith, the state and Church alike claimed Latin as their official tongue.

Virgil's (70–19 B.C.) *Aeneid*, written under the aegis of Augustus, is a monumental myth that links the history of Rome to the fallen city of Troy and thus, to the lineage of the goddess Venus herself. Virgil's romantic vision of Rome's past is shattered by Lucretius's (100–55 B.C.) *On the Nature of the Universe* and Cicero's (103–43 B.C.) devastating critique of ancient Roman mythology, *The Nature of the Gods*. With the exception of

Ovid's (43 B.C.–A.D. 17) account of Roman myths and stories of the gods in his *Metamorphoses*, most of the major works that followed Cicero discussed contemporary politics and military conquests. The veristic accounts and war commentaries in Tacitus's (A.D. 55–117) *Annals of Imperial Rome* and *The Agricola and the Germanica* remain classics of historical and anthropological study. Plutocracy's (A.D. 46–120) *The Makers of Rome* and Ammianus Marcellinus's (A.D. 330–390) *The Later Roman Empire* continue the historical literary tradition. Roman Christian philosophical thought is seen in Augustine's (354–430) classic *The City of God* and Boethius's (475–525) *The Consolation of Philosophy*, which contains the reflections of a devout Christian in an unjust world.

The fall of the Roman Empire, successive barbarian invasions, and the ensuing unstable political situation from 500 to 1000 contributed to a dearth in authorship and introduced different languages into Italy. While Latin was used more infrequently, a variety of spoken dialects rose throughout the peninsula. The popularity of these dialects (called the "vernacular") and the appearance of 13th-century Sicilian and Tuscan vernacular poetry remedied the lack of Italian literature and the loss of classical Latin. It was the Tuscan, or Florentine, vernacular that Italy eventually adopted as its common language. For the time being, Latin distinguished itself only as a language of the Church.

Writing in the Florentine vernacular, it is Dante (1265–1321) who gave birth to modern Italian literature and language. His *Divine Comedy* is a classic of satire and Christian reflection. Dante's journeys through hell, purgatory, and heaven are voyages of faith, politics, philosophy, and love.

It is unrequited love that Francesco Petrarca (1304–74), better known as Petrarch, is most remembered for. In his *Il Canzoniere,* Petrarch examines this unrequited love and his yearning soul to express a new emotive and literary tone in poetry.

Giovanni Boccaccio (1313–75), a contemporary and friend of Petrarch, offers a glimpse into everyday Florentine life and experience. In his *Decameron*, a group of seven gentlemen and three ladies seeking refuge in the Tuscan countryside from a plague devastating Florence tell 100 tales of life, death, love, and scandal.

Italy's literary renaissance began with Dante, Petrarch and Boccaccio, whose works pervaded 14th, 15th, and 16th century Europe. With the subsequent rediscovery of Greek and Latin and the rising interest in classical antiquity—its literature, art, philosophy, and language—in the 15th century, this renaissance flourished. In a culture now defined by humanism, Italian thought and learning emphasized the dignity of man, the integrity of the individual spirit, and the beauty of earthly life. The interest in man as the measure of all things opposed the medieval view of humanity as insignificant before God.

Significant works from this period explore the ideals of beauty and harmony and express faith and optimism in man's potential. In his *Oration on the Dignity of Man*, Pico della Mirandola reevaluates man's importance in the spiritual and temporal world. The theme of man and his potential is similarly explored in works by Leonardo Bruni, Marsilio Ficino, Leonardo de'Medici, Ludovico Ariosto, and Angelo Ambrogini Poliziano.

Leon Battista Alberti (1404–72) and Leonardo da Vinci (1452–1519) are model Renaissance men; both were artists, mathematicians, scientists, and philosophers whose life, work, and writings reflect the embodiment of a spiritual, moral, and worldly man.

Political writings of the period assert man's potential and power as ideal only when politics are free from the constraints of religion and morality. *The*

Prince, Niccolò Machiavelli's (1469–1527) analysis of human nature and political ethics (or rather, unethical politics), emphasized the principles of and struggle between *virtu* (power) and *fortuna* (chance). Influential and widely read from the time of its first publication to today, *The Prince* is practically the guidebook for Mafia conduct.

In contrast, courtly and noble conduct is articulated in Baldassare Castiglione's (1478–1529) *The Courtier*. Here Renaissance moral aspiration is expressed through the courtly ideals of grace, harmony, and decorum.

Italian literature declined in the late 16th and the 17th centuries as the modern European world struggled with the ideas of man and nature and moved away from humanism and towards the Church. Literary satire defines the turbulent era. Of note is Paolo Sarpi's (1552–1623) *The History of the Council of Trent*, a critical analysis of conflict, reformation, and faith.

The Enlightenment in the 18th century encouraged an awakening of Italian historical and social consciousness. Giovanni Battista Vico, Lodovico Antonio Muratori, and Giuseppe Panini exemplify this new intellectual and psychological awareness.

The 19th century Romantic movement in Italy emphasized calm, simplicity, and harmony; the period's writers emphasized a balance between human and spiritual expression. These thoughtful, powerful, and poetic writers included Ugo Foscolo, Giacomo Leopardi, and Alessandro Manzoni (1785–1873), whose *I Promessi Sposi* explores the Catholic faith and the meaning of existence.

The Italian Risorgimento produced writers who contributed nationalistic, didactic histories; among these authors are Vincenzo Gioberti and Giuseppe Mazzini. A literary movement away from Romanticism towards Realism in the works of Giovanni Verga, Antonio Foggazzaro, Giovanni Pascoli, and Gabriele D'Annunzio complemented the nationalistic interests.

Luigi Pirandello (1867–1936), recipient of the Nobel Prize for Literature in 1934, transformed the verism of the realist writers into a cynical and ironic view of Italian life. In his popular *One, Nobody, One-hundred thousand*, Pirandello explores the vacuousness of life. A similar spirit is seen in the works of Italo Svevo and Benedetto Croce (1866–1952), who examined man's freedom, spirituality, and individuality.

While Fascism stifled Italian intellectualism, major writers including Ignazio Silone, Corrado Ivaro, and Alberto Moravia continued to publish and oppose the dictatorship. The post-war period gave rise to a profound neo-realistic voice among writers. Post-war Italy is vividly recalled in the works of Leonardo Sciascia, Pier Paolo Pasolini, Primo Levi, Carlo Levi, Giorgio Bassani, and Guiseppe Tomasi di Lampedusa.

Numerous contemporary Italian authors also enjoy international acclaim; the most remarkable among them are Italo Calvino, Elsa Morante, and Umberto Eco.

ITALIAN MUSIC

Few nations, with the possible exception of Germany, have contributed so much to the enjoyment of music as Italy. Although Italian music proper begins with the reforms of Pope Gregory (540–604), whose "chants" continue to enchant the world, it was not until the 16th century that Italy emerged as a major musical nation. Opera developed here in the 16th century when Jacopo Peri (1561–1633), who worked for the famous Medici family in Florence, composed the world's first operas, the *Dafne* and the *Euridice*. Since then Italians haven't stopped singing. During the 18th century Vivaldi (1678–1741) wrote numerous concertos, operas, and religious works. In the 18th century Italy created the overture and sinfonia. In the 19th century, Puccini (1858–1924) transformed opera from the realm of the rich and famous to the world of everyday reality. Rossini (1792–1868) and Verdi (1813–1901) contributed to this transformation to make opera one of the world's most popular art forms. While many Christians recoil at the overt immorality of many operatic scripts, behind almost all of them lies a deep morality and sense of justice that reflect a profound Christian worldview expressed in dramatic musical form.

ITALIAN ART

Leonardo DaVinci claimed that art was the "grandchild of God"; certainly, nowhere more than in Italy, in both secular and sacred art, was this child so divinely nurtured.

Any investigation of Italian art reveals that it is indebted to many sources but in servitude to none. Italy's geography, history, and culture distinguish her from the rest of Europe; she was a mediator between the ancient civilizations of the East and the burgeoning culture of the West and is the matron of a peninsula characterized by its own struggle with diversity and unity.

Italy's earliest artists were the Etruscans. Religion and death occupied Etruscan minds. Stirred by their deities, magic, and divination, the Etruscans built elaborate temples to house their gods. Concerned with mortality and the afterlife, the Etruscans built vast cities of decorated underground tombs (*tumuli*) to house their dead. While the Etruscans depicted scenes from Greek myths on their temples, sarcophagi, and funerary urns, they chose to decorate their tombs with objects and scenes from everyday life, with common images depicting eating, drinking, merriment, hunting, and physical contests.

While the Romans borrowed many of the Etruscan cultural practices, the art of ancient Rome is indebted in part to Greek artistic production and heritage and to Roman sensibilities, which were shaped largely by the state. Roman art served the state. It celebrated the history of both the real and the mythical Rome. The city's roads, aqueducts, amphitheaters, baths, and forums praised Rome's greatness. Narrative scenes on public monuments recalled military glory, and the ubiquitous image of the emperor promulgated the belief in his divinity and the worship of his image as proof of loyalty to Rome.

Though Christian art would eventually echo the imagery of Imperial Roman art, early Christian art sought much humbler representations. Pre-Constantine Christian art consisted mainly of symbols decorating catacombs. A favorite among these simple representations is the vision of Christ as the Good Shepherd protecting his faithful flock.

In 313 Constantine (312–337), the first Christian emperor, issued the Edict of Milan granting Christians the right to worship freely. Post-Constantinian art reflects this freedom, and the early Christians begin to use art in the service of their new churches. The veneration of martyrs, the accumulation and proliferation of relics, and the rise of the cult of saints mark the rise in didacticism of Christian art. Sacred images became the bible of the illiterate.

As the Church slowly assumed more administrative responsibility from the Roman Empire, it also began to absorb Imperial imagery. Byzantine artistic activity in Italy reflects this imperial influence. Constantine founded Constantinople in 330, marking the transference of the Imperial court from the Western world to the Eastern world. Two centuries later, the Emperor Justinian (527–65) would bring his court and his art to Ravenna. Byzantine art and architecture would soon flourish in Italy due to an influx of craftsmen fleeing hostile iconoclast emperors (8th century and 9th century).

While influence from the East waned in the 10th century, Western stimuli in Italy surged. Pilgrims traveling to Italy in the 11th and 12th centuries helped to share and transmit images and ideas throughout the peninsula. In keeping with the pilgrim's ultimate goal, religious imagery emphasized man's salvation through the Christian church.

Imagery focused around the devastation of the plague and the Cult of the Virgin Mary mark the 13th century. Death and salvation weighed heavily on the medieval mind. In the Gothic period images of the austere and otherworldly Mother of God are replaced by maternal, human, and humble representations. She is the protector of and intercessor for humankind, offering hope and mercy to those who seek her through the Church.

During the 13th and 14th century in Italy, an increased demand for painting among the developing middle class necessitated greater art production. Political, cultural, religious, and individual concerns were placed on art and artists.

Cultural rivalries among developing city-states resulted in propagandistic civic and private art. The growing merchant classes were considerable art patrons. As individuals amassed more disposable income, they spent more money on art. Through art, collectors and patrons revealed their wealth and sophistication to the world. The pride and accomplishment of a city was expressed through its painting, sculpture, and architecture.

The Renaissance revived the great cultures of ancient Greece and Rome. This renewed study of antiquity, its literature and art, gave rise to humanism. Humanism led to an increasingly human treatment of Christian subject and images in art. Philosophers, humanists, and artists formed the Renaissance understanding of man as equal to and independent from his Christian faith. Man was the master of his own destiny and through his free will could "attain the state of angels" (Pico della Mirandola).

Renaissance art appeals to the intellect. Order, harmony, symmetry, and proportion were a reflection of the divine. The numinous was found in a greater understanding of nature and the principles of mathematics and geometry.

Sacred art was increasingly represented as a synthesis of Christian theology and classical humanism. However, while the greatest gift of humanism was freedom—freedom to challenge, to inquire, and to investigate—it is this freedom, in art and in the Church it served, that laid the foundation for the Protestant Reformation.

The Catholic Church established the Council of Trent (1545–63) in response to the Protestant revolution. The council's function was to attack everything that weakened the Church's authority; Church doctrine became more dogmatic than ever.

In 1563 the Council of Trent laid down rules and regulations governing religious art. Sacred art required decency, decorum, and clarity. Art was to be dramatic and appeal to the viewer's emotions and rouse their faith and fervor. Nudity was not acceptable in public religious works of art. Pope Pius IV (1559–65) had Daniele da Volterra paint loincloths over some of Michelangelo's *Last Judgement* nude figures. His work earned Daniele the nickname "the panty painter."

The Council recognized that art was a powerful propagandistic tool, and the Church used it to emphasize the glory of the Catholic Church, Rome, and the pope. The Church was once again the measure of all things, and its art stimulated religious zeal.

Italian art began slowly to decline at the end of the 17th century. The age of great art patronage moved to France, and fewer Italian patrons commissioned grand works of art.

In the 18th century, Italy redefined herself as an influential art center. Rome attracted European painters, sculptors, and architects eager to learn from the treasured legacy of Rome's artistic past. These neoclassicists sought to evoke the ideals of ancient Greece and Rome.

The *Macchiaoli*, a school of Florentine painters formed in 1855, define Italian art in the latter half of the 19th century. Painting in patches (macchia) of pure color, the group is often associated with the Impressionists. The *Macchiaoli* art was a reaction against the mimicry of the past and the academy, and it inaugurated the modern Italian art movement.

Two significant movements arose in Italy in the early 20th century, futurism and *pittura metaphysica*. The Futurists strove to eliminate tradition, destroy museums and libraries, glorify industry and mechanization, and deify war. The Metaphysical painters emphasized the enigmatic and the dreamlike, and their works exerted a significant influence on the French surrealists. Art between the two World Wars and under Mussolini fell into decline. However, contemporary Italian art enjoys an international stage, contributing to and vitalizing current trends and tastes.

ARCHITECTURE STYLES

THE EARLIEST CHURCHES (TO 800)

Christians originally met in private homes or secret hiding places. Eventually, when Christianity became an accepted religion in the Roman Empire, Christians adapted the Roman basilica, or assembly hall, as their meeting place. From the 2nd century to the 6th century the basilica was the standard form of church building in Western Europe (figure 1).

Figure 1

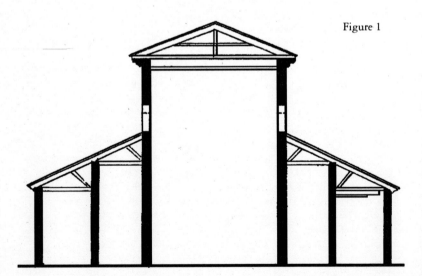

The Pantheon

In 313, with the *Edict of Milan,* Emperor Constantine granted toleration and the protection of the state to Christianity. Following this development, the Roman Empire, which until then had sporadically persecuted Christians, gradually became Christian. Consequently, many formerly pagan buildings and places of worship were converted into churches. One such architectural conversion was the Roman temple of the Pantheon in Rome. The circular plan of the Pantheon and similar buildings provided Christian architects with the basic layout of many churches.

Thus, the circular church, like the Neonian Baptistry in Ravenna, became the basis of what was later to be known as the Byzantine style. It was this circular style that became very popular throughout the Eastern Roman Empire, providing the basis for the ground plan of the Church of the Holy Sepulchre in Jerusalem and the greatest of all Byzantine churches, Hagia Sophia, in Constantinople.

Byzantine art flourished in various Western outposts of the Eastern Empire, including Ravenna in Italy, where Byzantine-style churches were built in a circular pattern.

THE ROMANESQUE STYLE (9TH–13TH CENTURIES)

Strange as it may seem, the other great inspiration for the development of churches in Europe was the abundance of Roman ruins such as those of the Arch of Constantine and the Colosseum in Rome, which inspired awe in all who saw their magnificent ruins for centuries after they had fallen into disrepair and disuse. Thus

Arch of Constantine

ancient Rome provided the inspiration for Christian architects for over a millennium. The basic designs were incorporated into church buildings to create what became known as the Romanesque style.

Notice the massive nature of the stonework and the rounded arches in both the Arch of Constantine and the Colosseum that became a feature in what is known as the Romanesque style. These ruins clearly influenced later builders, both in providing them with a basic style and often with the raw materials out of which to build churches.

Romanesque churches have very thick walls reinforced by buttresses. Buttresses are specially thickened sections of wall which look like a smaller second wall. They are necessary to help carry the weight of the walls and roof. Although the Romans knew how to make concrete, the secret of this valuable aid to building was lost from the 4th century to the early 19th century. Therefore, medieval

builders had to rely on porous mortar and carefully placed stone slabs which interlocked with each other.

Most Romanesque churches were built to a cruciform plan. Normally the altar, or communion table, in such churches always faced east while the entrance, known as the West End, is at the other end of the church.

Romanesque shapes for arches, doors, roofing, and windows were very distinctive. If you learn to recognize these shapes, you will soon know whether a church or part of a church is Romanesque. Below are several examples of typical Romanesque shapes.

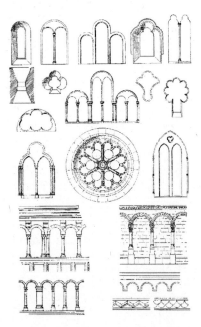

Colosseum, Rome

THE GOTHIC STYLE (12TH–16TH CENTURIES)

"Gothic" was originally used as a term of contempt by the Italian art historian Giorgio Vasari (1511–74) for what he regarded as the "barbaric" nature of Northern European architecture. By associating this style with the Goths who had helped destroy ancient Rome, Vasari implied that it was unworthy of civilized people. Today, the Gothic style is regarded as one of the greatest architectural achievements of the Middle Ages and the high point of Christian civilization. The overall impression created by Gothic buildings is one of unbelievable lightness. The whole structure points to heaven and reminds the worshiper of God.

Notice the flying buttresses in the Milan Cathedral, below. These are the arches used to strengthen the upper walls of the nave. They deflect the weight of the roof from the nave walls to the outer walls, making it possible to build the walls both higher and thinner. Along the roof, gutters and open spouts conduct rain water well away from the walls. These spouts are often decorated with animal figures and heads known as gargoyles.

Several phases of the Gothic style can be distinguished: the Early, High, and Late, as well as the Gothic revival of the late 18th and early 19th century. Gothic cathedrals were built over centuries; consequently, the styles often changed even within one building. When visiting a Gothic cathedral, look for the fan vaulting or roof supports, which have veins like those of a fan. This is often very beautiful and a masterpiece of craftsmanship.

Gothic churches are recognizable by their pointed arches and windows. The following diagram provides some examples to help you recognize them.

25

Milan Cathedral, Milan

THE RENAISSANCE STYLE (14TH–17TH CENTURIES)

From the mid-14th century to the late 17th century, a style best described as Renaissance art and architecture developed in Italy and spread to the rest of Europe. In Rome, St. Peter's Basilica incorporates the main features of the early Baroque style known as the Renaissance style. It combines straight lines, corners, and curves in a far more sophisticated manner than the heavy solidity found in Northern European buildings of the same period. Thus, Italian Romanesque architecture led directly to the development of the semiclassical Renaissance style that is characterized by its sharp edges and angular, geometric features.

St. Peter's Basilica, Rome

THE BAROQUE STYLE (17TH–18TH CENTURIES)

For many years, Baroque was used as a term of contempt for what was thought to be a degenerate form of art. Such attitudes were changed by the Swiss art historian and critic Jacob Burckhardt (1818–97), who argued that contrary to popular opinion, particularly in Protestant Northern Europe, Baroque was an important artistic movement and a legitimate development of the Renaissance style. The Baroque style proper was essentially found among Roman Catholics.

Baroque churches are intended to symbolize the Holy Trinity and God's revelation of himself in the world. It is almost impossible to provide a cross-section of a typical Baroque church. Similarly, one cannot point to specific Baroque designs except to say that they involve twists and turns, cherubs and angels, in a profusion of colors. The Age of the Baroque coincided with the revival of Roman Catholicism and Protestant Pietism and the flowering of a rich musical tradition.

NEOCLASSICISM AND NOSTALGIC NATIONALISM (18TH–20TH CENTURIES)

In his *A History of Architecture,* Sir Banister Fletcher points out that in Europe the neoclassical style of the 19th century, which was inspired by Greek temples, was closely connected with a growing nationalism and a form of neo-paganism.

The new master problem for late 18th-century and early 19th-century architects was the creation of civic pride and national consciousness through museums and cultural monuments. The rediscovery, even reinvention, of ancient Greek culture coincided with a decline in church construction in favor of secular buildings that proclaimed the rise of humanity and national pride. Instead of creating great churches to the glory of God, aspiring architects were busy creating temples to man.

It is interesting to note that although nostalgic nationalism inspired artists and architects throughout the 19th century, most Italian architects remained fairly distant from the wave of nationalistic fervor that swept much of northern Europe. This is probably because the Italians were conscious of their own rich artistic heritage and felt no need to recreate an imaginary past based on either the Middle Ages or ancient Greece and Rome. On the other hand, during the 1920s and 1930s, Italian Fascists capitalized on the grandeur of ancient Rome, giving some Italian buildings the same nationalistic designs as those used by architects in the north.

HOW TO ENJOY YOUR VISIT TO AN ITALIAN CHURCH

Visiting Italian churches can be quite confusing for anyone used to thinking about a church as simply a place to hear a sermon and meet fellow Christians. Even guidebooks are often not very helpful because they are full of unfamiliar terms like *chancel, sanctuary,* and *transept.* Unless you grew up in Europe, you will probably be overwhelmed with this mass of information and seemingly endless detail. So to make things easy, we have provided a brief introduction to the layout of a typical church and cathedral.

Below is the layout of a typical parish church.

The structure of this church would be familiar to most people. There is a TOWER and MAIN DOORWAY, or NARTHEX, a baptismal area represented by the FONT, the main body of the church known as the

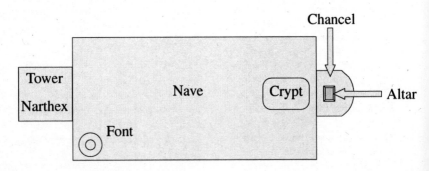

NAVE, and a place for the communion table, or ALTAR, known as the CHANCEL. Finally there is a CRYPT, or underground chapel used for burying people. Although this structure looks familiar, the way it was understood by medieval people is far from familiar.

Now let us examine a more advanced and complex design, below.

To the basic church design, transepts have been added and the tower has been moved. The narthex is also called the PORCH. There are also two altars plus an ALTAR SCREEN, which separates the nave from the chancel, where the choir would be located. The screen also separated lay-

people from the monks and priests who sang in the choir. The VESTRY was a small room used by the priest to change from his ordinary clothing into the special church clothing, or vestments, used during the service.

Now we must look at the most developed version of a church, which would be found in a cathedral. It is important to remember that in medieval churches the altar, not the pulpit, was the focus of worship. The congregation was separated from the high altar by a screen and could not even see what was happening. Most people stood in the nave or aisles, often conducting daily

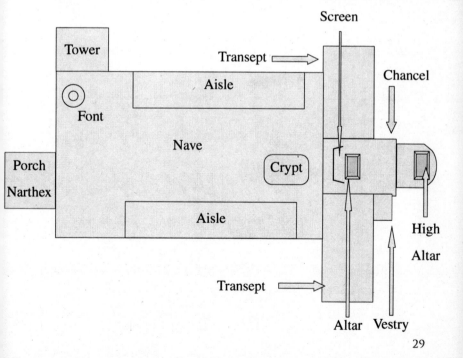

business or exchanging gossip while the priests performed the Mass. Pews were not added until after the Reformation, when people sat to hear the preaching of the Word.

Below is the layout of a typical cathedral. Let us go through these various areas in turn. First the worshiper entered the church through a doorway with a porch or NARTHEX. In Roman basilicas, the narthex was a long porch at the west end of the church. It was the place where women, people awaiting baptism, or those who were under some form of discipline waited before being allowed into the church itself. Symbolically the narthex

was associated with the cleansing waters of baptism and the womb where the child waits before its birth.

In some churches there is also a PARADISE PORCH. It is so named because it was decorated with sculptures and frescoes, or wall paintings, of the Garden of Eden. It often contained a fountain where unbaptized people and sinners could wash themselves before entering the church.

Beyond the narthex one enters the NAVE. This is the main body of the church and is the Latin word for "ship." It represents the ship of salvation, Noah's Ark, and the invisible church of Christ

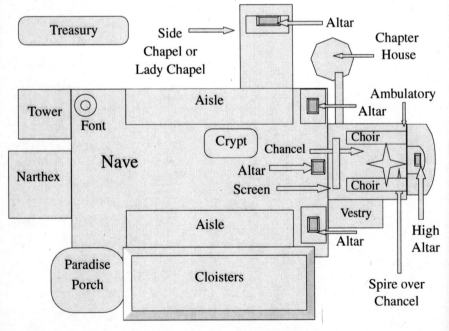

to which all saved souls belong and where humans are protected from the storms of life and material temptations. The nave was both a place of worship and general meeting place. Not until after the Reformation were seats added. Before then everyone had to stand, and people often wandered around selling food and other goods in winter.

In large churches there may be more than one nave and most have AISLES, which are separated from the nave by pillars.

Near the nave is a BAPTISMAL FONT. Originally these were wide, low stone basins where new converts stood while water was poured over them. Later, as the general population became Christian, fonts were smaller, raised vessels suitable for baptism.

Near the font and the narthex there is often at least one TOWER. This functioned both as a landmark and a watchtower in isolated villages. Bells were added to call people to worship and warn of danger.

At the end of the nave was an ALTAR, where the death of Christ was ritually reenacted with each service.

Until the 10th century, worshipers partook in communion before the SIDE ALTARS, where they received both bread and wine. Later they received only bread. Originally this change was made to prevent drunkenness, but later it gained theological importance as only priests were allowed to receive communion in both kinds, bread and wine.

Beyond the altar was a SCREEN, which prevented ordinary people from entering the chancel.

The CHANCEL was where the choir, which consisted of men only, was located. The CHOIR STALLS are often richly decorated with wood carvings.

Beyond the chancel was the HIGH ALTAR, where the most solemn Masses were performed. In medieval churches the celebration of the Mass was the central event.

Near the high altar is the CRYPT. Originally crypts were underground chambers where Christians met for worship in secret and where they buried their dead. Crypts are often the earliest part of a church building.

The VESTRY is the small room where priests changed from their normal garb into ecclesiastical robes, which were selected on the basis of their color depending on the season in the church year.

Many large churches have a walkway leading behind the choir, chancel, and the high altar. This is known as the AMBULATORY and was used, particularly in pilgrimage churches, to allow worshipers to file past relics.

The LADY CHAPEL, which is often located behind the high altar, was devoted to the Virgin Mary. It was often the most important side altar in a church and usually survived after the Reformation, when many altars were removed from churches.

To one side of large churches, usually the south side, one finds the CLOIS-TERS. This is an enclosed rectangle with a high outside wall and roof, often with very beautiful stonework and ceiling vaulting, surrounding an open garden, usually a grassy lawn, that is enclosed by a low wall and pillars. Here monks and other clergy could walk in bad weather, reciting the Scriptures or praying. In time cloisters became more elaborate and served both as a general meeting place for monks and as a place where copyists transcribed the Scriptures or wrote sacred theological treatises.

Above the chancel it became the practice to build a tall church SPIRE. The spire served as a local landmark and replaced, or at least supplemented, church towers.

Cathedrals also have a CHAPTER HOUSE, which is the meeting place of clergy during synods and other important functions. Here the business of a diocese was discussed.

Finally, don't miss the TREASURY. Here the treasures of the church are kept, such as ancient crosses, Scriptures, rare books, relics, and vestments.

PART 3

CHRISTIAN HERITAGE SITES IN ITALY

TOP 10 CHRISTIAN SITES IN ITALY

1. **ST. PETER'S BASILICA IN THE VATICAN CITY:** This is the heart of the Roman Catholic faith, the burial place of Christianity's first pope, and one of the most stunning churches in Christendom.

2. **BASILICA OF ST. FRANCIS IN ASSISI:** It is truly a humbling experience to relive, through the church's marvelous frescoes, the life of one of the most pious men in the history of Christianity, St. Francis of Assisi.

3. **LEONARDO DA VINCI'S** *LAST SUPPER* **IN MILAN:** Stand before the world's most famous vision of the Last Supper, in which Leonardo captures each disciple's character and emotion as Christ reveals the news that one of them is his betrayer.

4. **HOLY SHROUD IN TURIN:** A marvel of faith, mystery, and skepticism, the Holy Shroud (a cloth imprinted with what appears to be Christ's form) is a possible physical link to the Savior at the end of his mortal life.

5. **DOME OF THE FLORENCE CATHEDRAL:** Soaring over 300 feet above the ground, this heavenly dome is the pride of Florence, the crowning achievement of Brunelleschi, and the symbol of the Florentine Renaissance.

6. **PICCOLOMINI LIBRARY IN SIENA:** A delight for the eyes and the mind, this library is rich in humanist learning, theological belief, and vibrant artistry.

7. **SAN CLEMENT IN ROME:** Experience almost 2000 years of mysticism and faith, visit the 3rd-century Mithraeum in the church foundations, see the 12th-century apse mosaics in the upper church, and attend an English mass.

8. **SANTA MARIA DEI FRARI IN VENICE:** Visit this still and somber church if only to see Titian's sublime altarpiece, the *Assumption of the Virgin*,

and contemplate the Virgin's heavenly glory.

9. SAN BRIZIO CHAPEL IN THE CATHEDRAL OF ORVIETO: Luca Signorelli's fantastic vision of the *Last Judgement* frescoed on the chapel walls is so vivid and effective, all who see it are moved to contemplate their own salvation and are deterred, at least for a moment, from wrongdoing.

10. BASILICA OF SAN VITALE IN RAVENNA: Herein lies the artistic link to Constantinople and the Byzantine glory achieved by the Emperor Justinian as he ruled the Roman Empire from its glorious eastern Mediterranean capital.

KEY TO THE TEXTS

All entries in the Christian Travelers Guides are written according to the following outline.

The name of each place is given in alphabetical order. Places are listed according to the local spelling, followed by the English spelling if needed, e.g., **Torino (Turin).**

Background: a short history of the area explains its religious, cultural, and intellectual significance.

Places to visit: individual sites are mentioned with recommendations about things that deserve close attention. Different places are identified in BOLD.

Throughout the text we have given people's names using the Italian spelling because when you look for a tomb, or at an inscription, what you will see is the Italian spelling. For example, Torre della Fame (Tower of Hunger).

Most dates are A.D. and are given as a plain number, e.g., 800. Only when there might be some doubt about the exact time are B.C. or A.D. used.

Map of Key Christian Heritage Sites in Italy

Switzerland

Austria

France

Milano (Milan)

Certosa di Pavia

Torcello

Torino (Turin)

Padua

Venezia (Venice)

Loreto

Ravenna

Pistoia

Prato

Lucca

Camaldoli

Empoli

Firenze (Florence)

Urbino

Pisa

Arezzo

Sansepolcro

Abazia di Fossanova (the Abbey of Fossanova)

Cortona

Citta di Castello

San Galgano

Siena

Pienza

Foligno

Volterra

Perugia

Gubbio

Montepulciano

Assisi

Todi

Chiusi

Spoleto

Sant'Antimo

Monte Olivento Maggiore

Roma (Rome)

Subiaco

Monte Cassino

Bari

Napoli (Naples)

Ravello

Sardegna

Massafra

Palermo

Monreale

Sicily

ABAZIA DI FOSSANOVA
(ABBEY OF FOSSANOVA)

The oldest Cistercian convent in Italy, the Fossanova abbey complex was a model for architects throughout southern Italy. In the 12th century the monks worked to reclaim the spiritual institution from the surrounding marshland. They triumphed by digging a canal, named the "Fossa Nova" (new canal), from which the abbey took its name.

First recorded in the 11th century as the Benedictine abbey, Santo Stefano, Innocent II ordered that it be transferred to the Cistercians in 1134–35. Situated along the route from Naples to Rome, it was here that the great Christian philosopher and apologist, St. Thomas Aquinas, died in 1274, enroute from Naples to Lyons. In the 15th century, the once wealthy and learned institution fell into moral decay, was abandoned, and its archive was dispersed.

PLACES TO VISIT

The CHURCH was consecrated in 1208. A massive rose window dominates the facade, glittering above a Gothic portal with delicately carved capitals. The interior is typical of Cistercian architecture with large interior arches and an octagonal tower atop the crossing.

The CLOISTER, to the right of the church, features Romanesque architecture on three sides and Gothic architecture on the fourth side. On the ground floor of the complex are the chapter hall, sacristy, refectory, and kitchen. The monks' cells occupy the second floor.

Separate structures include the infirmary and guesthouse, where St. Thomas died. The room was transformed into a chapel and displays an 18th-century relief depicting St. Thomas's death.

AREZZO

A terraced hill surmounted by a citadel rises above the intersection of three valleys, the Valdarno, the Casentino, and the Valdichiana, and marks the agricultural town of Arezzo. Throughout its lifetime, the surrounding fertile plains have produced grains and fruit for the Aretines. Its industrious citizens complement the plentiful land. Ancient Arezzo (Arretum) was

ST. THOMAS AQUINAS (1224/27–74). Known by his contemporaries as *Doctor Angelicus,* Aquinas is the most important philosopher and theologian of the Roman Catholic tradition and possibly the greatest Christian philosopher of all time. Educated by the Benedictines and Dominicans, he studied in Paris and Köln (Cologne). Later he taught in Paris 1252–59, 1269–72; and Italy 1259–69, 1272–74. He was responsible for "baptizing" the philosophy of Aristotle which he made the basis of Roman Catholic theology and apologetics. His Aristotelianism was opposed by the Franciscans, but his teachings were made the official doctrine of the Dominican Order. He was canonized in 1323 and made a Doctor of the Church in 1567. Finally, the study of Thomas Aquinas was made part of all theological training in 1366. Aquinas was made patron of all Roman Catholic universities in 1880. His authority as teacher was reaffirmed in 1923. In his thought the relation of reason to faith is one of subalternation, in which the lower (reason) accepts principles of the higher (faith). He rejected Anselm of Canterbury's ontological argument, preferring the cosmological and teleological arguments for the existence of God. For Aquinas there is a level of knowledge attainable by reason alone; another level attainable by reason for skilled thinkers and by faith for unskilled thinkers; the highest level, however, is attainable only by faith. The system Aquinas developed is called "Thomism," his followers "Thomists." Reformers like Martin Luther (1483–1546) and John Calvin (1509–64) rejected the teaching of Aquinas, although Philipp Melanchthon (1497–1560) and Thedore Beza (1519–1605) embraced his work in their educational work. In recent years evangelicals, influenced by Cornelius van Til (1895–1987), have rejected Aquinas's work, while others like Norman Geisler have embraced Aquinas's views in books like *Thomas Aquinas: An Evangelical Appraisal.*

THE CHRISTIAN TRAVELERS GUIDE TO ITALY

A

known c. 50 B.C. for producing a fine, bright red Aretine pottery called *corallino*. Today the city is known commercially for its jewelry production.

Ancient Arretum was the center of a large craft industry. It grew in size and importance in the Roman period as a strategic military outpost (294 B.C.); the town was conveniently situated on the Via Cassia, the Roman road from Rome to Florence. In A.D. 270 it became the see of a bishop. By the 10th century it was a free commune with Ghibelline sentiments, thus making Arezzo a natural enemy of Guelf Florence. The Florentines in the Battle of Campaldino defeated Arezzo in 1289, and by 1384 it was subject to Florence.

Arezzo is distinguished not only by its medieval character and artistic production but also as the birthplace of renowned men of arts. Some of its most famed men include the craftsman Marcus Perennius (born c. 70 B.C.), who invented Aretine pottery; the Etruscan nobleman Gaius Maecenas (69–8 B.C.), a poet and patron of the arts and friend of Augustus Caesar; the poets Virgil and Horace; the Benedictine Guido Monaco (Guido d'Arezzo), credited with inventing musical notation; the Byzantine painter Margarito (13th century); the writer and poet Pietro Aretino (b. 1492); and the painter and art historian Giorgio Vasari (1511–74).

Arezzo's famed citizens and golden periods can be experienced through the city's art and architecture. It is a pleas-

ant tour through a quiet town whose historic center is closed to traffic.

PLACES TO VISIT

The splendidly frescoed interior of SAN FRANCESCO more than compensates for the church's barren facade. It was built in 1322 by Fra Giovanni da Pistoia. A vast open structure, this church was designed to house the masses coming to hear Franciscan sermons.

Above the doorway is a stained glass oculus (1520) by the French artist Guillaume de Marcillat showing Pope Honorius III approving the Rule of St. Francis. Marcillat, who fled France to escape murder charges and became a Dominican monk, worked solely in Italy. His glass is abundant in Arezzo. Vasari praised his works, describing them not as "stained-glass windows but marvels, dropped from heaven to give consolation to man."

Of great consolation to the faithful are the images in fresco seen throughout the church including *Annunciations* by Spinello Aretino, Neri di Bicci, and Luca Signorelli; *Two Saints* by Andrea del Castagno; works by Lorentino d'Andrea; and a triptych of the *Madonna of the Girdle* (15th century) by Niccolò di Pietro Gerini.

The sanctuary houses the church's most celebrated works. A painted crucifix showing *St. Francis at the Foot of the Cross* (1250) hangs in the apse vault. On the walls behind the crucifix is the frescoed *Legend of the True Cross* (1453–64)

38

by Piero della Francesca. The Bacci family originally commissioned Bicci di Lorenzo to paint the apse, but he left Arezzo only having completed the *Evangelists* and the *Last Judgment.* Piero took up the commission, illustrating the walls with stories from the *Golden Legend* (13th century).

The **PIEVE DI SANTA MARIA** is a 12th-century church built above an earlier church that was destroyed in 1111. Vasari altered the new church in the 16th century. It is Arezzo's oldest surviving church and bears the artistic touch of many of its sons.

The Romanesque facade is Pisan in inspiration; four tiers pierced by arcades supported by colonnades rise above the square. Each of its decorative column capitals is unique. Rising above the church is the campanile (1330), called the "One Hundred Holes" for the 40 bays that pierce the structure and make its height possible.

The central portal and entrance to the church is decorated with symbols of the *Twelve Months of the Year* (1216). The use of the two-headed pagan god Janus to represent January is an interesting inclusion in the series.

An unrealized architectural project has left the simple church without a dome. Notice the delightful pillars and capitals within, decorated with representations of humans and animals. Also of note are two marble reliefs, a Byzantine *Epiphany* (11th century) and a *Nativity* (13th century). The carved baptismal

font in the baptistery chapel by Agostino di Giovanni includes scenes from the life of St. John the Baptist. On the high altar is an altarpiece commissioned by Bishop Guido Tarlati in 1320. This polyptych (1320–24), painted by Pietro Lorenzetti, portrays the *Madonna and Saints* in fashionable Tuscan attire. San Donato's gilt-silver reliquary bust (1346) is by a local craftsman, and the polychrome terracotta *Madonna* (15th century) is the work of Andrea da Firenze.

Arezzo's **DUOMO** crowns the city and overlooks the Parco del Prato and the 16th-century ruins of the Medici fortress. Dedicated to Arezzo's patron saint, San Donato, the cathedral stands upon the site of the former Benedictine church, San Pietro Maggiore. The Gothic structure was constructed between 1276 and 1511, the campanile was erected between 1857 and 1860, and the facade was faced between 1900 and 1914.

Windows and tombs stand out among the interior decorations. Guillaume de Marcillat's stained-glass windows (1519–23) shed light on one of the artist's few surviving complete cycles. The glass decoration illustrates the *Pentecost* (rose window), the *Calling of St. Matthew,* the *Baptism of Christ,* the *Expulsion of the Merchants from the Temple,* the *Adulteress,* and the *Raising of Lazarus.* This glassworker's artistry also includes frescoes in the nave vaults.

The 14th-century Gothic **HIGH ALTAR** entombs the martyred remains of

Arezzo's patron saint, San Donato, bishop of Arezzo, who was killed in 361 during Diocletian's reign. Next to it, a 4th-century Roman sarcophagus holds the mortal remains of Pope Gregory X (1205–76). The enclave that chose Gregory X as pope was the most time-consuming in recorded history, a lengthy three years! It convened in Viterbo between 1268 and 1271, ending only when the citizens cut off the enclave's food supply.

BISHOP GUIDO TARLATI'S TOMB (1327), in the north aisle, depicts his life's work as a zealous warrior and church hero. Near this noble bishop's tomb, Piero della Francesca painted *St. Mary Magdalene* as a noble peasant woman.

The LADY CHAPEL, to the left of the entrance, boasts several della Robbia ceramics including an *Assumption,* a *Crucifixion,* a *Madonna and Child,* and a *Madonna and Child with Saints.*

In the MUSEO DEL DUOMO, on the east end behind the cathedral, is a small collection of notable works. They include three painted 12th–13th-century wood *Crucifixes,* a terra-cotta *Annunciation* (1434) by Bernardo Rossellino, and three frescoed *Annunciations* by Spinello Aretino, his son, Parri di Spinello, and his master, Andrea di Nerio. Do not miss Bartolomeo della Gatta's *St. Jerome in the Desert* (15th century) and Vasari's *Preaching of the Baptist* and *Baptism of Christ* (1549).

Lime trees line the square facing the church of SAN DOMENICO (1275).

Inside, a painted wood *Crucifix* (1265) by Cimabue adorns the main altar. The walls in this aisleless structure are lined with fragmentary 14th- and 15th-century frescoes. The most complete works are Parri di Spinello's *Crucifixion* and *Life of St. Nicholas* (west wall), Luca di Tommè's *Christ with the Doctors* (south wall), and Spinello Aretino's *Annunciation* (east end). Giorgio Vasari's great-grandfather, Lazzaro Taldi Vasari, might have contributed the fresco of *St. Vincent Ferrer* (left wall). If so, it is the artist's only known work.

SANTISSIMA ANNUNCIATA, the church of the Virgin Annunciate, is a Renaissance structure begun by Bartolomeo della Gatta (1491) and completed by Antonio da Sangallo the Elder (1517). Built atop a 14th-century oratory, the unfinished facade of the new church incorporates recycled ruins from the oratory. Remnants of the earlier structure are visible in the right portal above an *Annunciation* (1370) by Spinello Aretino.

Inside, the main altar is decorated with silver-plated statues (16th century) and a venerated *Madonna* by Michele da Firenze. A *Madonna and St. Francis* by Pietro da Cortona adorns the chapel to the right of the main altar. To the left of the main altar are Matteo Rosselli's *Annunciation* and Niccolò Soggi's *Nativity.* A *Deposition,* in the first altar on the left, is by the hand of an 18-year-old Vasari.

The BADIA or church of SANTISSIME FLORA E LUCILLA IN BADIA was built in

1278 by the Benedictine order. In 1565, Vasari remodeled the church's structure and contributed to the interior decoration. His *Calling of St. Peter* on the main altar and his *Assumption* on the right choir wall were originally intended for the Vasari family tomb in Pieve di Santa Maria. Bartolomeo della Gatta contributed a lively *St. Lawrence* (1476) on the west wall. Along the south wall are a notable *Crucifixion* by Baccio da Montelupo and a painted crucifix by Segna di Bonaventura. Giuliano da Maiano designed the wooden intarsia ornament in the sacristy.

A long flight of steps rising before the entrance gives the church of SANTA MARIA IN GRADI (SAINT MARY OF THE STEPS) its name. The present church by Bartolomeo della Gatta (1592) stands above an earlier 11th-century Romanesque structure. Remains of the earlier church can be seen in the crypt, including a 13th-century painted wooden crucifix. Frescoes of the apostles (17th century) line the walls of the new church. Bernardino Santini (1629) and Salvi Castellucci (1633) crafted the wooden choir chapels. Be sure to see Andrea della Robbia's beautifully modeled terra-cotta group, the *Madonna del Soccorso.*

A lovely 15-minute stroll south of Arezzo leads to SANTA MARIA DELLE GRAZIE (1449), a delicate church built on the site of a sacred pagan spring, the "Fons Tecia." In 1428, San Benardino of Siena expunged all traces of heathen worship on the spot and ordered a church to be erected in its place. The building that rose on the site is enclosed in a walled garden adjacent to the Oratory of San Bernardino. An elegant loggia (1478) by Benedetto da Maiano leads into the church where you are greeted by Parri di Spinello's altarpiece, the *Madonne della Misericordia,* framed in a beautiful marble and terra-cotta altar panel by Andrea della Robbia.

The PALAZZO DELLA FRATERNITÀ DEI LAICI is home to the lay Fraternity of Santa Maria della Misericordia, a charitable Dominican organization established in 1262. The combination of the ornate Gothic first floor and Renaissance second floor is the result of 100 years of progress. It was begun in 1375 by Baldino di Cino and continued by Bernardo Rossellino (1433–60). Giorgio Vasari added the bell tower in the 16th century.

The CASA DI GIORGIO VASARI is the home of the art historian, painter, and architect Giorgio Vasari (1511–74). He purchased the house in 1540 and began an eight-year decorative program. It now houses the Museo e Archivio Vasariano, a collection acquired by the state in 1911. It features works by Vasari and his contemporaries. The family archives include correspondence from Michelangelo. The collection displays works by Aurelio Lomi, Franceso Vanni, Raimondo Zaballi, Alessandro Allori, Il Poppi, Il Doceno, and Andrea Sansovino. The most notable of Vasari's own works are the ceiling paintings in the

Camera D'Apollo of *Virtue, Envy, and Fortune* and a *Deposition*.

The **MUSEO D'ARTE MEDIOVALE E MODERNA** houses a collection of local and Tuscan art from the 14th century through the 19th century. The works are arranged chronologically, beginning with a courtyard of medieval sculpture including two 14th-century Madonnas taken from the city gates. The gallery displays a *St. Francis* by Margarito d'Arezzo and 14th-century works by locals Spinello Aretino and Parri di Spinello. Bartolomeo della Gatta painted a *St. Roch* as part of an offering for the saint's intercession during the Black Death. The collection includes art from the Renaissance to the 19th-century Macchiaoli painters. Highlights are works by Vasari, Signorelli, Dolci, Benvenuti, Fattori, and Signorini. On the

upper floor is the famous Aretine pottery and 14th- to 18th-century majolica ceramics.

A city park and former monastery mark the site of a **ROMAN AMPHITHEATRE AND MUSEO ARCHEOLOGICO MECANTE**. The small amphitheatre (117–38 A.D.) accommodated between 8,000 and 10,000 spectators. The curved ruins form the foundation for the Monastery of San Bernardo (1547). The convent now houses the archaeological museum. The collection includes Paleolithic, Neolithic, Archaic, Hellenistic, Etruscan, and Roman finds from the region. It also houses a collection of the famous Aretine *coralino* vases. Crafted locally from 50–70 A.D., the shiny red glazed ceramics and the tools used to produce them reveal the height of industry in Roman Arretium.

ASSISI

Long before Assisi experienced a spiritual awakening with the rise of monastic movements in the 11th century, the natural peace and solitude of the town on the rise of Mount Subasio offered spiritual serenity. Assisi was originally occupied by the Umbri (from whom the region gets its name) and later the Etruscans, the Romans, the Goths, and the Longobards. Today, Assisi's permanent occupants are outnumbered by pilgrims coming from all

over the world in devotion to St. Francis, the lover of nature and animals and patron saint of Italy (an honor he shares with St. Catherine of Siena).

While the Benedictine order attracted much development and growth to Assisi prior to 1000, it is to St. Francis (1182–1226) that the town owes its fame.

PLACES TO VISIT

The **BASILICA DI SAN FRANCESCO** was built in honor of St. Francis and the event of his canonization. The site

FRANCIS OF ASSISI (1182–1226) was the founder of the mendicant order

of the Franciscans to whom we attribute the glory of Assisi. Born to a wealthy merchant couple, St. Francis was christened Giovanni Battista. It is uncertain why he was called Francesco, but it was possibly in tribute to the source of his father's wealth; Pietro Bernardone traded cloth in France, or in honor of his French mother, Pica. In his youth Francis led a decadent, privileged life. At twenty years old he gained military experience fighting in a civil war against neighboring Perugia. Assisi was defeated, and Francis was captured and spent a year in prison. After his release he set out on another military campaign. The night before his command set forth, Francis had two dreams; the first was of a vast hall covered with armor decorated with crosses, and in the second dream a voice told him to turn back. Francis heeded the voice in his dream and in 1206, on his return home, he experienced a remarkable conversion. Francis stopped to pray at the small church of San Damiano just outside Assisi. While he was kneeling before the altar crucifix, a voice said to him, "Go, Francis, and repair my house, which is falling into ruin." Francis repaired the church and two neighboring churches, San Pietro della Spina and the Porziuncola. At the same time, he abandoned his father's wealth and devoted himself to a life of prayer and poverty. Twelve followers gathered around Francis, and together they dedicated themselves to the imitation of Christ's life.

In 1210, Pope Innocent III approved Francis's *Regula Prima* (the rule for the order's vows of poverty, chastity, and obedience). Franciscan influence quickly spread through Italy and beyond. In 1212, in collaboration with St. Clare, a nun moved by the spirit of Francis, he founded a female branch of the order, the Minoresses or the Poor Clares. In 1219, Francis joined the crusades in Egypt in hopes to convert the Saracens and the sultan Malek-el-Kamel. In 1223, Pope Honorius III officially recognized the order within the Church and approved Francis's *Regula Bullata*.

In the last years of his life Francis became gravely ill and increasingly blind; however, his physical limitations were compensated for by a spiritual climax. In 1224 he composed the Canticle of the Sun when visiting Clare, and on September 14 of the same year he received the stigmata on Mount La Verna.

On October 3, 1226, at age 45, Francis died. He was temporarily buried in San Gregorio, but in 1230 was transported to the newly finished lower church of the Basilica of St. Francis. Francis's biographers Tomaso da Celano in Vita Prima (1230) and St. Bonaventura in Legenda Maggiore (1263) outline the life of the saint, his devotion to poverty and obedience, and his works modeled on the life of Christ. On July 16, 1228, Pope Gregory IX canonized Francis. Pope Innocent IV consecrated the Basilica of St. Francis in 1253. In 1754 Pope Benedict XIV elevated the church to Patriarchal Basilica and Papal Chapel.

Francis chose for his tomb, also chosen for his church, was the city's place for executions known as "Hell's Hill." Now known as "Paradise Hill," Francis chose this spot to parallel the site of Christ's crucifixion, Golgotha (the place of the skull).

The two-story, T-shaped basilica was built in two phases; the lower church was built between 1228 and 1230, and the upper church was constructed from 1230 to 1253. The architect is unknown but it is likely that Brother Elia, one of Francis's closest followers, oversaw the construction. The Gothic facade of the upper church is decorated with simple, noble lions and a double rose window framed by carvings of the symbols of the Evangelists.

The facade of the lower church echoes the simplicity of the upper church facade. Above the double portal is a mosaic of Francis giving a blessing; this blessing is extended to all who enter his church. Inside the lower church the combination of Gothic and Romanesque construction conveys the solidity and weight of Francis's faith.

The walls of the lower nave are the first frescoes to decorate the basilica. Painted in 1236 by the "Master of St. Francis," they represent the story of Christ (right) and the story of Francis (left).

Midway along the nave are stairs that descend to the crypt. Francis's body was proudly transported here in 1230, and his sarcophagus was on display until the end of the 15th century. The crypt was closed during a Perugian onslaught and remained inaccessible until it was rediscovered in 1818. Ugo Tarchi transformed the crypt between 1925 and 1932. In a simple urn atop the crypt altar are St. Francis's remains. The surrounding niches hold the remains of his four faithful companions, the blessed Leone, Rufino, Masseo, and Angelo. The alabaster and bronze votive lantern was added in 1939 by the Comuni d'Italia (the Communities of Italy), a gift to the patron saint of the nation.

A window behind the main altar directly above the crypt provides a bird's-eye view of the saint's tomb. Columns with floral capitals and mosaic arches frame the altar. The decorated vault above is divided into four sections and represents the *Allegory of Poverty,* the *Allegory of Chastity,* the *Allegory of Obedience,* and the *Apotheosis of Francis.* The choir is splendidly decorated with intaglio and intarsia, and above it is a *Last Judgment* (1623).

Look for Cimabue's *Madonna and Child Enthroned with Four Angels and St. Francis* in the right transept and Pietro Lorenzetti's *Deposition and Crucifixion* in the opposite left transept. The side chapels are a later addition to the completed lower basilica. Giotto, Cimabue, Dono Doni, Cesare Sermei, and Pietro and Ambrogio Lorenzetti are a few of the artists who worked on these chapels. The CAPPELLA DI SAN MARTINO (1322–26) is a masterwork by Simone Martini depicting the story and life of St. Martin with mysticism and grace.

Proceed to the upper church from a staircase in the lower right transept. The ascension from the austere, dark lower church into the light upper church is both physically and spiritually uplifting. In the right transept is Cimabue's *Life and Crucifixion of St. Peter.* Cimabue's work continues through the apse with the *Story of Mary.* In the left transept five apocalyptic scenes are preceded by the famous negative image of Cimabue's *Crucifixion,* a dramatic composition that has unfortunately oxidized and turned black due to the white lead content in his paint.

The four evangelists decorate the vault above the main altar. Each is depicted writing the gospels with a fictive vista of the region they evangelized before them: Matthew (Judea), John (Asia), Luke (Greece), and Mark (Italy).

The nave decoration is divided into two tiers, the upper and lower walls. The upper wall, decorated by Jacopo Torriti and the "Isaac Master" includes 34 frescoes depicting Old Testament stories (right wall) and New Testament stories (left wall). Twenty-eight scenes of the life of St. Francis decorate the lower walls. (Vasari traditionally attributed the Francis cycle to Giotto; however, the authorship of the fresco cycle is controversial.) Man is the link between the three cycles of painting on the walls. In the Old Testament scenes Adam is the first man, in the New Testament scenes Christ is the second man, and in the Francis cycle, Francis is the model man who conformed his life to the life of Christ.

Visit the TREASURY and PERKINS COLLECTION to view relics, liturgical objects, and artworks. For a history of the basilica and the adjoining sacred convent, venture into the treasury. It also houses cherished relics, among them a chalice used by Francis, a stone on which Francis rested his head, the saint's sandals, and his robe. The Perkins Collection, which includes objects and paintings from the 14th–16th centuries, enhances these articles. Of note are works by Fra Angelico and Luca Signorelli.

The CATTEDRALE DI SAN RUFINO (12th century) is dedicated to the first evangelist in the area, Assisi's 3rd-century bishop and martyr, St. Ruffin. Originally erected in the 8th century, it was reconstructed in the 1100s and consecrated by Pope Innocent IV in 1253. The adjoining campanile is 11th century and abuts the house of St. Clare.

Carved lions and griffins guard the church entrance. A lunette above the imposing guardians depicts Christ enthroned between the sun and moon, flanked by the Madonna and San Rufino.

The Baroque interior contrasts the austere Romanesque facade. Renovated in 1571, chapels within the church were decorated by Giorgetti, Dono Doni, Giovanni Duprè, and Amalia Duprè. Fortunately, the original baptismal font remains and stands to the right of the

A

church entrance. St. Francis and St. Clare were both baptized here.

Fittingly, the BASILICA DI SANTA CHIARA (1257) is modeled on the forms of the upper Basilica of St. Francis, just as Clare herself chose St. Francis's life of poverty and humility as the model for her own life. Born in Assisi to a noble family in 1194, Clare renounced her wealth and status and ran away from home to enter monastic life.

As cofounder with St. Francis of the order of the Poor Clares, she devoted herself to God. Her order spread quickly through Europe, but her first followers were those closest to her, her mother and sisters. Clare died in 1253 and was canonized by Pope Alexander IV in 1255. Curiously, in 1958 Pope Pius XII named her the patron of television based on her accurate vision of the Christmas Mass in the Basilica of St. Francis while she was bedridden in her convent miles away.

Clare's Gothic church follows a simple Latin cross plan. The focal point is the 13th-century *Crucifix* behind the main altar by the "Master of St. Clare," creator of other significant icons in the church. The frescoed vaults above the main altar praise female models of Christian purity, among them the Madonna, St. Clare, St. Agnes, St. Catherine, and St. Lucy. In the left transept is a notable 14th-century *Nativity* and in the right transept is the *Story of St. Clare.* The church relics include the urn containing St. Clare's body and the crucifix that spoke to Francis.

The CHIESA DI SAN FRANCESCO PICCOLINO is built on the site traditionally believed to be St. Francis's parental home. According to legend, Francis's mother, Pica, was guided to the stall by a mysterious pilgrim and gave birth to her son in the straw. Inscribed before the antique entrance arch is the following: *Hoc oratorium fuit bovis et asini stabulum, in quo natus est B. Franciscus mundi speculum* (this oratory is the stall of a bull and an ass, in this place was born blessed Francis, mirror of the world).

The TEMPLE OF MINERVA AND ROMAN FORUM, the heart of 1st-century Assisi, remains the heart of the city today, opening out onto the main piazza. The Corinthian-columned temple was turned into a Baroque church. Within, the 11th-century crypt of San Nicolò (Nicholas) houses the archaeological collection that includes urns, inscriptions, and architectural fragments. The forum was discovered five meters under the ground level of the piazza in the 19th century. Traces of the wall, floor, cisterns, and stairs to the temple can be seen. On the supporting walls of the temple names of the various city magistrates can still be read.

Visit the PINACOTECA CIVICA, a collection of frescoes by significant Umbrian artists from the 14th to 16th centuries that was assembled late in the 1800s. Important artists include Ottaviano Nelli, Tiberio d'Assisi, Niccolò Alunno, and Dono Doni. The OSSERVATORIO CHRISTIANO documents the pres-

B

ence of Christ in literature, the figurative arts, music, and cinema. It boasts a 45,000-volume library and houses a collection of contemporary sacred art with works by Carpi, Carrà, DeChirico, and Pirandello, to name a few.

As you walk through Assisi's main streets, notice that the houses with steps leading off the main road have two doors. The first door is the main entrance, and the second door, often higher and narrower, is walled up and called the "door of the dead." According to tradition, it is opened to take the dead out of the house and then immediately resealed.

If you have time, venture 2.5 miles east of Assisi to the **EREMEO DELLE CARCERI** (Prison's Hermitage). This is where Francis and his followers came for solace and prayer. It is not a prison, but a spiritual retreat. The Franciscan friars living there are excellent guides through the site's small frescoed church and grotto.

BARI

Bari, a prized medieval seaport, is divided into two sections: the historically rich pre–19th-century city and the sprawling post–19th-century modern city. The labyrinthlike *Città Vecchia* (Old City) starkly contrasts the orderly grid plan that defines the *Città Nuova* (New City). Bari's indispensable port assured its growth and prosperity; it also meant all the European powers would seek to control it. The city thrived during the 11th century, rivaling Venice's cosmopolitan port. It emerged as an important religious center at the end of the century, hosting the Council of Bari in 1098. At the gathering, St. Inseam defended the Doctrine of the Procession of the Holy Ghost. Perhaps Bari is best known as the final resting place for the relics of St. Nicholas (Santa Claus).

Founded by the Illyrians, ancient *Barium* passed from the Romans to the Ostrogoths, to the Byzantines, to the Lombards, and to the Saracens before it was known as the "doorway to the East" in the 10th century. Confident in the city's commercial importance, Bari was both rival to and ally of Venice. In 1071, Bari fell to the Normans under Robert Guiscard and inaugurated its most prosperous period.

In 1087, 47 Barese sailors raided the city of Myra in Asia Minor and successfully abducted the relics of St. Nicholas of Myra (d. 326), the patron of Russia. The Myrans were outraged, as were the Venetians, who intended to pilfer the remains of this generous, child-loving saint for themselves. To celebrate the arrival of San Nicola and the sailors' cunning, the Baresi hold festivals on May 8 and December 6

B

(Nicola's feast day). The spring festival includes a parade through the streets and a procession on the sea, the Processione dei Pellegrini (the Procession of the Pilgrims) that culminates in a reenactment of the saint's arrival in Bari. St. Nicholas's legend soon merged with the Christmas tradition for three reasons: his feast day is near Christ's birth, his gift of three bags of gold to an impoverished nobleman's daughter was likened to the three Magi bringing gifts to Christ, and he showed many kindnesses to children.

When William the Bad retaliated against a local uprising in 1156 he demolished the city; all that remained standing was the shrine of St. Nicholas.

PLACES TO VISIT

The BASILICA DI SAN NICOLA (1087–1197) enshrines the remains of St. Nicholas of Myra, the patron saint of children more popularly known in the West as Santa Claus. Legend tells that St. Nicholas, while staying at an inn, discovered that the proprietor was stealing children, killing them, and serving them to his guests. Nicholas found three chopped-up bodies preserved in brine and returned them to life and wholeness by making the sign of the cross.

Frescoes within the church depict the above resurrection scene and other miracles attributed to St. Nicholas. The crypt contains the relics of St. Nicholas, which exude a miraculous fluid the Baresi call "manna." Since its construc-

tion, pilgrims to the church have included both Catholics and Orthodox Christians journeying to see Nicholas's venerable relics.

The beautifully carved *bishop's throne* (11th century) stands in the apse. It was likely carved for the Council of Bari. The medieval work depicts three figures supporting the throne in the front, while two lions carry the weight in the back.

The CATHEDRAL OF BARI (12th century) was reconstructed after William the Bad razed the city in 1156. It stands atop an early Christian basilica (8th–10th centuries); the remains of its mosaic pavement are seen in the south apse. Masterfully detailed rose windows and doors in the cathedral facade depict Oriental-inspired flora and fauna.

Inside is the unique circular basin called a *trulla*. Once used as a baptistery (11th century), it now functions as the sacristy (17th century). Do not miss the bishop's throne, ciborium, and pulpit, all reconstructed from original fragments after the Norman destruction.

The church archive houses precious documents, including an 11th-century *exultet* and numerous illuminated manuscripts.

The PINACOTECA PROVINCIALE contains Southern Italian art and a number of Venetian works. Of note are Giovanni Bellini's *St. Peter Martyr*, Paris Bordone's *Sacra Conversazione*, Paolo Veronese's *Virgin in Glory with Saints*, and Tintoretto's *St. Roch*.

CAMALDOLI

The Forest of Camaldoli provides the ideal setting for the Monastero di Camaldoli; its serene woods encourage contemplation and reflection—it is a haven for the hermetic life of the Camaldolese Order. The care of the Camaldoli woods and its variety of species (silver furs, beech, manna ash, and ilex among them) fell to the monks, and the area is now part of the national park, the Foreste Casentinesi.

In 1012, St. Romualdo, a Benedictine monk from Ravenna, founded the Order of Camaldoli, the fulfillment of a vision in which he was instructed to create a hermetic community in service to God. According to legend, while seeking a location St. Romualdo dreamed of white-clad men climbing a ladder from earth that reached the heavens. The beautiful and remote wooded hills of Casentino fulfilled the dream location. Here he founded the Monastery of Camaldoli (named after Count Maldoli who bequeathed the land) and clothed his monks in white robes.

PLACES TO VISIT

The EREMEO DI CAMALDOLI (Camaldoli Hermitage) built in 1012 is a complex with 20 separate living quarters, each with a private chapel and garden in order to ensure a secluded existence for each monk. The complex also included a church for communal worship. The church was rebuilt in the 13th and 18th centuries, and its rich Baroque decoration (1669) and elaborate ceiling frescoes (17th century) contrast the severe monk's cells. Atop the high altar is the *Crucifixion and Four Saints* by Bronzino. Look for Andrea della Robbia's tabernacle, the *Madonna and Child with Saints*. In the chapter house is a modern painting by Augusto Mussini of *St. Romualdo and His Disciples in the Forest* (1915).

By 1046, the popularity and beauty of the site as a layman's retreat rose and threatened the idyllic hermetic solitude. In response, St. Romualdo built a monastery and hospital one kilometer down the mountain for visitors and pilgrims, thus preserving his solitary community from the temptation and corruption of the outside world.

The cloister and church were built in 1100, and the church was subsequently rebuilt. Paintings by Giorgio Vasari including the *Deposition*, the *Nativity*, and the *Madonna with St. John the Baptist* decorate the church.

In 1046 a hospital was built; within its walls is the famed ANTICA FARMACIA (Old Pharmacy) from 1543. Here the monks sell products they have made for centuries: medicines, herbal teas, liqueurs, and natural toiletries—all part of their self-sufficient existence.

While visiting take advantage of the numerous pathways and trails carved through the forest. Perhaps a contemplative walk will encourage you to stay at the monastery for a spiritual retreat.

C

BENEDICT OF NURSIA (480–547) was the founder of Western monasticism and author of *The Rule of St. Benedict.* He was sent to Rome to study, but revolted by the degenerate life of the capital, he fled to a cave near Subiaco, where he became a hermit. Later he established the monastery of Monte Cassino, where he remained until his death.

CERTOSA DI PAVIA

Experience sacred splendor on a day's excursion from Milan at the Certosa, or Charterhouse of Pavia. Here, contemplation and opulence unite. The Carthusian vow of silence adopted by the monks originally occupying the complex is maintained by Cistercian monks who returned to the monastery in the 1960s after almost 200 years of vacancy.

PLACES TO VISIT

Commissioned by Gian Galeazzo Visconti, the **CHARTERHOUSE** construction continued 200 years after its patron laid the first cornerstone in 1396. A guided tour led by a resident monk is the best way to view the complex. The dazzling yet surprisingly incomplete church facade (1473) is a dizzying visual

feat. Designed by Giovanni Antonio Amadeo (lower section) and Cristoforo Lombardo (upper section), the elegant Renaissance structure stands alongside the Baroque Forestiera (1625), or guesthouse, by Francesco Maria Ricchino.

Works within the **CHURCH** are as sumptuous as the exterior. Among the masterful paintings and frescoes is Perugino's *God the Father* (1499), Bergognone's *Crucifixion,* and a *Virgin and Child* by Bernardino Luini.

The **SMALL CLOISTER** (1466) houses terra-cotta works and offers a beautiful view of the church dome. The large cloister is divided into 24 monks' cells each equipped with a private chapel and walled garden. While each monk's cell includes a dining area, the frescoed refectory is where they gather together to eat in silence.

CHIUSI

Today, rich Etruscan remains attract throngs of visitors to Chiusi, but in Roman times its attraction was as a seemingly safe haven for Christians fleeing pagan Rome. Its ancient Roman legacy is linked to the plight of the early Christians and the origins of the Church in Tuscany.

A powerful member of the League of Twelve, Chiusi (Etruscan Camar) rose in strength under King Porsenna (507 B.C.) to battle and subjugate Rome. Its Roman domination was brief, and by 296 B.C. it succumbed to Roman rule and was renamed Clusium. Its link to Rome was the catalyst for Tuscan Christianization.

In the 3rd century, Mustiola, a devoutly Christian Roman girl, fled Rome and the amorous emperor Aurelian, to Chiusi. She was accompanied by a priest and a deacon, Felice and Irenaeus. Their flight enraged the emperor and resulted in their persecution. In July 274, Mustiola was lashed to death with a studded whip. The local bishop rescued her body and buried it in the nearby catacombs. She was named patron saint of Chiusi.

PLACES TO VISIT

The oldest cathedral in Tuscany, SAN SECONDIANO dates to early Christian origins in the 4th century. It was destroyed and rebuilt in the 6th century by a local bishop. Destroyed a second time and rebuilt to its original plan in the 12th century, it was again restored between 1887 and 1894. The adjacent campanile (1585) was a medieval defense tower constructed over a Roman cistern.

Parts of the original Roman structure are incorporated into the interior columns and capitals. A monument was erected to Santa Mustiola in 1785, and during the 19th-century renovation, Arturo Viligiardi painted imitation mosaic on the nave walls and apses. Original Roman mosaics can be seen under the high altar.

The MUSEO DEL CATTEDRALE contains 3rd–5th-century inscriptions from nearby catacombs. Its most significant work includes 21 antiphonals (choir books) from the Abbey of Monte Oliveto Maggiore, illuminated in the 15th century by Liberale da Verona, Sano di Pietro, and others.

The 3rd–5th-century CATACOMBS are filled with early Christian inscriptions and art, attesting to the large Christian presence in Chiusi. The earliest and most intricate, the catacomb of Santa Mustiola, was discovered in 1634, while the catacomb of Santa Caterina was found in 1848.

CITTÀ DI CASTELLO

Legendary happiness has long been attributed to Città di Castello. It lies in the Umbrian valley enroute to Tuscany and benefits from the best of both regions; vineyards, olive groves, and farmhouses are abundant in the surrounding countryside. However, the abundance that contributes to its happiness may not be attributed to its agriculture but to its marvelous collection of art in its churches and museums.

Romans knew Città di Castello as *Tibernium*. It owes its Christian origins to the Roman soldier, Crescentius, who spread the word of Christ in the area and was later sanctified. Christian legend labels this event as the beginning of the town's true happiness. Bishop Florido, who helped rebuild the flourishing city in the 6th century, after Totila destroyed it, augmented this happiness. During this period of rebirth the city was called Castrum Felicitas—the castle of happiness. In the 10th century it was known as Civitas Castelli and was torn between Tuscan and Umbrian struggle for its ownership until it finally fell into the hands of the church.

PLACES TO VISIT

The 11th-century DUOMO, dedicated to Saints Florido and Amanzio, was enlarged in 1356 and completely reconstructed between 1466 and 1529. Carved representations of *Justice, Mercy,* and scenes of the *Life of Mary* grace the left facade of the church, while the true facade, begun in 1632, remains unfinished.

A wooden choir (1540) in the presbytery is decorated with stories of the patron saint of the city (San Florido) and stories from the Old and New Testaments.

A moving *Transfiguration* in the left transept is the work of Rosso Fiorentino.

The MUSEO DEL DUOMO is through the right transept. Within, a *Madonna and Child with the Infant St. John* by Pinturicchio hangs in a dark corridor that leads to one of the best collections of sacred art in Italy. The TREASURE OF CANOSCIO is a collection of Paleo-Christian liturgical objects found in 1934. Found in the nearby Sanctuary of Canoscio, it includes a 16th-century agate cross, a precious 15th-century altar frontal, and a tablet depicting *Christ Blessing, Symbols of the Eucharist, The Annunciation, The Visitation, The Epiphany, The Presentation in the Temple, The Flight into Egypt, The Betrayal,* and *The Crucifixion.* The treasure was taken to Rome and would have remained there if not for a local bishop who appealed to Mussolini for its return.

The **PINACOTECA** in the Palazzo Vitelli alla Cannoniera houses a collection of Umbrian art second only to the one in Perugia. While Città di Castello did not produce any notable local artists, its residents' love for art compensated for it. Early Sienese and Umbrian works include numerous representations of the *Madonna and Child* by Neri di Bicci, Bartolo di Fredi, Antonio da Ferrara, and Spinello Aretino. In a room dedicated to Luca Signorelli is one of the artist's earlier works, a *St. John the Baptist* accompanied by works attributed to Signorelli's school, including the *Eternal Father, The Martyrdom of St. Sebastian,* and the *Conversion of St. Cecelia.* Highlights in the collection include Raphael's *Creation of Eve* and *Crucifixion with St. Roch and St. Sebastian* and a *Coronation of the Virgin* by Ghirlandaio. A large ceramic *Nativity* and an *Adoration of the Virgin* by Andrea della Robbia are also of note.

CORTONA

Cortona commands a breathtaking view of the Chiana Valley and neighboring Umbria's Lake Trasimeno. Built atop a steep hillside surrounded by olive trees and grapevines, Cortona seems to hover on a cloud of groves and vineyards. Proud citizens can link their ancestry to the founders of Troy and Rome; tradition claims that Cortona is the "Mother of Troy and the Grandmother of Rome." According to legend, Dardanus, the founder of Troy, who dropped his helmet here while battling a rival, christened the city Corito. The word for helmet is *corythos,* and the subsequent town Corito grew up where the corythos fell.

Cortona's citizens, past and present, are known for their particular reverence for St. Francis and his companion, Brother Elias, a Cortonan native.

In the 4th century B.C., Cortona was one of the 12 cities of the Etruscan League. By the end of the 3rd century B.C., it was a Roman colony. During the Middle Ages it suffered both external and internal strife, intertwined in battles against neighboring Perugia, Arezzo, and Siena and in local squabbles between Guelf and Ghibelline families. In 1409, it was captured by the king of Naples and subsequently sold in 1411 to Florence.

During the 14th and 15th centuries, Cortona was a center for artistic production, attracting a wealth of artists, including Sassetta and Fra Angelico. The city is also the birthplace of three renowned artists: Luca Signorelli (1441–1523), Pietro da Cortona (1596–1669), and Gino Severini (1883–1966).

PLACES TO VISIT

C

Built primarily by Giuliano da Sangallo in 1560, the DUOMO stands atop the remains of an 11th-century Romanesque church. Ruins from the earlier church are incorporated into the facade.

Numerous artists contributed works to the beautiful barrel-vaulted interior. The treasure of works includes Rafaello Vanni's *Transfiguration*, Lorenzo Berrettini's *Death of St. Joseph*, Luca Signorelli's *Crucifixion*, Francesco Signorelli's *Incredulity of Thomas*, Bronzino's *Madonna of the Holy Girdle*, and Andrea del Sarto's *Adoration of the Shepherds*. Local talent includes an *Adoration of the Shepherds* by Pietro da Cortona and a mosaic by Gino Severini.

Across from the Duomo, the deconsecrated church of Gesù houses the MUSEO DIOCESIANO. The Jesuit structure, built between 1498 and 1505, is built atop another church. Among the museum's masterpieces is a Roman sarcophagus (A.D. 200) carved with a dramatic battle scene that was studied and copied by Donatello and Brunelleschi. The former church is graced with a number of works: Pietro Lorenzetti's *Crucifixion* (1320), Fra Angelico's *Madonna Enthroned with Saints* (1437) and *Annunciation* (1428–30), Bartolomeo della Gatta's *Assumption of the Virgin* (1475), and Luca Signorelli's *Deposition* (1502) and *Communion of the Apostles* (signed and dated 1512). According to Vasari, Signorelli's son was the model for Christ.

Brother Elias, who is entombed in its crypt, founded the church of SAN FRANCESCO in 1223. It was the first Franciscan church built outside Assisi. It was constructed to hold a priceless relic—a piece of the True Cross brought from Constantinople by Brother Elias. Encased in a Byzantine ivory reliquary inscribed in Greek, the relic rests atop the main altar. The church marks an end for more than one native son; not only is Brother Elias entombed here, but Luca Signorelli's (d. 1523) tomb is believed to be beneath the crypt. While he was not buried here, Pietro da Cortona's last and unfinished work, the *Annunciation*, hangs in the north aisle.

A custodian will let you into the small church of SAN NICOLÒ (15th century). An enclosed cypress garden faces the church's ionic columned porch, a 1930 addition. Inside is a two-sided altarpiece by Luca Signorelli depicting a *Deposition* (visible side) and a *Madonna and Child* (turned to view on request).

The neo-Gothic church SANTUARIO DI SANTA MARGHERITA (1856–97) was built atop an earlier church (1247–97) dedicated to St. Margaret of Cortona. Inside is the saint's vacant Gothic tomb (1362); her body lies encased on the main altar for all to view.

The descent from this church (the highest point in the city) to the town follows the VIA CRUCIS (Way of the Cross) built in 1947. A decorative mosaic winding alongside the street by Gino Severini represents the *Stations of the Cross*.

Gino Severini also contributed work to SAN MARCO. The facade of the lower church is decorated with his mosaic of ST. MARK. The upper church contains a beautiful altar (17th century) sculpted by Andrea Sellari.

The eclectic collection in the MUSEO DELL'ACCADEMIA ETRUSCA is far more broad than its name suggests. Works include Etruscan and Roman remains from the 6th to 1st centuries, Renaissance and Baroque paintings, Egyptian sarcophagi, and rare treasures from almost every century. It is also the site of the famed Accademia Etrusca (Etruscan Academy), founded in 1727 for archaeological and historical research and boasting Montesquieu and Voltaire among its early members.

The eclectic collection offers something for all. Do not miss the Paleo-Christian glass chalice (4th–5th century A.D.), the 15th-century ivories, a 12th-century mosaic of the *Madonna,* painted *Madonnas* by Pinturicchio and Signorelli, and Pietro da Cortona's *Virgin and Child with Saints.* The last room is dedicated to native Gino Severini's works.

Important sites lie just outside Cortona's walls. Built on the site of a former limestone quarry and tannery is SANTA MARIA DELLE GRAZIE AL CALCINAIO, an archetypal Renaissance church. The elegantly proportioned structure (1485–1513) is the only work certainly planned by the architect Francesco di Giorgio Martini. The church was commissioned by the Arte dei Calzolai (the shoemaker's guild) after a miraculous vision of the Madonna appeared on the wall of the tannery to a worker (calcinaio).

The venerated miraculous image of the Madonna stands over the main altar. In 1516, Guillaume de Marcillat contributed a rose window to the exterior representing the *Madonna of Mercy.* In the church, be sure to see Bronzino's 16th-century *Madonna and Child with Saints.*

Yet another model Renaissance structure is the church of SANTA MARIA NUOVA. Designed by Giovanni Battista Infregliati, construction was continued by Cristofanello (1550–54) and Vasari, who contributed the cupola. Bronzino's *Birth of the Virgin* crowns the altar and complements the serene interior.

Fra Angelico was a member of the Dominican friary originally housed in the church of SAN DOMENICO. Above the portal is a faded fresco depicting the *Madonna and Child Between Two Dominican Friars* by the monk's hand. A number of significant works within include Luca Signorelli's *Madonna with Angels and Saints,* Lorenzo di Niccolò Gerini's *Coronation of the Virgin* (signed and dated 1402), and an *Assumption* by Bartolomeo della Gatta.

Along the picturesque slopes of Monte Sant'Egidio is the CONVENTO DELLE CELLE, a hermitage likely founded by St. Francis in 1210 on return from Rome. The serenity of Le Celle appealed to St. Francis and his followers. The present building is a Capuchin convent built in 1537. It encloses and preserves the Franciscan structures, providing the visitor the opportunity to see Francis's small cell and stone bed behind the altar.

EMPOLI

E

Industrial Empoli is known for two things: its excellent art collection in the Museo della Collegiata, and its glassworks, specializing in green glass production. Visitors will recognize the wine *fiasco* (wine bottle with straw-wrapped base) produced locally. The city is the birthplace of the painter Jacopo Chimenti (1551–1640), known as Empoli, and Ferruccio Busoni (1866–1924), a composer and pianist to whom the citizens have dedicated an annual festival of piano music held in October and November.

First documented in the 8th century, Empoli's heart is the 12th-century church of Sant'Andrea. It benefited from the rise of wealth, industry, and Florentine allegiance. In 1260, after the Ghibelline victory at the Battle of Montaperti, it was in Empoli that Florentine deserter Farinata degli Uberti insisted Florence not be burned to the ground. As a result, the Guelfs soon regained power, and in 1283 they condemned Farinata of heresy. Dante placed Farinata in the sixth circle of hell, among the heretics, ironically in an eternally burning tomb (Inferno, Canto X).

PLACES TO VISIT

Begun in 1093, documents attest to the existence of the COLLEGIATA DI SANT'ANDREA in 780. Ironically, the part of the church that is truly revered and that receives most visitors is the museum! The MUSEO DELLA COLLEGIATA DI SANT'ANDREA was founded in 1859 and houses Tuscan sculptures, paintings, and frescoes. The collection offers a font (1447) by Bernardo Rossellino, the frescoed *Christ in Pietà* (1424–25) by Masolino, a *Madonna and Child* by Mino da Fiesole, a wooden statue of *St. Stephen* (signed and dated 1403) by Francesco di Valdambrino, the *Madonna of Humility with Four Saints* (1404) by Lorenzo Monaco, and the *Tabernacle of St. Sebastian* (1475) sculpted by Antonio Rossellino, with paintings by Francesco Botticini.

The Augustines in the 11th century founded the church of SANTO STEFANO DEGLI AGOSTINIANI (14th century). It houses prized fragmentary frescoes by Masolino depicting the *Legend of the True Cross* (1424). They were destroyed in 1792; fortunately the sinopia underdrawings remain. Do not miss two 15th-century statues of the *Annunciation* by Bernardo Rossellino and Bicci di Lorenzo's painting of *St. Nicholas of Tolentino Protecting Empoli from the Plague* (1445).

FIRENZE
(FLORENCE)

Florentine aspiration and achievement is truly represented by the city's patrons and symbols: Mars, Hercules, St. John the Baptist, David, and the lily. The bellicose god of war, the hero of antiquity, the messenger of Christ, the triumphant shepherd boy, and the Christian symbol of purity define the proud Florentine identity. Crowning civic pride is the glorious cathedral dome, dominating Florence and exalting not only God and the city but also man.

The belief in human potential, the aspiration to perfection, and the rediscovery and renewed study of ancient literature aligned with the privilege of prosperity in Florence furnished the apex of human creativity. The 15th-century Florentine Renaissance fostered an active intellectual and cultural environment where art, science, and philosophy flourished. Florence is the western link between the ancient and modern world.

In 59 B.C. Julius Caesar founded the Roman colony "Florentia," the city rich in flowers, which likely derived its name not from an abundance of flora but from the Roman general Florinus who died in an attack on nearby Fiesole. Florence asserted little influence in the Middle Ages; it was besieged by invaders and eventually fell under Lombard domination. In 786 Charlemagne visited Florence, and 100 years later the city's third circle of walls, the Carolingian walls, were completed. A fourth set of walls built in 1078 marks the patronage of Countess Matilda, the margrave of Tuscany, whose alliance with Pope Gregory VIII influenced the Florentines to rally with the pope against the Holy Roman Emperor, Henry IV.

In the 12th century, self-governing Florence prospered under the growing cloth and money-lending trades. Their success necessitated the rise of guilds in the interests of Florentine tradesmen, professionals, and artists. By the end of the 13th century, the major guilds ruled Florence.

Feuding Guelfs and Ghibellines also dominated the period's politics. The largely Guelf merchant classes aligned themselves with the pope in hopes of preserving their commercial interests from imperial interference. Conversely, the Ghibelline nobility supported the emperor and the prospect of exerting imperial control to subdue the rising merchant class.

Guelf and Ghibelline tension rose, and Florentine power passed between the two factions. The struggles were marked by the Ghibelline victory at the Battle of Montaperti in 1260 and the

> **GUELFS AND GHIBELLINES:** Guelf and Ghibelline are Italian corruptions of German words: Guelf was derived from the German family named Welf; Ghibelline from Waiblingen, the name of a fortress belonging to the House of Hohenstaufen. The Guelfs were identified as supporters of the papacy, the Ghibellines as the imperial, anti-papal party.

F

Guelf victory in 1289 at the Battle of Campaldino. Prosperity and growth continued despite political instability. Although internal and external wars plagued the city, Florence initiated a building program that would proclaim its glory.

The mendicant orders also came to 13th-century Florence. A renewed push towards piety and morality accompanied their arrival. In 1240 the popular Patarene sect sought to reform Florence; they named their own bishop and sought to eradicate evil and eliminate immorality. Four years later the Church condemned the Patarenes. St. Peter Martyr led his fellow Dominicans in zealous pursuit of the heretics and eliminated the sect.

In the 14th century calamity struck Florence. In 1306 a disastrous fire ravaged the city; famine visited from 1315–17; the Arno flooded in 1333; in 1339 King Edward III of England, unable to repay his debts, sent two of Florence's most lucrative banking families into bankruptcy; and in 1348 the Black Death decimated the population, only to return for more victims in 1350 and 1430.

Fortunately, by the beginning of the 15th century Florence had more than recuperated. It was recognized as the European center of artistic and intellectual activity. Medician power and patronage had been established with Giovanni di Bicci de' Medici (1360–1429), who founded the most successful bank in Florence. The Medici bank controlled papal finances, and the resulting Medician prosperity would soon embellish the city. Cosimo de' Medici "the Elder" (1389–1464) and his grandson Lorenzo de' Medici "il Magnifico" (1449–92) were civic leaders, foreign and domestic ambassadors, humanists, and art patrons whose guidance brought relative peace and great wealth to Florence.

While scholars and artists flocked to the bustling city, so too did those wishing to usurp Medician power. In 1478, after years of trying to take over alum mines in Imola from Medici control, Pope Sixtus IV ordered that the uncooperative parties be murdered. Lorenzo and Giuliano de' Medici were to be killed on Sunday, April 26, while they celebrated Mass in Florence's cathedral. Allied with the Pazzi family (longtime Medici rivals), the pope sent the two youngest Pazzi men to attack. They killed Giuliano, but Lorenzo escaped to safety in the sacristy. The conspirators were executed by nightfall.

After the death of Lorenzo, his son Piero (1472–1503) ruled for just two years. In 1494, he was driven out of Florence and died in exile. The political vacuum created in Florence allowed Savonarola to come to power. Savonarola's rise marked the suspension of Florentine luxury and immorality. The Dominican reformer was contemptuous not only of Florentine decadence but also of growing ecclesiastical decay, particularly in Rome. The Florentine public embraced Savonarola's moral crusade and adopted efforts to abolish evil and vanity in Florence. However, popularity soon shifted, and the zeal with which the Florentines participated in the Bonfire of the Vanities in 1497 was surpassed only by the fervor which accompanied Savonarola's burning at the stake a mere year later.

Medici leadership was restored and saw the rise of two popes from its familial line. Pope Leo X (1475–1521) and Pope Clement VII (1478–1534) ruled under the motto "God has given us the papacy, so let us enjoy it!" Enjoy it they did, commissioning in the meantime masterful Renaissance works from scholars and artists.

Medici favor fell again until Clement, allied with Emperor Charles V, restored permanent Medician domination. While the Medici dukes ruled, Florence declined. The banking and cloth trades no longer prospered, and artists and scholars sought work outside Florence. In the early 18th century, Florence passed into a favorable Austrian rule. Under Duke Leopold II in the 19th century, Florence capitalized on tourism and its rich past. For a brief period, during the unification of Italy, Florence became the nation's capital.

PLACES TO VISIT

The BATTISTERO DI SAN GIOVANNI (Baptistery of St. John), from 1059 and 1128, was built atop an earlier 6th-century building; beneath its foundations lies a 1st-century A.D. Roman palace, believed instead by the Florentines to be an ancient Roman temple dedicated to Mars (god of War). Responsible for the baptistery decoration, the medieval guild of the "Arte di Calimala" (the wholesale cloth importers) added the green and white marble striping to the exterior (11th–13th centuries) and in 1400 held a competition for the decoration of the north doors.

Andrea Pisano had already executed the bronze south doors (1336), decorating the 28 quatrefoil panels with scenes from the *Life of St. John the Baptist* and the *Cardinal and Theological Virtues*. Ghiberti won the commission to decorate the new north doors, and his winning *Sacrifice of Isaac* is on display in the Bargello alongside Brunelleschi's losing submission. The north doors (1403–24) depict the *Life of Christ, The Evangelists,* and *Doctors of the Church* in 28 frames

F

59

similar to Pisano's earlier work. Pleased with his work, the Calimala guild commissioned Ghiberti to create a second set of doors. Praised by Michelangelo as the "Gates of Paradise," the east doors (1425–52) depict scenes from the Old Testament in ten large panels whose design reveal a renewed interest in antiquity, emotion, and perspective. The scenes are (left to right and top to bottom): the *Creation and Expulsion of Adam and Eve, Cain and Abel, The Story of Noah, Abraham and the Sacrifice of Isaac, Jacob and Esau, The Story of Joseph, Moses and the Ten Commandments, The Fall of Jericho, Saul and David,* and *Solomon and the Queen of Sheba.* Notice Ghiberti's self-portrait in the second row on the left door (fourth from the top).

The decorative interior features an inlaid marble floor and stunning 13th-century mosaics. Christ's image dominates the glittering *Last Judgment* in the cupola. Four bands surround the scene and illustrate the stories of *Genesis,* of *Joseph,* of *Christ,* and of *St. John* consecutively. In the vault, above the altar, are the baptistery's earliest mosaics (early 1200s by a monk named Jacopo), which depict the *Agnus Dei Surrounded by Prophets.* On the pavement are geometric motifs and zodiac signs. To the right of the altar is the tomb of *Anti-pope John XXIII* by Donatello and Michelozzo.

Begun in 1334 by Giotto (*capomastro* = director of cathedral works), the CAMPANILE was completed in 1337 by Andrea Pisano and Francesco Talenti.

Four hundred and fourteen steps lead up the 276-foot-tall bell tower. The lower bas-reliefs, designed by Giotto and executed by Pisano (originals in the Museo dell'Opera), depict the *Creation of Man, The Fall of Man,* and *Redemption Through the Arts and Industry.*

The BASILICA DI SANTA MARIA DEL FIORE (St. Mary of the Flower) stands atop Florence's ancient cathedral, a 6th-century church dedicated to the Palestinian saint, Reparata. By the 13th century, citizens desired to erect a new and great cathedral worthy of Florentine piety, pride, and prosperity; in 1294 the sculptor Arnolfo di Cambio was appointed architect to the new dream. He died before its completion and work resumed under Francesco Talenti in 1335. By 1417 the nave was completed, and work on the glorious dome began three years later. Between 1420 and 1436 Filippo Brunelleschi and his crew labored, in record time, to complete the glorious dome. In 1436 Pope Eugenius IV consecrated the cathedral.

Brunelleschi's dome crowns the cathedral, its majestic aspect subjugating the church to a secondary appeal. The symbol of civic pride and a masterful architectural feat, Brunelleschi's dome was raised without the use of scaffolding. Brunelleschi created a double dome with an internal herringbone brick structure to support the outer shell. After spending many years in Rome studying antique ruins, Brunelleschi returned to Florence to avenge his reputation after losing the competition for the baptistery doors. He sought the commission for the dome and won it without revealing his plans or any of his newfound architectural and engineering expertise. According to Vasari, Brunelleschi challenged the jurors to make an egg stand on its point. Each attempted and failed. Brunelleschi then took the egg and smashed one end on the table; the point, now a cracked base, supported the egg. He proclaimed to the astonished crowd that if he had told them how to stand the egg on its point, anyone could do it; the same would follow with his plans for the dome. Thus, the commissioners should trust him and award him the project. They did. The resulting dome is the symbol of Florence and the Renaissance and the model of individual achievement.

While a full understanding of Brunelleschi's methods and techniques still eludes historians, architects, and engineers, visitors can gain an intimate understanding of the structure by climbing the dome's 463 steps to the top. Seven stained-glass windows (1443–45) can be viewed from the gallery that circles the inner drum. The windows depict the *Presentation in the Temple, Prayer in the Garden,* and the *Ascension* by Lorenzo Ghiberti; the *Coronation of the Virgin* by Donatello; the *Nativity* and the *Resurrection* by Paolo Uccello; and the *Deposition* by Andrea del Castagno.

Arnolfo di Cambio's original, yet incomplete facade was dismantled in 1587, and the church front was left bare until Emilio de Fabris designed and built the present face (1871–87). His work mimics the decoration on the cathedral's side walls. The *Porta della Mandorla* (Door of the Almond) on the north side of the cathedral is worth attention; it was sculpted between 1391 and 1405 by numerous artists. Atop the door gable within an almond-shaped frame is Nanni di Banco's *Assumption of the Virgin.*

Within the vast and somber interior, visitors can descend into the excavations of the cathedral's Paleo-Christian predecessor, Santa Reparata. At the bottom of the stairs lies Brunelleschi's humble tomb, discovered in 1972, seven years after the ancient church was discovered. The cathedral proper is full of tombs and monuments to non-Florentines; the most notable among them is Paolo Uccello's painted equestrian monument (1436) to Sir John Hawkwood, the English commander of the Florentine army (known as Giovanni Acuto by the Italians), and Andrea del Castagno's equestrian monument to Niccolò da Tolentino (1456). The frescoed cupola depicts the *Last Judgement* (1579) by Giorgio Vasari and Federico Zuccari. Beneath the dome, above the door of the south and north sacristies are terra-cotta lunettes by Luca della Robbia depicting the *Ascension* and the *Resurrection* respectively. Inside the north sacristy, delicate intarsia cupboards date between 1436 and 1445.

The MUSEO DELL'OPERA DEL DUOMO houses precious works from the cathedral, baptistery, and campanile. Established in

F

1891, the museum highlights include sculptures from Arnolfo di Cambio's original facade depicting the *Madonna and Child, Santa Reparata,* and the *Madonna of the Nativity.* Michelangelo's unfinished *Pietà* (1550–53) intended for his own tomb and originally in the Duomo stands on the landing of the stairs. Vasari claims that the representation of Nicodemus is a portrait of Michelangelo. Luca della Robbia's *Cantoria* (1430s) illustrates *Psalm 150;* a vision of gaiety, its dancing, singing, and playing children contrast with Donatello's racing *putti* from his contemporary *cantoria.* Donatello's emotive *St. Mary Magdalene* and his bald *Habakkuk* (called "lo zuccone" meaning pumpkin head) are housed in the room adjacent to Giotto's original bas-reliefs (carved by Andrea Pisano) from the campanile. Baptistery treasures include a gilt silver altar frontal and a cross by Betto di Francesco and Antonio del Pollaiuolo.

The ORSANMICHELE fulfills both a sacred and secular role. Built atop the 9th-century church of San Michele ad hortum (St. Michael in the Garden), the present palace-like structure, erected in 1336 by Francesco Talenti, replaced an earlier market, and its new upper stories were used to store the city's reserve grain supply.

Bernardo Daddi's *Madonna* (1347) replaced a miraculous image of the Virgin, which was destroyed when the earlier market burnt in 1304. The image is framed in Andrea Orcagna's Gothic *Tabernacle* (1349–59), commissioned by the survivors of the Black Death that ravaged Florence the previous year. In 1380, the main floor market was moved, allowing the church to occupy the entire ground level.

Eager to convey Florentine piety and prosperity, the city ordered each guild to erect a statue of its patron saint in the exterior niches of the Orsanmichele. Competition and rivalry between the guilds inspired leading Florentine artists to execute renowned and influential works. The fourteen guilds and their statues are as follows: The Calimala (wholesale cloth importers) commissioned Ghiberti to execute a *St. John the Baptist* (the first life-size bronze cast in the Renaissance); the Tribunale di Mercanzia (Merchant's Court) commissioned Verrocchio to portray the *Doubting Thomas* (1466–83); the Giudici e Notai (judges and notaries) commissioned a *St. Luke* (1601) by Giambologna; the Beccai (butchers) ordered a *St. Peter* (1408–13) attributed to Donatello (the first freestanding Renaissance marble statue); the Conciapelli (tanners) commissioned Nanni di Banco to execute a *St. Philip* (1415); the Maestri di Pietra e di Legname (stone masons and carpenters) commissioned *Four Warrior Saints* (1415) by Nanni di Banco; the Armaiuoli (armorers) commissioned a *St. George* (1417) by Donatello; the Cambio (bankers) ordered a *St. Matthew* (1419–22) by Ghiberti; the Lanaiuoli (wool manufacturers) commissioned Ghiberti to execute a *St. Stephen*

DONATELLO'S ST. MARK

Donatello (c. 1386–1466), one of the most influential artists of the 15th century, is considered the greatest Florentine sculptor to precede Michelangelo. His works were among the first to recall classical Roman forms, and he imbued these forms with a sense of drama, heroic spirit, and religious pathos. He worked in every sculptural medium including marble, bronze, terracotta, and wood.

The medium used in carving reflected the status and wealth of the patron commissioning the work. In 1411 the *Arte dei Linaiuoli* (Linen Merchant's Guild), a minor and less prosperous guild, commissioned Donatello to carve a statue in marble of their patron saint, St. Mark, for their niche in the Orsanmichele. They impressed upon Donatello that although they could not afford a more expensive bronze piece, they expected his marble statue to be as impressive as any bronze work.

Donatello set diligently to his task. However, when the Linen Merchants came to see the finished statue in Donatello's studio, they were outraged. They thought the statue was too crude, too ugly. Fearing ruin and humiliation should they display the statue, the Linen Merchants demanded it be recarved. Donatello convinced the merchants to wait until he could place the statue in its proper niche in the Orsanmichele and "finish" it there. Weeks later he unveiled the statue on site without having altered it. Immediately upon seeing it, the Linen Merchants admired the work and praised Donatello.

The 7-3/4-foot statue of *St. Mark* (1411–13) was revolutionary, representing a dramatic break with the immediate past. It is considered the first Renaissance figure demonstrating an excellent understanding of classical form. The pose, called *contrapposto* (Italian for counter-poise), represents a counterbalance between the axes of the hips and the shoulders while the weight of the figure is distributed upon one leg. The drapery emphasizes this form; the straight folds add solidity to the weight-bearing leg while the curved folds suggest weightlessness and movement. Here Donatello pays close attention to the body contours, both the exposed forms and those beneath the drapery. St. Mark appeared as though he were about to step out of his niche on his own volition. This lifelike and animated nature is reflected in Donatello's representation of the saint's face. St. Mark's visage is intense, emotional, dignified, and dynamic. In 1492 a young Michelangelo remarked that Donatello's St. Mark was "the most convincing representation of an honest man" that he had ever seen.

F

(1428); the Maniscalchi (ferriers) requested a *St. Eligius* (1408) by Nanni di Banco; the Linaiuoli e Rigattieri (linen and used cloth merchants) commissioned Donatello to create a *St. Mark* (1411–13); the Pelliccai (furriers) commissioned a *St. James the Greater* by Niccolò Lamberti; the Medici e Speziali (doctors and apothecaries) ordered a *Madonna and Child* (1399); and the Setaiuoli e Orafi (silkweavers and goldsmiths) commissioned a *St. John the Evangelist* (1515) by Baccio da Montelupo.

The Dominican church of **SANTA MARIA NOVELLA** (begun 1246) stands atop an earlier church dedicated to Santa Maria delle Vigne (1094). In 1221 the Dominicans received the property, and 50 years later, two friars turned architects, Sisto and Ristoro, began work on the nave. The 14th-century marble facade seamlessly incorporates two distinct building periods; the lower facade was finished in 1360 and the upper facade was executed between 1456 and 1470 by Leon Battista Alberti. The spacious piazza before the church was reorganized in 1245 to accommodate the devout throngs who came to hear St. Peter Martyr preach against heresy. His impassioned inquisitorial rampage led the people to turn on him, and a suspected heretic thrust a knife into the wrathful preacher's head.

Soaring stripped vaults define the expansive and sparse interior. In 1565 Vasari renovated the interior and whitewashed its original frescoes. Luckily, Masaccio's *Trinity* (1428) with the Virgin, St. John the Evangelist, and donors above a skeleton was left untouched. An inscription beneath the skeleton reads, *"io fu gia quel che vio siete, voi sarete ancor quel ch'io son"* (I was that which you are, you will be that which I am). Giovanni Tournabuoni commissioned masterful frescoes by Domenico Ghirlandaio behind the altar. They depict the *Life of the Virgin, St. John the Baptist,* and *Dominican Saints* and include numerous portraits of the Tournabuoni family, contemporary Florentine humanists and artists, and Ghirlandaio himself.

The church is rife with beautiful chapels. Owned by a renowned Florentine banker, the Cappella di Filippo Strozzi contains frescoes painted by Filippino Lippi (1502) near the end of his life. The scenes illustrate *The Crucifixion of St. Philip the Apostle, The Martyrdom of St. John the Evangelist,* and *The Raising of Drusiana.* According to legend, armed solely with faith and a cross, Philip removed an idolized dragon from the Temple of Mars. As the banished demon fled, it emitted a smell that killed much of the populace. Infuriated, the temple priests captured Philip and crucified him upside down. According to the *Golden Legend,* John was submerged in a pot of boiling oil only to emerge miraculously unharmed. Behind the altar is Filippo Strozzi's delicately carved tomb by Benedetto da Maiano. The Cappella Rucellai contains Nino Pisano's marble *Madonna and Child* and a bronze tomb for the Dominican Francesco Lionardo

Dati by Ghiberti (1425). The 14th-century Cappella Strozzi contains an altarpiece by Andrea Orcagna depicting the *Redeemer Giving the Keys to St. Peter and the Book of Wisdom to St. Thomas Aquinas* (1357). A loincloth was meant to cover Brunelleschi's wooden *Crucifix,* a powerful vision of the Redeemer, in the Cappella Gondi.

Famed frescoes decorate Santa Maria Novella's cloisters. The Chiostro Verde (Green Cloister) takes its name from the green pigment used by the artist Paolo Uccello. His work depicts stories from Genesis accompanied by biblical references. The scenes include the *Creation of Adam, The Flood,* and the *Drunkenness of Noah.* Frescoed by Andrea di Bonaiuto in 1365, the Cappellone degli Spagnuoli's (Spanish Chapel) monumental decoration illustrates the *Mission, Works and Triumph of the Dominican Order and the Catholic Church.* Notice St. Dominic releasing the hounds of the Lord, the *"Domini canes,"* a play on the role of the monks in the Dominican Order; they are militant, virtuous, and victorious over vice and heresy.

SANTA TRINITÀ (1250–60) stands atop the site of one of the oldest churches in Florence. The present church, built by the Vallombrosan Order, replaces an earlier 11th-century church. Founded in 1038, the Vallombrosan Order owes its existence to the Florentine San Giovanni Gualberto. Intent on avenging his murdered brother and killing the assassin, Giovanni captured the murderer. But remembering Christ's sufferings, Giovanni forgave him. Giovanni sped to the nearest church to thank God. As he prayed, the image of Christ on the crucifix before him appeared to bow its head; from that moment Giovanni's monastic life had begun.

The austere church owes its fame to the Sassetti Chapel. Francesco Sassetti, a prosperous Florentine merchant, commissioned Ghirlandaio in 1483 to depict the *Life of St. Francis* on the chapel walls. Ghirlandaio painted *St. Francis Receiving the Rule of Order from Pope Honorius* in Florence's Piazza della Signoria surrounded by 15th-century Florentine citizens, among them Lorenzo il Magnifico, his sons, Piero, Giovanni, and Giuliano, and the patron Francesco Sassetti with his son. Sassetti and his wife are also present in Ghirlandaio's *Adoration of the Shepherds.* To the right of the Sassetti Chapel is the *Crucifix* whose Savior bowed to San Giovanni Gualberto, who knelt before it in thanks and prayer.

Elegant church commissions also include the *Altarpiece of the Annunciation* (1422) by Lorenzo Monaco (in the south aisle) and the *Tomb of Benozzo Federighi, Bishop of Fiesole* (1454–57) by Luca della Robbia (in the second chapel in the choir).

The Medici parish church, SAN LORENZO, was rebuilt in 1420 by Giovanni di Bicci de' Medici and subsequently embellished by his descendants. It is a monument to Medici aspiration and a mausoleum for its most illustrious

F

members. Built by Brunelleschi (1425–46) and finished by Manetti in 1461, the early Renaissance basilica stands atop the earlier church of St. Zenobius (a famous Florentine bishop) consecrated by the Church Father St. Ambrose in 393.

Michelangelo designed the unfinished facade. Commissioned by Pope Leo X (Lorenzo de' Medici's second son) in 1516, the work never progressed beyond models and a rough brick facing. It is within this serene church that the Accademia del Disegno held a memorial service honoring Michelangelo on July 14, 1564.

Cosimo il Vecchio, named *Pater Patriae* (Father of the Nation) by the Florentines, is buried beneath the dome at the church crossing. This successful banker, humanist, and art patron is, in death, suitably surrounded by a wealth of fine art and a remarkable library harmonized within architectural splendor. Cosimo commissioned Donatello's last works, the cathedral's dramatic *Bronze Pulpits* (c. 1460). Savonarola preached at the first pulpit; its reliefs depict *The Agony in the Garden, The Flagellation, Christ before Pilate, The Crucifixion, The Lamentation,* and *The Entombment.* The second pulpit portrays *Mary at the Sepulchre, Christ in Limbo, The Resurrection, The Pentecost,* and *The Martyrdom of St. Lawrence.* Donatello rests entombed beneath a vault in the left transept near his magnanimous patron Cosimo. Within the vault is an *Annunciation* by Filippo Lippi, and nearby is Bronzino's fresco, *The Martyrdom of St. Lawrence.* Rosso Fiorentino's *Marriage of the Virgin* (1523) together with a *Tabernacle* by Desiderio Settignano embellish one of the minor church chapels.

The SAGRESTIA VECCHIA (1420–29), the Old Sacristy, is the oldest part of the new church. Entombed within the sacristy are Cosimo's parents and children: Giovanni di Bicci de' Medici, his wife, Piccarda Bueri, and their grandsons, Giovanni and Piero de' Medici. They too rest below a heavenly dome constructed by Brunelleschi and decorated by Donatello. Spirited apostles and martyrs enliven Donatello's *Bronze Doors.*

Ascend the staircase into the BIBLIOTECA LAURENZIANA created by Michelangelo in 1524 to house the vast manuscript collection amassed by Cosimo il Vecchio and his grandson Lorenzo il Magnifico. Commissioned by Pope Clement VII (1519–43), il Magnifico's nephew, the undulating Mannerist design is a celebrated prototype. The library contains over 10,000 Greek and Latin manuscripts, including a 5th-century codex by Virgil.

Enter the CAPPELLE MEDICEE (Medici Chapel) from the side of the church on the Piazza degli Aldobrandini. A stairwell leads up to the Chapel of the Princes, a mausoleum containing the remains of numerous Medici family members designed by Michelangelo according to plans based on the beloved Florentine Baptistery.

Michelangelo's greatest work for the church, despite his leaving it unfinished like much of the rest of his work for San Lorenzo, is the SAGRESTIA NUOVA (1520–24 and 1530–33), the New Sacristy. Inside, the two Medici tombs honor Lorenzo, duke of Urbino (1492–1519), and Giuliano, duke of Nemours (1479–1516); two tombs that were never completed would have honored Lorenzo il Magnifico and his brother Giuliano. The mood within the still and somber mausoleum reflects the quiet sleep of its occupants. Figures representing the times of day, *Day and Night* and *Dusk and Dawn,* recline atop the sarcophagi below noble and idealized statues of those entombed within. The *Virgin and Child,* Michelangelo's last statue of a Madonna, was to adorn il Magnifico's memorial.

A model Renaissance palace, the PALAZZO MEDICI-RICCARDI was erected by Cosimo il Vecchio in 1444 and subsequently bought by the Riccardi family in 1659; today it is the seat of the prefect. Visiting kings, Charles VIII of France among them, were treated to a masterful vision of three pious monarchs: Benozzo Gozzoli's *Procession of the Magi* (1459–60). The sumptuous cavalcade winds along the verdant landscape. Among the various processional participants are Medici family members; the third king might be a portrait of Lorenzo il Magnifico. Gozzoli depicted himself among the crowd, unmistakably identified by his monogrammed red cap.

Depictions of the Last Supper commonly decorate convent refectories. The vision of Christ dining with his disciples in SANT'APOLLONIA (1339) was a sight privy only to the cloistered nuns that dined before it until it was whitewashed and rediscovered in 1860. Andrea del Castagno's masterpiece, the *Last Supper* (*cenacolo* in Italian), was painted between 1445 and 1450. Castagno's unique marbled setting is serenely elegant, enriching the nun's dining hall. Also by Castagno are the frescoes of the *Crucifixion, Deposition,* and *Resurrection.*

The Dominican church of SAN MARCO is greatly overshadowed by the adjoining Museo di San Marco, which is housed in the remaining convent structures. Founded in 1299, the church and convent were rebuilt in 1442 by Michelozzo. Commissioned in 1437 by Cosimo il Vecchio, the enlargement accommodated Europe's public library with classical Greek and Latin texts that attracted humanists from afar—yet another Medici triumph! In 1491, the impassioned fundamentalist preacher Savonarola, who was soon to be condemned a heretic, became the church prior.

Fra Angelico, the pious monk whose frescoes are the convent's treasures, painted *St. Thomas, Christ as a Pilgrim,* a *Pietà,* and *St. Dominic at the Foot of the Cross* in the corners of the elegant Chiostro di Sant'Antonio (Cloister of St. Anthony). The adjacent Ospizio dei Pellegrini (Pilgrims' Hospice) now hospitably hosts a collection of Fra

F

Angelico's paintings gathered from Florentine churches. The most notable pieces include the *Deposition* (1435–40), the *Last Judgment* (1431), the *Madonna della Stella,* and the piece the Tabernacle of the Linaiuoli (flax workers) commissioned in 1433 depicting the *Madonna Enthroned with Saints.* Another Fra Angelico, his *Crucifixion with Saints* (1441–42), decorates the Chapter House.

A flight of stairs leads up to the monk's dormitory. On the wall of each simple cell is a fresco by Fra Angelico. The most famous of the angelic visions is the *Annunciation* at the top of the staircase. A contemplative focus within the sparse cells, Fra Angelico's most revered cell works are the *Noli me tangere,* an *Annunciation,* a *Transfiguration,* and a *Coronation of the Virgin.* Fra Bartolomeo also contributed work to the dormitory, most notably a portrait of Savonarola depicted with his head cleaved open like St. Peter Martyr, in the prior's cell.

In 1984 a *Crucifix* by Fra Angelico was transferred to the church, his only work within the structure. However, do not miss the work of convent second resident monk and painter, Fra Bartolomeo's *Madonna and Six Saints* (1509).

The Servite order founded the church of the **SANTISSIMA ANNUNCIATA**, dedicated to the Virgin Annunciate in 1250. Heavily renovated in the Baroque style during the Counter-Reformation, Michelozzo built the church and cloister from 1444 to 1481. His Chiostrino dei Voti (Cloister of Votives), or atrium, welcomes visitors with inviting 16th-century frescoes depicting the *Assumption* by Rosso Fiorentino, the *Visitation* by Pontormo, the *Marriage of the Virgin* by Franciabigio, the *Birth of the Virgin* and *Visit of the Magi* by Andrea del Sarto, and the *Nativity* by Baldovinetti.

Votives and candles and flowers engulf the Annunciata's revered image of the Virgin. According to legend, a 13th-century monk executed this miraculous painting of the Annunciation accompanied by an angel, who painted the Virgin's face. The church honors this painting in its name. Two intriguing works within the sacristy, both by Andrea del Castagno, depict the *Holy Trinity with St. Jerome* and *St. Julian and the Savior.*

Ask the sacristan to let you into the Chiostro dei Morti (the Cloister of the Dead) to see Andrea del Sarto's *Madonna del Sacco* (1525), curiously named for the sack upon which St. Joseph rests.

Dante would first lay eyes on the object of his unrequited love, Beatrice, in the courtyard of the **BADIA FIORENTINA,** a Benedictine abbey founded in 978. Dante recalls the importance of the abbey's bell in his *Paradiso,* canto XV.

The abbey was rebuilt in 1284 and almost entirely remodeled in 1631. Inside is Mino da Fiesole's tomb (1469–

81) of Count Ugo (d. 1001), margrave of Tuscany. Ugo's mother founded and generously funded the church. In 1485 Filippino Lippi painted one of the few frescoes to survive the 17th-century renovations, the *Madonna Appearing to St. Bernard.*

Italy's most illustrious citizens, Ghiberti, Michelangelo, Machiavelli, Galileo, and Rossini, to name a few, are buried within the splendid medieval church **SANTA CROCE**. Rebuilt by Arnolfo di Cambio in 1294, according to legend the church was founded early in the 13th century by St. Francis himself.

While the grand neo-Gothic facade built between 1557 and 1563 clothes the exterior, an open timber roof protects celebrated 13th–15th-century works within the immense church. The tomb monuments commissioned for Italy's who's who inspired a wealth of remarkable art. Along the right aisle Antonio Rossellino's milking Madonna, the *Madonna del Latte* (1478), rests above the tomb of Francesco Nori, a conspirator and victim in the Pazzi conspiracy. Michelangelo chose in life to live in Rome and in death to rest in his hometown Florence. His tomb by Vasari (1570) stands alongside a memorial to Dante (1829), who died in exile in Ravenna in 1321, never to return to his native Florence. The *Life of St. Francis and Five Virtues* is depicted on Benedetto da Maiano's pulpit (1476) facing the nave. Donatello's evocative *Annunciation Tabernacle* (c. 1430) stands near the simple 18th-century tomb of Niccolò Machi-

avelli. The effigy of humanist and scholar Leonardo Bruni (1447) by Bernardo Rossellino is a fittingly noble and tranquil depiction of the city chancellor and author of *The History of Florence.*

Along the left aisle, facing Bruni's tomb, is his successor to the position of chancellor of the republic, also a humanist and scholar, Carlo Marsuppini. While Bruni influenced his successor, Marsuppini's tomb (1453), created by Desiderio Settignano, imitates Bruni's tomb. Further along the aisle is Galileo's tomb (1737), built almost 100 years after his death upon receiving a church pardon and being granted a Christian burial.

Resplendent 14th-century frescoes embellish Santa Croce's famous chapels. The Castellani Chapel was decorated by Agnolo Gaddi with scenes from the *Lives of St. Nicholas of Bari, St. John the Baptist, St. Anthony Abbot, and St. John the Evangelist.* The Baroncelli Chapel, frescoed by Giotto's pupil Taddeo Gaddi between 1332 and 1338, depicts the *Life of the Virgin* with a *Coronation of the Virgin* by Giotto and his assistants.

Enter the sacristy chapels through a door and corridor designed by Michelozzo. Within, frescoes by Taddeo Gaddi, Spinello Aretino, and Niccolò Gerini illustrate the *Crucifixion,* the *Way to Calvary,* and the *Resurrection,* respectively. Giovanni da Milano adorned the Rinuccini Chapel with scenes from the *Life of the Virgin and St. Mary Magdalene.* Michelozzo's Medici Chapel (1434) contains a terra-cotta altarpiece of the

F

Madonna and Child (1480) by Andrea della Robbia.

Giotto decorated two chapels for Florence's most prosperous families, the Peruzzi and the Bardi families. Giotto painted the walls using the dry fresco technique, painting on dry plaster as opposed to painting on readily binding wet plaster. As a result the works are poorly preserved, suffering further damage when they were whitewashed in the 18th century. Scenes in the Peruzzi Chapel depict the lives of two saints, John the Evangelist and John the Baptist. The Evangelist's wall illustrates the *Vision at Patmos*, the *Raising of Drusiana*, and his *Ascent into Heaven*. The Baptist's wall illustrates *Zaccharias and the Angel*, the *Birth of St. John*, and *Herod's Feast*. The story of St. Francis adorns the Bardi Chapel walls. Giotto depicts *Francis Receiving the Stigmata*, representations of *Poverty, Chastity*, and *Obedience*, the *Triumph of Francis*, the *Death of Francis*, and *Francis Being Tried Before the Sultan*. A second Bardi Chapel in the left transept contains Donatello's marvelous wooden *Crucifix*, which Brunelleschi insulted by calling it a less-than-marvelous depiction of a "peasant on a cross."

The *Legend of the True Cross* (1380) by Agnolo Gaddi decorates the vaulted sanctuary. This medieval legend accounts for the history of Christ's cross from the Creation until the 7th century. The wood of the cross grew from a branch of the Tree of Knowledge that passed from Adam to Moses and finally took root in Jerusalem, serving as a bridge across a

stream. While visiting Solomon, the Queen of Sheba prayed at the bridge after receiving a vision which foretold of its future use. As prophesied, the cross was eventually used to crucify Christ. Constantine's mother, Helena, discovered the cross in Jerusalem; a Jew named Judas knew its whereabouts. The cross was subsequently stolen by the Persian king and was not recovered until the 7th century when the Emperor Heraclius defeated the Persians and returned to Jerusalem carrying the cross in triumph.

Adjacent to the church, the MUSEO DELL'OPERA DI SANTA CROCE houses water-damaged works from the devastating 1966 flood and salvaged frescoes and works from the church, including Cimabue's *Crucifix* and a bronze statue of *St. Louis* (1424) by Donatello. The entire complex suffered damage on the fateful November 4th when the Arno's water levels rose to nearly $16\frac{1}{2}$ feet. The water also reached the famed CAPPELLA PAZZI, the serenely decorated and harmoniously conceived chapter house (1430–46) by Brunelleschi. The architect translated the simple geometric forms of the square and the circle into an elegant structure. Inside, simple terra-cottas by Lucca della Robbia depict the *Twelve Apostles* (c. 1442–52).

Harmony, elegance, and balance describe the church of SANTO SPIRITO. An 18th-century facade masks Brunelleschi's rhythmic interior, designed by the architect from 1428 to 1435. Work did not begin until after his death in 1444 and was completed 44 years later. The Augustinian church and convent replaces two earlier structures from 1250 and 1292.

The church is often filled with architecture students on pilgrimage to study what most call Brunelleschi's greatest Renaissance creation. Perfect perspective and mathematical harmony are the church's secondary saints. The elaborate barrel-vaulted *Vestibule* and octagonal *Sacristy* by Cronaca and Giuliano da Sangallo, respectively, are architectural delights. The few great works that interrupt the serene architectural details include Filippo Lippi's *Madonna and Child with St. John,* Verrocchio's *St. Monica and Augustinian Nuns,* a sculpted *Altarpiece* by Andrea Sansovino, and a *Trinity with Saints Mary Magdalene and Catherine.*

The REFECTORY, to the left of the church, houses Andrea Orcagna's ruined *Last Supper* and above it, the well preserved and much celebrated dramatic *Crucifixion* (c. 1360–65). The dining hall also contains a collection of 12th-century to 15th-century sculptures.

Fresco cycles by Masolino and Masaccio attract throngs to the medieval church of SANTA MARIA DEL CARMINE. The two chapels painted by the early Renaissance masters survived a devastating fire in 1771. The Carmelite convent was founded in 1250 and its church built 18 years later; after the 18th-century fire, the church was rebuilt in an unimpressive Baroque style.

Providence insured that the Cappella Brancacci (Brancacci Chapel) not only survived the consuming flames in 1771 but also endured a threat by city authorities in 1690 to demolish and replace the chapel with something more contemporary. Thanks to divine intervention, the fresco cycle depicting the *Life of St. Peter* and executed by Masolino (1425 and 1427) and his pupil Masaccio (1428) still survive today. When the chapel's patron, Felice Brancacci, a wealthy merchant and statesman, was exiled by the Medici in 1436, the chapel remained incomplete until Filippo Lippi completed the decoration around 1480. Despite being executed by three different artists, the frescoes appear to be painted by the same hand. Lippi meticulously studied the work of the earlier masters, giving a seamless unity to the finished cycle. The most celebrated scenes depict *St. Peter Baptizing* (Masaccio); the *Tribute Money* (Masaccio), which illustrates three events: a city official asking Christ to pay the tribute money, Christ showing Peter a lake from which he extracts money from the mouth of a fish, and Peter paying the tribute money; the *Expulsion of Adam and Eve* (Masaccio); *Peter's Release from Prison* (Lippi); *Peter Healing the Sick* (Masaccio); and *Peter Enthroned* (Masaccio). The chapel altarpiece by Coppo di Marcovaldo depicts the *Madonna del Carmine.*

The Umiliati (a branch of the Benedictine Order) are responsible for founding the church of the OGNISSANTI (All Saints) and credited with establishing the wool-working trade in Florence. Without these humble monks-cum-wool-crafts-men, perhaps the successful Florentine wool economy would not have existed. Built in 1256, the Franciscan Order assumed church ownership in 1561.

The sanctuary was also the parish church of Amerigo Vespucci (1451–1512), a Medici salesperson who followed Columbus's route to America in 1499 and 1501. Above the Vespucci family tomb (1471) is Ghirlandaio's *Madonna della Misericordia;* Amerigo is allegedly in the painting as the young boy protected by the Madonna.

On the refectory wall in the church convent is Ghirlandaio's exotic *Last Supper* (1481). Notice the two opposing visions by Botticelli and Ghirlandaio (both painted c. 1481) depicting *St. Augustine's Vision of St. Jerome* and *St. Jerome* respectively.

The OSPEDALE DEGLI INNOCENTI (1445), Europe's first foundling hospital, continues to operate as an orphanage and nursery. Brunelleschi's elegantly designed portico with its slender colonnade and serene arches is embellished with Luca della Robbia's *Medallions* (1487) depicting babies in swaddling clothes. At the left end of the building is the "rota," a rotating door used as a baby deposit. Added in 1660, the door was sealed shut in 1875. The Hospital Pinacoteca houses some important works; notice Botticelli's *Madonna and Child,* Domenico Ghirlandaio's *Adoration of the Magi,* Piero di Cosimo's *Madonna and Saints,* and Luca della Robbia's *Madonna and Child.*

After spending some time in the city's major churches, explore some of its smaller ones. The notable artworks in the ancient church of SANT'AMBROGIO (rebuilt 13th century) include a *Madonna Enthroned with Saints John the Baptist and Bartholomew* by Orcagna's school, a *Tabernacle* (1481–83) considered to be the finest work of Mino da Fiesole, and a fresco by Cosimo Rosselli that includes portraits of 15th-century Florentines. The convent of SANTA MARIA MADDALENA DEI PAZZI is dedicated to a Counter-Reformation nun and saint born into the wealthy Pazzi family. Inside the Chapter House is one of Perugino's masterpieces, the *Crucifixion and Saints* (1493–96). Legend claims that Charlemagne founded the city's oldest church, SANTI APOSTOLI (1075), in 786. Inside is a beautiful tabernacle by Andrea della Robbia. The square before it, Piazza del Limbo, is so named because it occupies a former graveyard for unbaptized children. The first Christian cemetery stood before the church of SANTA FELICITÀ (St. Felicity, a 5th-century Roman martyr), founded by Christian merchants from Syrian Greece. The renovated 18th-century church houses Pontormo's masterful Mannerist *Deposition* (1525–27), with *Evangelists* in the cupola by Pontormo and Bronzino.

A beautiful walk from Porta San Miniato up to the Romanesque basilica of SAN MINIATO AL MONTE (St. Minias on the Mount) is worth the effort. The ascent is lined with cypresses and a delicate rose garden for the nature lovers and the Stations of the Cross for the pious. Atop the monumental staircase and past the cemetery is a glorious church that commands a stunning view. Constructed from 1013 to 1207 atop an earlier church, the edifice is dedicated to the Florentine warrior-deacon Minias, who was martyred around 250 and buried in the hillside. The white and green facade (1090) shines atop the city like a meticulously cut gem. Atop the window is a 13th-century mosaic depicting *Christ Flanked by the Virgin and St. Minias.*

The interior (1018–63) has luckily remained virtually untouched. Seven intarsia panels (1207) on the marble pavement depict the zodiac and animal motifs. Within the Cappella del Crocifisso is a tabernacle (1448) by Michelozzo constructed to hold the crucifix that spoke to San Giovanni Gualberto. (The crucifix was later moved to the Church of Sta. Trinità.). The painted panel doors are the work of Agnolo Gaddi, and the terra-cotta roof and ceiling are by Luca della Robbia.

The funerary Chapel of the Cardinal of Portugal enshrines the remains of the 25-year-old Cardinal Iacopo Lusitania. Antonio Rossellino carved the Cardinal's delicate tomb (1461–66). The sepulchre rests below five terra-cotta ceiling medallions (1461) with representations of the Cardinal Virtues and the Holy Ghost by Luca della Robbia. Atop the bishop's throne is Alesso Baldovinetti's *Annunciation* (1466–73).

A mosaic in the choir apse depicts the same subject seen in the facade, *Christ Between the Virgin and St. Minias* (1297). In the Sacristy are Spinello Aretino's *Evangelists* and *Life of St. Benedict.*

Since the Middle Ages generations of Florentines have assembled in the PIAZZA DELLA SIGNORIA to discuss politics and participate in public ceremonies. Although today tourists flood the square and surrounding cafés, the piazza is still the stage for Florentine politics. The square is best known for two fires fueled by the politics of faith: The square was host to the Bonfire of the Vanities in 1497 and an Inquisitorial roast on May 23, 1498. At the first fire Savonarola feverishly incinerated books, art, and all other immoral vanities he could accumulate. At the second fire the Catholic Church burned Savonarola.

The UFFIZI (offices) was designed by Vasari in 1550 to house the Grand Duke Cosimo's administrators; if the rooms retained their original purpose they would be among the most marvelously decorated offices in the world. The superb collection houses some of the world's greatest masterpieces. The chronologically arranged collection deserves more than one attentive visit.

The first frescoes visitors encounter on the ground floor are Botticelli's *Annunciation* (1481) and Andrea del Castagno's *Illustrious Florentines* (c. 1450), including Boccaccio, Petrarch, and Dante. On the second floor the GABINETTO DEI DISEGNI E DELLE STAMPE (Prints and Drawing

F

F

GIROLAMO SAVONAROLA (1452–98).

Born to a family of Ferrarese court physicians, Girolamo Savonarola renounced the courtly splendor; instead, he observed strict moral principles and severe asceticism. As a young man he left Ferrara for a monastic life in Bologna. In 1481 he came to Florence to live and preach at San Marco.

His famous reforming sermons attracted thousands. His reputation as a zealous and fiery preacher gained him the privilege in 1491 to speak in Florence's duomo. During the Lenten service Savonarola proclaimed that Florentine decadence and immorality were leading the citizens away from the kingdom of God and into the consumptive fire of evil. He urged the Florentines to repent, reject all vanity, and aspire to be governed by the will of God. He portrayed the invading king of France, Charles V, as a minister of God, a vehicle of God's vengeance. The Florentines, fearful of the French threat and facing political uncertainty after the death of "il Magnifico," looked to Savonarola as their spiritual and political leader.

After the French passed through Florence, Savonarola continued his quest for virtue. He demanded that the populace fast and give their possessions to the poor. He sent bands of children to roam the streets and become spies for virtue, informing Savonarola of every vice and transgression. In 1497, Savonarola ignited his Bonfire of the Vanities in the Piazza della Signoria. Immoral paintings and books, jewels, clothing, cards, and dice were burned, despite an offer by a Venetian to purchase the entire pyre.

In June of 1497, Pope Alexander VI excommunicated Savonarola for disobeying papal orders and claiming, "I can no longer place any faith in your Holiness." Though he was instructed to preach no more, during Lent in 1498 Savonarola preached to a large crowd. In his fervor he claimed to be ablaze with the Spirit of the Lord. By May 28 Savonarola was literally aflame, condemned to hang and burn as a heretic in the Piazza della Signoria. He and two of his followers were tortured and charred, and their ashes were thrown into the Arno to ensure no remains be found or relics be preserved.

Rooms) is open only to scholars. Fortunately, occasional exhibits allow the public a glimpse at the exquisite works.

The first corridor on the third floor contains Roman statues and busts. The often-closed room 1 houses Hellenistic and Roman works, much studied by Renaissance artists. Room 2 holds the three celebrated 13th-century Tuscan *Maestàs*. These paintings of the Madonna enthroned by Cimabue (c. 1285), Duccio (1280s), and Giotto (c. 1310) offer a comparative glimpse at the evolving stylistic treatment of similar subject matter, a visual transition from the Byzantine to the early Renaissance. Notice a second Giotto, the polyptych *Madonna and Four Saints*. Works by 14th-century Sienese artists in room 3 include Ambrogio Lorenzetti's *Presentation in the Temple* (1342) and Simone Martini's *Annunciation* (1333). The 14th-century Florentine works in room 4 highlight Nardo di Cione, Bernardo Daddi, and Giovanni da Milano. In rooms 5 and 6 are Gentile da Fabriano's *Adoration of the Magi* (1423) and the same subject by Lorenzo Monaco. Room 7 houses Domenico Veneziano's *Madonna Enthroned with Saints Francis, John the Baptist, Zenobius, and Lucy* (1448), Piero della Francesca's portraits of *Federico di Montefeltro and His Duchess Battista Sforza* (1465), and Paolo Uccello's *Battle of San Romano*. Room 8 contains two famed works by Filippo Lippi, his *Coronation of the Virgin* (1447) and *Madonna and Child with Two Angels* (1465). Notice Alesso Baldovinetti's *Annunciation*. Room 9 features Pollaiuolo and his *Labors of Hercules* (1478) and *Saints Vincent, James, and Eustace* (1492). Botticelli dominates rooms 10 to 14. *The Annunciation, Adoration of the Magi, La Primavera* (Spring), *Calumny, Pallas and the Centaur, The Birth of Venus,* and *The Madonna of the Magnificat* absorb visitors, who linger in these rooms for hours at a time. A Medici agent commissioned the 14th room's greatest import, the *Portinari Altarpiece* depicting the Adoration of the Shepherds by Hugo van der Goes. Room 15 highlights Verrocchio and his famed pupil Leonardo da Vinci with *Tobias and the*

Three Angels by the former and the *Annunciation* and the *Adoration of the Magi* by the latter. Room 18 contains the famed *Medici Venus* (1st century B.C.). Room 19 houses works by Perugino and Signorelli. Notice the former's *Madonna Enthroned with Saints John the Baptist and Sebastian* and two tondos depicting the *Madonna and Child* and the *Holy Family*. Dürer's *Portrait of His Father* and *Adoration of the Magi* accompany Cranach's *Adam and Eve* in room 20. Room 21 highlights Giovanni Bellini's *Sacred Allegory*. Room 22 contains works by Holbein and Joos van Cleve the Elder. Mantegna and Correggio are exhibited in room 23. Michelangelo's *Tondo Doni* in room 25 depicts the Holy Family and was painted for the occasion of a wedding. Room 26 contains Raphael's vivid *Portrait of Pope Leo X with Cardinals Giulio de' Medici (Clement VII) and Luigi de' Rossi* and his delicate *Madonna del Cardellino* (Madonna of the Goldfinch). Andrea del Sarto's *Madonna of the Harpies* is also housed in this room. Room 27 contains works by Pontormo and Bronzino. His *Knight of Malta* and *Portrait of a Sick Man* accompany Titian's *Flora* and *Venus of Urbino* in room 28. Sixteenth-century Emilian works in rooms 29 and 30 feature Parmigianino's long-necked Madonna, the *Madonna "dal collo lungo."* Room 32 houses Sebastiano del Piombo's *Death of Adonis*. Room 34 contains an *Assumption* and *Holy Family with St. Barbara* by Veronese. Alongside the Tintorettos in room 35 are Rubens's *Henry IV Entering Paris* and *Henry IV at*

Ivry, both from a larger cycle. Room 43 contains Caravaggio's *Sacrifice of Isaac.* Room 44 houses Rembrandt's *Self-Portrait, Portrait of an Old Man,* and *Self-Portrait as an Old Man.*

The Corridoio Vasariano (Vasari Corridor) is replete with artists' self-portraits. It begins with Vasari and continues chronologically with Agnolo, Taddeo Gaddi, Andrea del Sarto, Bronzino, Bernini, Pietro da Cortona, Rubens, Rembrandt, Velasquez, Hogarth, David, and Delacroix, to name a few.

Founded by Pietro Leopoldo I in 1784, the GALLERIA DELL' ACCADEMIA was a place for students to study art; today it seems a place for tourists to jostle for position to view Michelangelo's *David.* Certainly the museum's greatest attraction, the *David* (1501–04), symbol of civic triumph and pride, deserves a heroic audience. Standing 16 feet high, the statue is carved from a single block of marble. The stone was quarried in 1464 and left abandoned until Michelangelo took on the task. Andrea Sansovino and Leonardo da Vinci were previously offered the stone but declined the prospect. At 29 years old, Michelangelo masterfully transformed the stone into a resolute hero seen moments before his triumph (1 Samuel 17:32–37). Commissioned in 1501 and erected in 1504 in the Piazza della Signoria, the *David* symbolized the Florentine victory over Charles VIII, the victory of Republicanism over tyranny, and the victory of the underdog over the favorite. In 1873

the statue was transferred to the Accademia and replaced with a copy.

Intended for the tomb of Pope Julius II, Michelangelo's four *Slaves* (1531–23) now stand in the Accademia. The unfinished figures struggling to break free from their stone prisons were given to the Medici by Michelangelo's nephew in 1564.

Important paintings in the Accademia collection include Filippo Lippi's *Descent from the Cross,* Fra Bartolomeo's *Madonna Enthroned with Saints,* Botticelli's *Madonna and Child with the Young St. John,* Lorenzo di Credi's *Adoration of the Child,* and Giovanni da Maiano's *Pietà.*

Once a prison, the MUSEO NAZIONALE DEL BARGELLO'S only current captives are some of the city's art treasures. The Bargello rooms are filled with sculpture, vivid stone figures whose vitality exceeds the building's previous occupants.

The museum houses Michelangelo's *Tondo of the Madonna and Child with the Infant St. John, Bust of Brutus,* and his *Apollo.* On display are both Michelangelo and Jacopo Sansovino's *Bacchus;* the latter was influenced by the former representation. Notice De' Rossi's *Dying Adonis* and Giambologna's bronze *Mercury.* In the Cortile is Cenni's *Cannon of St Paul.*

On the first floor is Donatello's statue of *St. George* and bas-relief of *St. George Slaying the Dragon,* both from the Orsanmichele. The story of George slaying the evil dragon to rescue the Libyan king's daughter who was offered for sacrifice comes from the *Golden Legend;* the victo-

FLORENCE AND HER "DAVIDS"

David, the king of Israel, the hero of the Old Testament, and the personification of courage is the symbol of the city of Florence. The Florentines likened themselves to their protector; they were the modern Davids able to overcome any adversity, military, political, civic, or technological. Representations of the biblical figure often depict David's combat with Goliath (1 Samuel 17:38–51) or David's triumph over Goliath (1 Samuel 18:6–7). Three Davids in particular are of interest: those of Donatello, Andrea del Verrocchio, and Michelangelo.

Donatello carved many Davids. His most famous depiction, however, is one cast in bronze in the Museo Nazionale (Bargello). Donatello's *David* (1430s) was the first free-standing nude statue since the Fall of Rome. The life-sized nude (5 feet) represents a youthful David standing triumphantly over Goliath's head. The svelte adolescent is noble, dignified, and beautiful.

Andrea del Verrocchio cast a bronze David that is also housed in the Museo Nazionale (Bargello). Verrocchio's *David* (1470s) is a vision of a mere shepherd boy, an unlikely yet verdant hero, proud of his achievement.

Michelangelo's sculpture is unquestionably the most famous David (the original resides in the Accademia and a copy stands in the Piazza della Signoria). On August 16, 1501, Michelangelo received the commission to carve a gigantic David to serve as a symbol of the renewed republican government. With the Medicis in exile since 1494 and the execution of the heretic Savonarola in 1498, the Florentines wished to proclaim their newly gained freedom.

Michelangelo's colossal *David* (16 feet), if for no other reason than its technical achievement, was a source of immense pride for the Florentines. *David* is the embodiment of strength, an idealized and perfect athlete. If it were not for the sling on his left shoulder, *David* would easily be mistaken for Hercules. The mythological hero Hercules, the symbol of fortitude, was considered a sort of spiritual twin to David and a coprotector of Florence. Michelangelo in his *David* combines the idea of these two protectors of Florence into one symbol of moral and physical strength—Man as hero responsible for his own actions and master of his fate.

F

rious saint and martyr symbolizes the triumph of faith over the infidel. Other Donatello works include a bronze *David with the Head of Goliath* and a marble version of *David*. Ghiberti and Brunelleschi's reliefs of the *Sacrifice of Isaac* for the Baptistery door competition are displayed together. Stunning Madonnas include Agostino di Duccio's *Madonna and Child with Angels*, Michelozzo's reliefs of the *Madonna and Child*, Luca's *Madonna and Child in a Rose Garden*, and Luca della Robbia's *Madonna of the Apple*.

The second floor includes Giovanni della Robbia's *Tondo of the Madonna and Child and Young St. John* and his father Andrea's *Madonna of the Cushion* and *Madonna of the Stonemasons*. Verrocchio's bronze *David* is a stunning interpretation of the favorite Florentine subject.

The grand **PALAZZO PITTI**, built by a wealthy Florentine merchant and banking family in 1458 and enlarged through to the 19th century, houses eight separate museums including the famed **GALLERIA PALATINA**. The Palatina collection houses Medici acquisitions, 16th–18th-century works which include Titian's *Concert*, his portrait of *Pietro Aretino*, and his *Portrait of a Lady*. Notice Rosso Fiorentino's *Madonna Enthroned with Saints*, Andrea del Sarto's *Deposition*, and another Titian, his *Mary Magdalene* in the Hall of Apollo. Fittingly decorating the Hall of Mars is Rubens's allegory of the *Consequences of War*; nearby is his *Four Philosophers*. Both are among his most cel-

ebrated works. Within the Hall of Jove, Raphael's intimate *Portrait of a Lady* (La Fornarina), Verrocchio's *Head of St. Jerome*, Fra Bartolomeo's *Deposition*, and Andrea del Sarto's *Young St. John the Baptist* are highlights in a room full of masterpieces. The Hall of Saturn contains Raphael's *Madonna della Seggiola* (Madonna of the Small Seat) and his *Madonna del Granduca (Madonna of the Grandduke)*, named after it was purchased by Ferdinand III of Lorraine. Do not miss Perugino's *Deposition*. The Hall of the Education of Jove includes Cristofano Allori's *Judith and Holofernes* and Caravaggio's *Sleeping Cupid*. The Hall of Ulysses contains Filippino Lippi's *Death of Lucrezia*. The Hall of Justice displays Titian's *Portrait of a Man*.

Other collections in the palace include a costume gallery, a modern art gallery, and a museum of silver objects.

Florence is full of spectacular museums, often too many to digest in one visit. If time allows, visit the **HORNE MUSEUM** with 14th–16th-century painting and sculpture from the collection of the English art historian Herbert Percy Horne (1864–1916). Giotto's *St. Stephen* and Beccafumi's *Tondo of the Holy Family* are not to be missed. The **CASA BUONARROTI**, purchased by Michelangelo in 1508 and owned by the Buonarroti family until 1858, houses Michelangelo's earliest work, the *Madonna of the Steps* (sculpted at age 15), an early battle relief, a torso, and some of the master's drawings.

FOLIGNO

Nestled in a plain surrounded by hills, Foligno is one of the few Umbrian towns not placed atop a hill. This quiet, prosperous town is famous for spreading the written word throughout Italy. On April 11, 1472, a local printer, Emilio Orfini, with the help of a German printer, produced 33 copies of the 1st edition of the *Divine Comedy*. It was the first book printed in the Italian language in Italy.

Originally an Umbrian center, Roman *Fulginiae,* situated along the Flaminian Way, was an important commercial municipality. The modern city retains its ancient commercial importance, and its parallel streets are characteristic of Roman urban planning. Long after the secular origins of Foligno were established, its sacred genesis began. In A.D. 251 the body of martyr and bishop San Feliciano was buried at Foligno, and his tomb became a site of pilgrimage. A church was built on the spot, and it became the nucleus of successive towns named *Castellum San Feliciani, Civitas Feliciani,* and *Civitas Nova Fulginii.* After devastation under the hands of the Saracens and Hungarians, Foligno became a free commune under the church (12th century). In 1227 the Guelfs were chased out by Frederic II's imperial captains, but internal struggles between papal and imperial supporters continued. In 1310, the pontifical vicar, Rinaldo Trinci, defeated the Ghibellines. Between 1420 and 1439, Foligno reached a cultural and political climax and dominated its neighbors including Spello, Assisi, Bevagna, Montefalco, Trevi, and Norcia.

PLACES TO VISIT

The DUOMO (1133), dedicated to San Feliciano, continues to be the heart of the city. It was enlarged in 1201 and radically transformed in the 16th and 18th centuries. A mosaic of *Christ Enthroned Between Saints Felician and Messalina with Pope Leo XIII* was added during the 1904 facade restoration. (Messalina is a local 3rd-century martyr who was killed while bringing food to Feliciano.)

Within the Baroque interior, notice the gilt baldachino, an imitation of Bernini's work in St. Peter's, Rome. Spiraling columns and a canopy surmounted by figures stand above a 12th-century crypt and catacombs.

Inside the sacristy is a relief *Crucifixion with the Virgin and St. John* by Nicolò Alunno. Look for a copy of Raphael's *Madonna di Foligno,* which hangs in the left transept, and exit the church from here to glimpse the church's secondary facade. Carved in 1201, cosmic symbols including sundials, crescent moons, and the signs of the zodiac decorate the ornate Romanesque arch. Statues of Emperor Frederic (Barbarossa) and Anselm (local bishop) frame the portal.

The **PALAZZO TRINCI** (1389–1407) is the site of Foligno's library, gallery, state archive, and archaeological museum. Inside the courtyard are various Roman remains and a staircase to the **PINACOTECA**. On the ceiling in the vestibule are Pope Sixtus IV's coat of arms. The story of Romulus and Remus decorates the loggia that leads into a chapel covered with frescoes by Ottaviano Nelli that cover themes from the *Marriage of Anne* to the *Life of the Virgin* and ending with the *Crucifixion.*

The **HALL OF THE LIBERAL ARTS AND THE PLANETS** depicts representations of *Grammar, Dialectics, Music, Geometry, Philosophy, Astrology, Arithmetic,* and *Rhetoric* among the *Moon, Mars, Mercury, Jupiter, Venus, Saturn,* and the *Sun.*

The **HALL OF THE GIANTS** by Ottaviano Nelli depicts 15 heroes from Roman history. Among them, *Augustus, Tiberius, Scipius Africanus,* and *Nero.*

The following rooms run from 14th- and 15th-century Umbrian art, through the High Renaissance, and into the Baroque with works by Niccolò Alunno, Pier Antonio Mezzastris, Benozzo Gozzolli, and Dono Doni.

The numerous votive frescoes on the walls and pilasters of **SANTA MARIA INFRAPORTAS** (11th or 12th century)

form a gallery within the church. The most notable works include a *Crucifixion with St. Jerome* by Mezzastris and a *Madonna and Child with St. John* (1500) by Ugolino di Gisberto. Byzantine frescoes (12th century) in the Cappella della Assunta depict *Christ Blessing with Saints Peter and Paul,* the *Angel Gabriel,* and *Dismas, the Good Thief.*

Inside the 14th-century church of **SAN NICOLÒ** is an elaborate decorative polyptych representing the *Nativity, Resurrection,* and *Saints* by Niccolò Alunno (1492); the predella with five scenes from the Passion is in the Louvre.

The **CHIESA DELLA NUNZIATELLA** seems to be two churches. This Renaissance structure is divided in half by two iron gates with an altar on either side. Above the left altar is a richly decorated tabernacle by Lattanzio di Nicolò, and in a niche above the right altar is a *Baptism of Christ* and an *Eternal Father* by Perugino (1507).

Lack of funds dictated that **SAN SALVATORE** would not have the decorative extravagance of other Foligno churches; however, the Flemish tapestry behind the altar compensates for sparse ornamentation. It is a 16th-century work decorated with Old Testament scenes.

The **MONASTERY OF SANT'ANNA** is a convent school for girls decorated largely by Mezzastris. In the courtyard is a cycle of evangelical stories by Lattanzio di Niccolò and Feliciano de'Muti

(1578). The convent is best known for a work that is no longer here. Raphael's *Madonna di Foligno* hung here for over 200 years until it was taken by Napoleon's troops in 1798. In 1816 it was returned not to Foligno but to the pope and has remained in the Vatican collection since then.

GUBBIO

Prehistoric man called the site at the foot of Mount Ingino home long before the Umbri claimed it as their religious and political center in the 3rd century B.C. Legend tells that Gubbio (ancient Iguvium) was one of the first five towns built after the Great Flood. Perhaps it was the flood that destroyed the Neanderthal residents, whose remains were recently unearthed.

In the 3rd century A.D., Gubbio developed a strong alliance with Rome and flourished until it was destroyed by the wrath of Totila. In the Middle Ages it was a strategic outpost between Ravenna and Rome. With a populace of Ghibelline supporters, the Holy Roman Emperors favored it. A period of artistic and cultural development came under the rule of the Montefeltro (Dukes of Urbino) and the della Rovere. Under the power of these wealthy families the populace developed Guelf sympathies, and in the 16th century Gubbio came under papal rule.

While many people and the traditions of many periods left their mark on Gubbio, its medieval glory prevails. The city remains almost unaltered since the Middle Ages, and its greatest traditions, art, and legends originate in that period. The *Corsa dei Ceri* (the Race of the Ceri) is the most famous and possibly most ancient festival. It is an enduring festival that requires the physical endurance of many men to carry out the celebration. Held annually on May 15, the eve of Sant'Ubaldo (11th-century bishop and patron of the city), the festival may predate the very saint it honors. Legend claims the festival is a vestige of the pagan worship of the Goddess Cerere; some say it is a tribute to Ubaldo, who saved the city from Barbarossa in 1155; others believe it symbolizes civic power.

The Ceri (meaning waxes) are three heavy, 16½-feet-tall wooden statues representing respectively Sant'Ubaldo (patron of masons), San Giorgio (patron of merchants), and Sant'Anthony the Abbot (patron of farmers). On the first Sunday of May, the Ceri are carried from their home on the peak of Mount Ingino, the Basilica of Sant'Ubaldo, down to the city. The statue bearers are called Ceraioli, and they descend with the statues, in three groups of about twenty men, to the Chiesa dei Muratori (church of the masons).

G

81

A celebratory Mass is held for the Ceraioli on the morning of the 15th, followed by a leisurely procession of the Ceri through the streets. At 2 o'clock a celebratory banquet of fish is served, and at 5 o'clock the excitement resumes. The procession takes the form of a furious race as the men who carry the Ceri run through the city to the top of the mount. Here the statues are returned to the basilica until the following year. Miraculously, Sant'Ubaldo always wins the race, followed by St. George, and finally St. Anthony the Abbot.

PLACES TO VISIT

If you happen to miss the festival you might choose to reenact your own version of the Corsa dei Ceri by climbing up Mount Ingino to see the BASILICA DI SANT'UBALDO. Or take the cable car up and simply enjoy the view. The medieval church was reconstructed and enlarged in 1524 by the della Roveres. An urn on the main altar holds the relics of Sant'Ubaldo, and the windows decorating the nave show episodes from the life of the saint. On the left side of the nave stand the Ceri, in anticipation of their yearly sport. Notice the statue of Sant'Ubaldo is missing three fingers; they were cut off by a former devout custodian as a keepsake.

Return to the lower city and make your way to the PIAZZA QUARANTA MARTIRI (Square of the Forty Martyrs). The square's public gardens are a great place to have a picnic and reflect on those who gave up their lives for both religious and political liberty (a statue at the entrance is a monument to the town's fallen heroes from World War I). Across from the gardens is the Gothic church of SAN FRANCESCO (St. Francis), once thought to be designed by Fra Bevignate of Perugia.

Inside is the CAPPELLA DELLA MADONNA with its beautifully preserved frescoes discovered only in 1942. The work of Gubbio's most celebrated painter Ottaviano Nelli, the 17 frescoes recount the *Life of the Virgin.*

Locals claim that a small chapel in the SACRISTY is the room where St. Francis slept while visiting Gubbio. This chapel was once part of the medieval residence of the Spadalonga family, the family with whom Francis boarded. Legend tells that during Francis's stay a pack of wolves was terrorizing Gubbio. One wolf in particular was most vicious. Francis brought it upon himself to save the town from this menace. He found the wolf and brought it to town, where, before all the citizens, he made a pact with the wolf. Gubbians promised to feed the wolf regularly in exchange for an end to the terror. Francis and the wolf sealed the agreement with a handshake. Recently, while repairing a nearby church, a skeleton of a giant wolf was discovered under a stone marker—might these be the remains of the "terror" of Gubbio?

The adjacent cloister houses the RACCOLTA DI OGGETTI D'ARTE, a small collection of art objects. The collection includes fragments of a cross, possibly the work of the father of painting in Gubbio, Oderisi da Gubbio (d. 1299). Few of his works still exist and he is referred to in few written sources; the most notable reference is by Dante, who called him "l'onor d'Agobbi" (the honor of Gubbio) (Purgatory XI, 80).

The MUSEO AND PINACOTECA COMUNALE houses works by the Gubbian school of artists and other Umbrian treasures. The collection, in the Palazzo dei Consoli, was designed and constructed by Gattapone and Angelo da Orvieto (1332–37). Over the main entrance is a *Madonna and Child with Saints John and Ubaldo* (1495) by Bernardino di Nanni. Within, the first room is dedicated to Roman archaeological remains found in Umbria. The museum actually begins in the second room that holds the celebrated Tavole Eugubine (the Eugubine Tables), seven tall bronze tablets from 270–200 B.C. that refer to ceremonial cult practices. Found in 1444 in the environs of the Roman theatre, they are written in a combination of Etruscan and Latin characters to express the Umbrian language (for which no written alphabet existed) phonetically. A fresco representing *The Madonna and Child and Saints John the Baptist, Anthony, Francis, Ubaldo, and the Standard Bearers of the City* by Palmerucci

(Gubbio's oldest known painter, influenced by the Sienese) decorates the walls.

The Pinacoteca upstairs documents 13th–16th centuries. Gubbian art includes works by Palmerucci, Nucci, and Damiani. The beautiful blonde *Madonna del Melograno* (Madonna of the Pomegranate) disputably attributed to Caporali, Lippi, and Pier Francesco Florentino and the *Noli me Tangere* by Timoteo Viti (Raphael's first teacher) are among the most notable in the collection.

In-situ frescoes in the Gubbian tradition abound in the city's churches. The 13th-century Gothic DUOMO is faced with a 16th-century facade that incorporates the symbols of the evangelists supporting a rose window surmounted by the figure of a mystical lamb. The arcade's ceiling within is an excellent example of Gubbian "wagon vaulting," meant to imitate hands clasped in prayer.

The decorative simplicity of the church of SAN DOMENICO (originally dedicated to St. Martin, 1186) typifies Dominican church construction. The facade is bare, and the delicate floral designs carved in the ceiling are unpainted. The chapels are frescoed by artists from the early Umbrian school and from the period of Baroque restoration. Ottaviano Nelli's work is seen in the chapel of St. Peter Martyr.

The tiny structure of SANTA MARIA NUOVA (no longer a church) contains beautifully preserved frescoes; they

G

include the *Madonna del Belvedere* (1403) by Ottaviano Nelli, a moving *Crucifixion* by the local Giovanni Pintali, and a *Madonna Giving Milk to the Child with Saints* by Bernardino di Nanni. Two massive coffins (in left nave) once held the sacred remains of St. Ubaldo. The first is a wooden coffin secured with seven locks that did not escape the intrusion of a robber's drill, and the second is a later coffin enclosed in metal and secure from robbers seeking treasures.

The 13th-century church of SANT' AGOSTINO has a unique modern facade and unusual cylindrical buttresses for support. The interior was almost entirely decorated by Ottaviano Nelli. The beautifully decorated presbytery deals with themes of the Last Judgment, Christ and the apostles, and stories from the life of St. Augustine.

Pilgrims literally following in the footsteps of Christ flock to the church of SAN PIETRO. In the corner of a small chapel is an inscription, *Vestigia Pedum Christi* (a trace of Christ's foot), and opposite it is the shape of a foot imprinted on the stone. To the faithful, the shape is clearly the impression of a foot, while others are skeptical that the impression represents any form.

"La Vittoriana," the Franciscan church of SANTA MARIA DELLA VITTORIA, is built on the spot where Francis encountered the wolf. Come prepared with a bit of food; the wolf's descendants still roam the area.

Gubbio was christened "patria dei matti" (the land of the crazies) by foreigners visiting the city during the Race of the Ceri; the visitors were amazed that anyone would continue such a physically demanding tradition. If you find the festival appealing, be sure to acquire a *patente da matto* (a certificate of madness) by running around the FONTANA DEI PAZZI (the fountain of the insane) three times while local "nuts" splash water on you. Interestingly, a part of the Ceri festival and procession includes splashing the three statues with buckets of water. Certifiably mad? You decide.

LORETO

Pilgrims worldwide journey to Loreto to venerate the Santa Casa, the Holy House of the Virgin Mary. A choir of angels miraculously transported the sacred abode to Loreto in the 13th century. Its relocation to a laurel grove (*laure-* tum), from which the town derives its name, was not inadvertent. Symbolizing triumph, eternity, and chastity, the imperishable and verdant laurel leaf is a fitting symbol to surround the house of the Virgin, herself the personification of purity and the indefatigable church. The laurel, the Virgin, her church, and its followers are "a wreath that never fades" (1 Corinthians 9:25–26).

The Holy House was relocated twice. Turkish destruction threatened to destroy the humble Nazarene house, thus necessitating its removal by angels to Dalmatia in 1291. On December 10, 1294, angels once again transported it, this time to Loreto. Pope Innocent VII inaugurated the celebratory mass for the Feast of the Transportation of the Holy House (December 10), and Pope Benedict XV named the Madonna of Loreto, undoubtedly the world's first frequent flyer, the patron saint of aviators.

PLACES TO VISIT

A bronze statue of Pope Sixtus V (1585–90) commands the Piazza della Madonna. His effigy stands on the stairs before the SANTUARIO DELLA SANTA CASA (c. 1460–1560), built to house the Holy House. Its architects include Giuliano da Maiano, Giuliano da Sangallo, Bramante, Sansovino, and San-

gallo the Younger. The church facade (1587) features a bronze statue of the *Virgin and Child* by Girolamo Lombardo above three bronze relief portals by the same artist. The adjacent campanile is a neoclassical addition (1750) designed by Luigi Vanvitelli.

Works by Domenichino, Guido Reni, Barocci, and Carlo Maratti decorate the interior. Napoleon plundered the majority of the church decorations; fortunately, he left the fresco cycles by Melozzo da Forli and Luca Signorelli.

Beneath the dome is the Holy House, encased in a marble screen begun by Donato Bramante in 1468. Sansovino, Sangallo, and Della Porta executed relief carvings depicting *Scenes from the Life of the Virgin Mary.*

The house itself is a plain brick structure (28ft x 12.5ft x 13.5ft). Within a niche is a small black representation of the *Virgin and Child* in Lebanon cedar. The Lebanese cedar tree symbolizes Christ's beauty and majesty: "His countenance is as Lebanon, excellent as the cedars" (Song of Solomon 5:15).

LUCCA

From afar, Lucca looks like Eden sprouting from a rock. Lush trees crown Lucca's massive 17th-century ramparts, softening the once imposing and necessary defense walls.

The idyllic tranquillity is a reward after centuries of unrest. Lucca was the first Tuscan settlement to accept Christianity. The Word was spread in A.D. 47 by Paulinus, Lucca's first bishop and St.

85

Peter's disciple. Today visitors to Lucca, faithful and nonbeliever alike, must enter into this paradise through St. Peter's gate.

Known for creating heavenly music, Lucca hosts the Sagra Musicale Lucchese (Festival of Sacred Music) annually from April through June, offering classical and religious music concerts in local churches. It is no surprise that this melodious Eden would produce two musical masters, natives Luigi Boccherini (1743–1805) and Giacomo Puccini (1858–1924).

Inhabited over 50,000 years ago, Lucca has long been considered a prime location. In 56 B.C. Caesar, Pompey, and Crassus chose it as the location of the First Triumvirate. It was the first Christianized Tuscan settlement and became the favored commune of the Holy Roman Emperor. It fought fiercely for its independence from Pisa and Florence. Lucca was subject briefly to the Pisan Ghibellines in 1314. Two years later it emerged independent and strong under the rule of a native nobleman, Castruccio Castracani, who secured the city's supremacy and prosperity (and his own) until his death in 1328. It fell again into Pisan control until 1369, when Emperor Charles IV granted it autonomy. In 1799 Lucca fell to Napoleon, and from 1805 to 1815 his sister Elisa Baciocchi ruled the city. It later passed into the control of Napoleon's widow, the city's favorite ruler, Marie Louise de Bourbon.

PLACES TO VISIT

The cathedral of SAN MARTINO is dedicated to the 4th-century Hungarian soldier, Martin of Tours, who fought in the Roman army and who, when chastised for choosing his faith over fighting, vowed to battle his enemy armed only with the Cross. The present church is built atop the site of a 6th-century church that was elevated to the seat of a bishop in the 8th century. In the 11th century the bishop of Lucca, Anselmo da Baggio, rebuilt the structure. He would soon be elected Pope Alexander II (1061–73). He consecrated the new church in 1070, but the newly aggrandized form did not satisfy the Lucchesi, who redesigned the interior in the 13th, 14th, and 15th centuries.

The asymmetrical facade was built to accommodate the pre-existing defense tower and transform it into a bell tower (1261). On the transitional pillar between the church and tower is a 12th-century carved labyrinth, a symbol of the arduous journey towards salvation.

The delicate, triple-tiered facade (1204) by Giudetto da Como rises above a richly ornamented portico (1233). Flanking the central doorway are reliefs depicting the *Labors of the Months* and the *Life of St. Martin*. Atop the left doorway are a *Deposition and Adoration of the Magi* by Nicola Pisano. Crowning the right doorway is *St. Martin Meeting the Arians* and *The Beheading of St. Regulus*.

Inside the church on the facade wall is the 13th-century Romanesque statue depicting *St. Martin Dividing His Cloak* (copy outside). The sculpture illustrates the event that transformed Martin's life and led him to devote his days to religion. According to the story, as a cavalryman posted in Amiens, France, Martin came across a beggar suffering from the cold. Martin immediately cut his cloak in two and gave half to the beggar. That night Martin received a vision of Christ and was forever changed.

Along the right aisle is a *Last Supper* attributed to Tintoretto and his school. Along the same aisle, a door leads into the sacristy with an altarpiece by Domenico Ghirlandaio of the *Madonna Enthroned with Saints,* surmounted by a lunette depicting the *Dead Christ* by Filippo Lippi.

In the right transept are two works by the local sculptor, Matteo Civitali: the tomb of Pope Nicholas V's secretary, Pietro da Noceto (1472), and the tomb of Domenico Bertini. Civitali also contributed two angels that flank the tabernacle in the chapel of the Holy Sacrament and the altar of St. Regulus (1484).

In the north transept is the serene funerary masterpiece, Jacopo della Quercia's tomb of Ilaria del Carretto Guinigi (1405–06). On the altar is Gianbologna's *Risen Christ with Saints Peter and Paul.* In the Cappella del Santuario

is Fra Bartolomeo's *Virgin Enthroned with Saints* (1509).

The Holy Image is the most precious and popular piece in the church. Encased in Civitali's marble Tempietto (1484) is the *Volto Santo,* a cedarwood portrait of Christ carved by Nicodemus after the Crucifixion. According to legend, this holy relic was concealed during iconoclast destruction and set adrift on a boat that landed in Luni in 782. The local bishop was told by angels to place the effigy in an ox-driven cart, and the relic was to remain where the oxen took it. The beasts headed straight to Lucca.

The image was greatly revered in the Middle Ages, attracting throngs of pilgrims to Lucca. The locals struck coins depicting the sacred image; cults devoted to the image arose in England, while King Rufus of England went so far as to swear oaths by the image. Soon, thousands of *Volto Santo* replicas were carved and spread throughout Europe. Celebrated yearly on September 13, the *Volto Santo* is adorned with jewels and paraded through the streets. No one seems to mind that the statue is probably a 13th-century copy of an 11th-century work modeled on an 8th-century Syrian image.

The MUSEO DELLA CATTEDRALE houses Francesco Vanni's *Crucifixion* (17th century) and Jacopo della Quercia's monumental statue of *St. John the Evangelist* (15th century). Do not miss the *Croce dei Pisani* (the cross of the

L

Pisans), a master goldwork by Vincenzo da Michele, portraying a golden Christ hanging on the Tree of Redemption flanked by the Virgin and St. John the Evangelist.

The CHIESA E BATTISTERO DI SAN GIOVANNI E SANTA REPARATA attests to centuries of worship on this Lucchesan site. The present structure was built between 1160 and 1187 with a facade dating to 1589. Visit the recent excavation that exposed five previous buildings. The layers reveal Lucca's original cathedral (715); below it, an early Christian church decorated with geometric mosaic pavement (4th–5th centuries); further underground, a Roman bath (2nd century A.D.); and finally, a Roman temple (1st century B.C.).

A huge stone Archangel Michael stands atop the towering facade of the church of SAN MICHELE IN FORO (11th–14th centuries). The winged sword-bearer looks down on Lucca's ancient Roman forum from his lofty perch in the heart of the city. Spiraling columns, carved figures, and beasts and delicate inlaid marble ornament the facade. On a pillar to the right is Matteo Civitali's *Madonna and Child* (1476–80), erected by the city in thanksgiving for deliverance from the plague.

Certainly citizens would have invoked the protection of a number of plague saints, as is evidenced by Filippo Lippi's work inside the church of *Saints Helena, Jerome, Sebastian, and Roch.*

Its past illustrious organists, Giacomo Puccini's father and grandfather, embellish the church history. Puccini himself also sang in the choir as a boy.

Giacomo Puccini's organ debut was held in the church dedicated to Lucca's patron saint, the church of San Paolino (1515–36). Here he practiced and played professionally.

In the 12th century, a small 6th-century basilica was rebuilt and rededicated to an Irish pilgrim, the builder of the original church on site. THE CHURCH OF SAN FREDIANO (1112–47) is dedicated to the 6th century bishop of Lucca, the abbot Finnian. He was an Irish pilgrim passing along the pilgrim's way in 588 who was cajoled by local clergymen to stay. He worked many miracles, including saving the city from flooding by diverting the nearby River Serchio. This and other miracles led to his canonization and were the impetus for renaming the church in his honor.

A 13th-century mosaic by Berlinghiero Berlinghieri decorates the facade. It is a radiant vision of Christ ascending into a golden-leafed heaven flanked by two angels with the 12 apostles below.

Scenes from the *Life of Moses and Christ as the Good Shepherd with Apostles and Prophets* decorate the Romanesque baptismal font (12th century) within. A Tempietto carved with allegorical representations of the months crowns the font. Behind it is Andrea della Robbia's lunette of the *Annunciation*. In a darkened corner, a coin-operated bulb will illuminate Matteo Civitali's *Virgin Annunciate*.

The 17th-century chapel of *Santa Zita* houses the mummified body of the saint (d. 1278). Paintings of her life and miracles by Francesco del Tintore decorate the chapel. The patron saint of maids and ladies-in-waiting, Zita was a 13th-century servant who took food scraps from her employer to give to beggars. When caught by her master, demanding to know what she was hiding in her apron, she responded, "roses and flowers." To both their surprise, when she opened her apron, the scraps of food had miraculously transformed into flowers. On her feast day, April 26, her shriveled body is removed from the chapel for adoration and the church piazza is strewn with flowers.

A single block of carved marble in the Cappella Trenta by Jacopo della Quercia and his pupil Giovanni da Imola depicts the *Madonna and Child with Saints* and the *Legend of the Saints*.

Amerigo Aspertini's frescoes (1508–09) in the chapel of Sant' Agostino portray the pride of Lucca; they depict the *Life and Miracles of San Frediano* and the *Legend of the Volto Santo*.

Incorporated into the growing city in 1260, the CHIESA DI SANTA MARIA FORISPORTAM (13th century) once stood outside Lucca's ancient walls. Inside, an early Christian sarcophagus carved with scenes of *Christ as the Good Shepherd* and *Daniel in the Lions' Den* serves as a font. Works by Guercino include *St. Lucy* and an *Assumption* altarpiece. A golden *Dormition and Assumption of the Virgin* (1386) by Angelo Puccinelli hangs in the sacristy.

The church of SAN FRANCESCO was constructed in 1228 and rebuilt in the 14th and 17th centuries. To the right of the high altar are the notable early works, the *Presentation of the Virgin in the Temple* and the *Marriage of the Virgin*. Seventeenth-century works include Passignano's *Noli me Tangere* and Federico Zuccari's *Nativity*. Famed local composers, Francesco Geminiani (1687–1762) and Luigi Boccherini (1743–1805), are buried here.

Lesser-known churches throughout Lucca contain notable treasures. Originally an oratory, the Pisan-Gothic SANTA MARIA DELLA ROSA (1309–33) was built against the town's Roman walls, incorporating the ancient blocks in its structure. The now deconsecrated SAN CRISTOFORO (12th–13th centuries) is the burial place of Lucca's greatest artist, Matteo Civitali (d. 1501). It also serves as a war memorial; the names of the town's dead are carved on its walls. Inside the seldom open church of SAN ROMANO (13th century) is the beautifully carved tomb of San Romano (1490) by Matteo Civitali. *Christ Handing the Keys of Heaven to St. Peter* (1203) by Guido da Como crowns the entrance to the church of SAN PIETRO SOMALDI (12th–14th centuries).

L

The **PINACOTECA NAZIONALE,** housed in the 17th-century Palazzo Mansi, offers a glimpse at Renaissance and Baroque art and 17th- and 18th-century palace decoration. Flemish tapestries (1665) and frescoes depicting mythological subjects (1688) decorate the sumptuous rooms. The paintings are beyond the breakfast and music rooms. The collection includes numerous Medici portraits by Bronzino and Pontormo; Domenichino's *Samson;* Vignali's *Tobias and the Angel;* Manetti's *Triumph of David;* battle scenes by Salvatore Rosa; and works by Sodoma, Andrea del Sarto, Jacopo Bassano, and Tintoretto.

The **MUSEO NAZIONALE DI VILLA GUINIGI** provides a survey of the local artistic history. Lucca's origins can be discovered in archaeological remains from the Etruscan to Late Roman period. The popularity of and reverence for the Volto Santo is evidenced in the medieval coin collection. Collected paintings and sculpture feature Matteo Civitali's reliefs of the *Annunciation* and *Ecce Homo,* Ugolino's *Madonna and Child,* and Fra Bartolomeo's *Madonna della Misericordia* and *God the Father with Saints Mary Magdalene and Catherine.*

A 20 km drive north leads to Borgo a Mozzano and the legendary **PONTE DEL DIAVOLO** (Devil's Bridge), an ancient footbridge over the Serchio River. According to legend, the townspeople made a pact with the devil; he would construct the bridge in exchange for the first soul to cross it. The clever and faithful villagers kept their bargain and relinquished the first soul to traverse the bridge to Satan—a small dog.

MASSAFRA

Two bridges span a deep ravine, the Gravina di San Marco, which divides Massafra into two parts: the old town called the Terra and the newer town called Borgo San Caterina. The ravine is lined with caves that served as chapels-caves *(laure)* for Greek monks during the Middle Ages. The monks devoted their lives to prayer in stunning surroundings; their numerous cave-churches are decorated with colorful frescoes.

PLACES TO VISIT

Descend a monumental staircase on the outskirts of the old town to the sanctuary of the **MADONNA DELLA SCALA** (1731). The church contains a cave-crypt (8th–9th centuries) decorated with a 12th-century fresco of the *Madonna and Child with Two Deer* called "La Vergine della Scala."

The **CRYPTA DELLA BONA NOVA,** adjacent to the sanctuary, contains a 13th-century fresco of *Christ Pantocrator.*

Descend 200m to the valley bottom to reach the FARMACIA DEL MAGO GREGURO (Pharmacy of the Magician Greguro), a complex of over 100 small adjoining caves. Tradition holds that this maze of subterraneous chambers served as storage rooms for the monk's medicinal herbs.

A stairwell carved from the rock on the east side of the ravine leads to another well-preserved cave-crypt. The Chiesa-crypta di San Marco contains a simple baptismal font and a fresco depicting St. Mark. Greek and Latin inscriptions are carved into the church structure. In the apse, 13th-century frescoes of saints Cosmas and Damian are all that survive of the once fully frescoed wall.

MILANO

(MILAN)

B ehind Milan's modern facade— its finance towers, industry, and smog—is a culturally rich metropolis. Profuse artistic, architectural, and cultural legacies reveal its lengthy and diverse history. The cosmopolitan commercial center offers an astonishing wealth of wondrous churches and spectacular museums. While the prosperous ruling families of the Visconti, Sforza, and Hapsburgs contributed significantly to Milan's worldly and spiritual heritage, it was Milan's bishops, Sant' Ambrogio and San Carlo Borromeo in particular, whose piety and vision encouraged a profusion of sacred art.

Settled by an ancient Celtic tribe, the *Insubri* (c. 388 B.C.), Milan was conquered by the Romans (2nd century B.C.) and renamed *Mediolanum* (the central place). Its centrality gained the city favor with the Roman emperors, who moved the imperial court to Milan. In February 313, Emperor Constantine I proclaimed the Edict of Milan, legislating tolerance for Christianity, enabling Christians to freely congregate, worship, and erect churches. In the 4th century, the Roman prefect Ambrogio was sent to Milan to resolve a conflict between the Catholics and the Arians (a heretical sect who denied the divinity of Christ). The local bishop, an Arian follower, had died and a new Milanese bishop was to be elected; however, the two feuding factions could not agree on a suitable candidate.

When Ambrogio stepped up to address the crowd, a child cried out, "Ambrogio shall be bishop"—and so, curiously, he was. The new bishop, though not yet baptized, became a model of devotion and piety and excelled

91

as an eloquent statesman and theologian. He unified the church against Arianism, converting St. Augustine along the way. He is also credited with conceiving the Ambrosian chant. Today, Ambrosian rites are still celebrated in Milanese churches (the service differs from the Roman rite), a reminder of the Milanese period of ecclesiastical independence from Rome (5th–11th centuries).

In the 11th century, Bishop Heribert established a citizen parliament and army under the new Milanese commune. The group fought foreign occupation for both the city and its church. In 1294, the Visconti family gained rule over Piedmont, Lombardy, and Emilia. In the 14th century, beginning with Gian Galeazzo Visconti's (1351–1402) rule, through Francesco Sforza's (1401–66) control, and ending with Lodovico il Moro's (1451–1508) reign, Milan realized two prosperous centuries and the acquisition and patronage of splendid artworks.

In 1535, Milan fell to the Spanish, renewing ecclesiastical rule. During the Counter-Reformation, under Archbishop Carlo Borromeo (1538–84), the sacred arts flourished. In 1712, the Austrian Habsburgs gained control; Milan experienced the enlightened dictatorship of Empress Maria Teresa, who encouraged social and moral reform. She encouraged art and learning at the Jesuit College and constructed its library, garden, observatory, art school, and gallery.

Napoleon continued Maria's vision by expanding the art gallery and commissioning the completion of the facade of Milan's Duomo.

PLACES TO VISIT

Twenty-two-hundred stone saints and 95 gargoyles inhabit the heart of Milan; they are the earthly witnesses to a city that sprawls around its heavenly DUOMO, Milan Cathedral. The cathedral was begun in 1386 by Gian Galeazzo Visconti, the first duke of Milan. The edifice, an outstanding example of Italian Gothic architecture, was an offering to the Virgin, a pious bribe in hopes of insuring the birth of a son. Two years later, in 1388, the duke received an heir, and the church was subsequently dedicated to "Maria Nascente," the nascent Mother.

The emergent structure was borne on the duke's fortune, state taxes, and the sale of indulgences. Its construction spans seven centuries. While a functional cathedral was in use by 1399, rebuilding continues today. Numerous architects contributed to the massive structure (518 feet long x 305 feet wide), among them Simone da Orsegnio, Giovannino de'Grassi, Bonino da Campione, Marco da Carona, Giovanni Antonio Amadeo, Pellegrino Tibaldi, Francesco Maria Richini, and Francesco Croce, to name a few.

Enter through the stunning bronze cathedral doors (19th–20th centuries) depicting the *Edict of Constantine, The Life of St. Ambrose, Milan Versus Barbarossa,* and the *History of the Cathedral.* Inside the spacious five-aisle church, intricate statuary and luminous stained-glass windows abound. Among the multicolored glass panes are the *Life of St. John the Evangelist* (1473–77), *Scenes from the New Testament,* the *Life of St. Eligius* (1480–89), the *Life of St. James the Elder* (1554–64), the *Life of St. Catherine of Alexandria* (1543), and representations of the *Prophets* (15th century).

The variety of statuary portrays *St. Bartholomew* (carrying his flayed skin) by Marco d'Agrate, the *Tomb of Giacomo Medici,* "Il Medeghino" (d. 1555) by Leone Leoni, the statue of *Martin V* by Jacopo da Tradate, the bronze *Trivulzio candelabrum* (13th–14th centuries), and representations of the *Doctors of the Church, Prophets, and Sibyls* atop the pinnacles.

The cathedral TREASURY is below the main altar, adjacent to the crypt of San Carlo Borromeo. The treasury contains precious ivory, gold, and silver from as early as the 4th century.

Archaeological excavations in the 1960s revealed the BAPTISTERY OF ST. AMBROSE. Properly called the Baptistery of San Giovanni alle Fonti (A.D. 378), it is the alleged spot where St. Augustine baptized St. Ambrose. Ambrose was named bishop of Milan before he was even baptized!

Much of the cathedral's eclectic artistic history survives in the MUSEO DEL DUOMO. The chronological arrangement of models, statues, tapestries, and stained glass adds to the cathedral's already overwhelmingly rich collection.

Milan's beloved St. Ambrose's church, SANT' AMBROGIO, is surrounded by a variety of religious edifices and structures dedicated to the bishop. They include an imitation medieval city gate (1939) decorated with its original statues of patron saints (1360) called the *Pusterla di Sant' Ambrogio* and the Università Cattolica del Sacro Cuore with cloisters (1497–1513) from a structure originally intended to be a convent by Bramante. It was reconstructed using original materials after suffering World War II damage.

Founded in A.D. 379, the church of Sant' Ambrogio, both basilica and martyrium, was constructed atop the burial site of two martyrs, Gervase and Protase. St. Ambrose's remains were added to the church's venerable relics. The church was rebuilt in 1080 and restored between 1859 and 1890.

Enter the church complex through the atrium (1088–99); inside the arcaded enclosure, the church facade and bell towers are revealed. Greater building advances and more wealth, not church hierarchy, distinguish the short *Torre dei Monaci* or Monk's Bell tower (9th century) from the more delicate, taller *Torre dei Canonici* or Canon's Bell tower (1144).

St. Ambrose is represented in relief on the bronze portals (10th century) that lead into the church. The early Christian presence is still the highlight

M

93

of Ambrose's church. Notice the beautifully carved pulpit that stands atop the *sarcophagus of Stilicho*, a 5th-century early Christian tomb. Master goldsmith Volvino contributed the two sanctuary treasures, a 9th-century *ciborium* and a golden altar, *Altare d'oro* (835), with gilt scenes from the lives of Christ and St. Ambrose.

Golden visions continue in the dome of the south apse with the *Sacello di San Vittore in Ciel d'Oro* (6th century), dedicated to St. Victor in the golden sky. Heavenly mosaics depict St. Ambrose among radiant saintly companions.

Beautiful frescoes throughout the church include Tiepolo's *Martyrdom of St. Victor and the Shipwreck of San Satiro* and Bernardino Lanino's *Madonna and Child.*

Pass through Bramante's *Portico della Canonoca* (1492–99) into the Museo di Sant' Ambrogio, which provides a church history and houses precious church relics.

Founded in 1463, the church of SANTA MARIA DELLE GRAZIE (1466–90) stands atop an earlier church site dedicated to the Virgin Mary of Grace. The fame of Leonardo da Vinci's *Last Supper* or *Cenacolo* (1495–97) draws thousands of pious pilgrims and inquisitive tourists to what was once the site of Northern Italy's Inquisition headquarters. Between 1553 and 1778, the adjacent Dominican cloister was the administration center for the Milanese Inquisition.

At the core of the church and cloister is the *Cappella della Maria delle Grazie,* with the venerated image of the *Madonna delle Grazie.* Within her church are numerous frescoed Dominican saints and scenes of Christ's life. At the elegant church crossing and elongated choir (1492) by Bramante is the tomb of Lodovico il Moro's wife, Beatrice d'Este (d. 1497).

Housed in the refectory is Leonardo da Vinci's *Last Supper* (1495–97). It covers the end wall of the dining hall. Christ's table is a pictorial extension of the monks' dining table—symbolically, they dine and commune together. On the opposite wall is a *Crucifixion* (1495) by Giovanni Donato Montorfano.

Unfortunately, Leonardo's experimental fresco techniques began to deteriorate almost immediately after the work's completion. Attempts to restore and preserve it were nearly lost during a World War II bombing raid. While restorers continue attempts to reclaim its original beauty, the *Last Supper's* enigmatic power and appeal need no revival.

The oldest church in Milan, SAN LORENZO MAGGIORE (rebuilt in the 16th century) recalls its former early Christian form and 12th-century remodeling. Known as the "Roman Temple," 16 imperial Roman columns (2nd–3rd centuries) stand in front of the basilica, before a copy of a statue of the Emperor Constantine, commemorating the Edict of Milan (313).

LEONARDO DA VINCI'S *LAST SUPPER*

In early 1482 Leonardo da Vinci left Florence for Milan; there he was engaged under the services of Lodovico Sforza, the duke of Milan. When, a decade later, the Sforza family decided to convert the Dominican church of Santa Maria delle Grazie into a family museum, they commissioned Leonardo to execute a painting in the refectory. Leonardo frescoed an enormous *Last Supper* (c. 1495–97) measuring 13 feet 9 inches by 29 feet 10 inches.

In the *Last Supper*, Leonardo represents the moment when Christ foretells his betrayal. His revolutionary depiction is an examination of human psychology, a study in how each disciple—the 11 innocents and the one guilty—react to the shattering news.

Posture, gesture, attitude, behavior, and appearance express each apostle's state of mind, their bond to Christ, and their knowledge of Christ's pronouncement. Every gesture and action links the figures into rhythmic groups. To Christ's immediate left, the ever-doubting Thomas raises a challenging finger; James the Greater draws back in horror; and gentle Philip leans forward inquiringly. Behind them, Matthew turns his face in dismay; Thaddeus (Jude) shows surprise, doubt, and suspicion; and Simon sits troubled. To Christ's right, John falls away from the Lord; Peter, boldly, knife in hand, demands if it is he Christ suspects; and Judas sits in shadow, seemingly unresponsive and staring at Christ while clutching the purse with its 30 pieces of silver. At the far right of the table Bartholomew inquiringly leans forward on the table; James the Less reaches out and places his left hand on Peter's strong shoulder; and Andrew raises his arm, hands outspread in disbelief.

Amid the confusion, Christ sits calmly. He is noble, dignified, serene, and majestic; he is the center of space, light, and life.

M

Reminiscent of the church of San Vitale in Ravenna, the interior of San Lorenzo recalls imperial splendor with galleries, numerous exedrae, and a spectacular dome crowning the centralized plan.

The *Cappella di Sant' Aquilino* (5th century) is a sumptuously decorated imperial mausoleum with mosaics depicting *Christ with the Apostles* (4th century). Near the entrance is an early Christian sarcophagus (3rd century), and atop the altar is a 16th-century urn containing the relics of St. Aquilinus.

St. Ambrose founded SAN NAZARO MAGGIORE in the 4th century. It was subsequently renovated in the 11th century and by Carlo Borromeo in 1571. The main church attraction is the peaceful mausoleum of the condottiere Giangiacomo Trivulzio. The simple tomb by Bartolomeo Bramantino (1512–50) features a Latin inscription by the busy condottiere that reads, "Qui numquam quievit quiescit; tace" (He who never knew rest now sleeps; silence).

Danielle Crespi, Giuseppe Nuvolone, and Bernardino Luini decorated the church proper. Look for the 16th-century *Cappella di Santa Caterina d'Alessandria*, decorated with frescoes of her life and martyrdom.

The basilica of SANT' EUSTORGIO was built in the 4th century and frequently remodeled with significant additions in the 13th, 14th, and 19th centuries. Its clock tower (1305) is the world's first towering timepiece.

Possibly founded by Bishop Eustorgio, the church was originally built to house the relics of the three Magi, which Eustorgio brought to the city in the 4th century. In 1164, Barbarossa transferred the relics to Cologne, and in 1903, only part of the threesome were returned. A Roman sarcophagus in the *Cappella dei Magi* holds the kingly remains.

Numerous tombs and painted chapels feature a *Madonna and Child* (15th century) by Ambrogio Bergognone, the tomb of Protaso Caimi (1360) by Francesco Croce, the tomb of Stephano Visconti, and a *Crucifixion* (14th century). Atop the main altar is a *Crucifixion*, possibly by Mattteo da Campione.

The church's greatest attraction is the early Renaissance *Cappella Portinari* (1462–66), long attributed to the Tuscan Michelozzo, but disputed to be by a Lombard architect. Delightful festooned angels line the drum that supports the dome. Frescoes by Vincenzo Foppa depict the *Life of St. Peter Martyr* (1336–39) by Giovanni di Balduccio. The funerary monument entombs a Dominican priest, Pietro da Verona, who was killed in 1252 for his fanatical extermination of heretics.

The small MUSEO DI SANT' EUSTORGIO houses 17th- and 18th-century paintings. Its underground rooms are believed to be Roman and early Christian crypts.

The second largest church in Milan, SANTA MARIA DELLA PASSIONE, was constructed according to a Greek cross plan in 1486, domed in 1530 by Cristoforo Lombardo, extended and transformed into a Latin cross plan in 1573 by Martino Bassi, and finally completed with the facade construction between 1692 and 1729.

Within, beautiful paintings include several works by Danielle Crespi, among them the *Fast of St. Charles*. Significant works also include a *Last Supper* (1543) by Gaudenzio Ferrari, a *Crucifixion* (1560) by Giulio Campi, and a *Deposition* by Bernardino Luini. The Museo della Basilica features more works by 17th-century Lombard artists.

SANTA MARIA PRESSO SAN CELSO is a large 16th-century church dedicated to the *Miraculous Virgin* and is also known as Santa Maria dei Miracoli (St. Mary of the Miracles). It was named a basilica in 1950. Adjacent to it is the smaller Benedictine structure of San Celso (11th–12th centuries).

The basilica's ornate facade is preceded by a delicate atrium with sculptures by Annibale Fontana depicting the *Stories of the Gospels.* Fontana also contributed statuary to the interior, including the statue of *Our Lady of the Assumption* (1586) situated atop the altar of the Madonna. Tradition requires that brides pray at this altar on their wedding day.

Significant works throughout the church include Bordone's *St. Jerome,* Ferrari's *Baptism of Christ,* and a *Virgin Adoring the Christ Child.*

Bramante's contribution to SANTA MARIA PRESSO SAN SATIRO (1476–86) made the edifice Milan's prized early Renaissance church. The structure incorporates the Basilica di Ansperto, built by Archbishop Ansperto in 879. The assumed church is now called the *Cappella della Pietà* with a terra-cotta *Pietà* group (1482–83) by Agostino De Fondutis.

The most famous attraction is Bramante's illusionistic apse behind the main altar; it convincingly adds a third dimension to the otherwise flat wall.

In 1809 Napoleon assembled the world-famous collection in the PINACOTECA DI BRERA as an aid to study for the Accademia delle Belle Arti and as a center for cultural studies. Works pilfered from Northern Italian churches and monasteries highlight 15th–18th-century Lombard artists. The gallery's numerous masterpieces include Raphael's *Marriage of the Virgin* (1504), Andrea Mantegna's *Dead Christ* (c. 1480), Giovanni Bellini's *Pietà,* and Piero della Francesca's *Brera Altarpiece* (1472–74) depicting the Virgin and Child enthroned with saints and the painting's patron, the Duke of Urbino. The collection also offers Titian's *St. Jerome,* Tintoretto's *Discovery of the Body of St. Mark,* Vincenzo Foppa's *Madonna and Saints,* and Ambrogio Lorenzetti's *Madonna and Child.* Other attractions by masters Vittore Carpaccio, Lorenzo Lotto, Jacopo Bassano, Gentile da Fabriano, Annibale Carracci, Anthony van Dyck, and El Greco feature a host of saints, angels, and venerated Virgin and Child representations. The recently acquired collection of 20th-century works includes the artists Modigliani, Severini, Carrà, De Pisis, Picasso, and Braque.

Founded in 1609 by Cardinal Federico Borromeo (1564–1631), the AMBROSIANA library and art gallery are a cultural and literary guide to Christian learning. Devoted to collecting documents that illuminated biblical study, the cardinal amassed 32,000 manuscripts, texts, and codices.

In 1618, Cardinal Borromeo donated his art collection to the center. Among the works are Ghirlandaio's *Nativity,* Botticelli's *Tondo of the Madonna and Child,* Raphael's *Cartoon for the School of Athens,* Caravaggio's *Basket of Fruit,* and Titian's *Epiphany.*

M

MONREALE

Towering atop a hill that overlooks the valley of the Conca d'Oro and surrounded by a sea of orange groves, the Duomo of Monreale looks to the Tyrrhenian.

The cathedral is a symbol of William II's (the Good) greatness and power. The last massive Norman church built in Sicily, the magnificent structure made concrete the rivalry between its secular patron and neighboring Palermo's archbishop. However, built between 1174 and 1183, the plan proposed to include both spiritual and temporal powers, and combined the royal palace, bishop's palace, and convent in one complex. While the structure united the sacred and secular, its construction also brought together a variety of skilled craftsmen—Muslims, Romans, Pisans, and Frenchmen among them.

PLACES TO VISIT

The unfinished facade of the DUOMO, dedicated to the Virgin of the Assumption, offers no hint of the splendor within. Passing through one of the fine bronze portals into the church is like being assumed into another realm. Golden mosaics (1182) illustrate the Triumph of Christ and the Church with scenes from the Old and New Testaments, the Acts of the Apostles, and the lives of various saints and popes. Notice the depictions of William II, receiving a crown from Christ and offering the cathedral to the Virgin. At the heart of the church, in the apse, is the imposing *Christ Pantocrator.*

Ornate inlay decoration continues in the CLOISTERS (1166), once part of a Benedictine monastery. Delicate twin columns are inlaid with island limestone and lava. The volcanic stone was quarried from Sicily's active volcano, Mount Etna.

A short trip from Monreale, surmounted on a similar hill overlooking the same fertile valley, is San Martino delle Scale and the ABBEY OF SAN MARTINO. Legend claims that Gregory the Great founded the Benedictine monastery in the 6th century. It was rebuilt in the mid-14th century and renovated in 1762. The monumental main staircase by Venanzio Marvuglia is part of the 18th-century expansion. The church decoration includes works by Pietro Novelli, Filippo Paladino, Annibale Carraci, Guercino, and Pietro di Spagna.

MONTE CASSINO

The famous Benedictine abbey dominates the hilltown of Cassino. Throughout its existence the Abbey of Monte Cassino was of primary importance to the monastics and the Church. Ironically, the two cannot agree on a feast day to celebrate the founder, Benedict; the monks insist on March 21 while the Roman Catholic Church commemorates July 11.

In the Middle Ages Monte Cassino was known as Castel San Pietro or San Pietro al Monastero. In 886 it succumbed to Benedictine popularity and was renamed Eulogomenopolis (Town of St. Benedict). In 1871 it took the name Cassino, derived from its original Latin name, *Casinum*.

Three ravens led St. Benedict from Subiaco (where he founded a monastery with his sister) to Cassino in 529. St. Benedict founded 12 monasteries for his followers; Monte Cassino was his greatest. Here, the father of Western monasticism formalized the rule of monastic life. His widespread European influence led Pope Paul VI to name him the patron saint of the continent.

At Monte Cassino, Benedict converted the pagan countryside. However, his self-sufficient monastery attracted all peoples. The nobility sent their sons, who, in turn, fostered an environment of erudition and learning. Here, scholar monks copied books, Bibles, and church writings. However, the solemn and learned environment was not free from misfortune. The monastery has been destroyed five times: by the Lombards in 589, by the Saracens in 884, by the Normans in 1030, by an earthquake in 1349, and by Allied bombing in 1944.

PLACES TO VISIT

Enter the ABBEY through the reconstructed 16th-century small cloister. Within is a modern bronze sculpture by Attilio Selva of the *Death of St. Benedict.*

Statues of saints, popes, and monarchs line the Chiostro dei Benefattori (Cloister of Benefactors), designed by Antonio da Sangallo the Younger.

Bronze doors on the ABBEY CHURCH depict all but the fifth ruinous assault on the monastery. The Baroque interior includes works by Cavaliere d'Arpino and Francesco Solimena. Beneath the high altar rest the sacred relics of the devoted twins, St. Benedict and St. Scholastica.

Fortunately, the abbey library was moved to the Vatican one year before the World War II bombing. Its treasures included the Biblia Hebraica (11th century) of St. Gregory the Great and the Liber Moralium.

MONTE OLIVETO MAGGIORE

A massive black cypress grove and olive orchard provides a break in the barren Sienese countryside and marks the site of the isolated Abbey of Monte Oliveto. It is one of Tuscany's most famous monasteries; its monks were host to both Pope Pius II in 1463 and to Emperor Charles V and his entourage of 2,000 men in 1536. In 1866 the monastery was named a national monument. Monks that run the abbey today are master book restorers and producers of a miracle herbal elixir, Fiora di Monte Oliveto.

A Sienese hermit, Giovanni Tolomei, founded the monastery in 1313. A wealthy nobleman, Giovanni abandoned his privileged life when he lost his sight and began receiving spiritual visions. He took the name of Bernardo and began a branch of the Benedictine order—the Olivetans—devoted to restoring St. Benedict's original rule.

PLACES TO VISIT

The great draw to the monastery is the GREAT CLOISTER (1426–74). Scenes from the life of St. Benedict, as recorded by St. Gregory the Great in his *Dialogues,* decorate its walls. Nine frescoes (1497–98) were executed by Luca Signorelli (west wall), while the remaining 27 frescoes (1505–08) were painted by Sodoma. The masterpieces deserve close attention. Look for Sodoma's self-portrait in the scene of Benedict miraculously mending a broken tray. He is the well-dressed, white-gloved man accompanied by two badgers.

While visiting Monte Oliveto Maggiore, stay in BUONCONVENTO and take in some masterpieces at the MUSEO D'ARTE SACRA (Museum of Sacred Art). The collection includes Duccio's (attributed) *Madonna and Child,* Andrea di Bartolo's *Madonna,* Sano di Pietro's *Annunciation,* and Matteo di Giovanni's *Madonna and Saints* and *Coronation of the Virgin.*

MONTEPULCIANO

N obly perched atop one of Tuscany's highest hills, set between the Orcia and Valdachiana valleys, Montepulciano commands a spectacular view. Its dignified air invokes images of relaxing in one of the numerous Renaissance palaces and sipping the famous local wine, Vino Nobile di Montepulciano. Its most famous cultured and erudite citizen was Angelo Ambrogini (1454–94), known simply as Poliziano. A humanist scholar and poet, he was friend to both Leonardo da Vinci and Botticelli, saving the former from assassins and inspiring the latter to paint the *Birth of Venus* and *Allegory of Spring* with his poem *Stanze per la Giostra.* Other distinguished natives include the Jesuit scholar and author of the *Catechism of Christian Doctrine,* Cardinal Roberto Bellarmino (1542–1621), Giovanni Maria del Monte, who would become Pope Julius III (1550–55), and his successor, Ricardo Cervini, Pope Marcellus II (1555), who holds the record for the shortest papal term, a mere 21 days.

Montepulciano first appears on record books in the 8th century as *Mons Policianus,* a Latin term from which the present name originates and with which the locals identify, calling themselves Poliziani. Subject alternately throughout the Middle Ages to Florence and Siena, it passed into final domination under Florence in 1511.

PLACES TO VISIT

The DUOMO stands atop the site of the earlier church of Santa Maria, built for the bishop of Chiusi when his see was transferred to Montepulciano. The adjacent bell tower is the only remnant of the earlier parish. Ippolito Scalza constructed the present unfaced Duomo from 1592 to 1630.

Inside, fragments of the tomb of Bartolomeo Aragazzi (1427–36) are dispersed throughout the vast interior and can only be assembled in the viewer's mind. The tomb was dismantled in the 17th century, disturbing the eternal rest of the secretary to Pope Martin V. His effigy remains at the church entrance; while other original elements found elsewhere include two statues flanking the main altar, the frieze below the main altar, and a statue in a niche to the right of the main altar. Unfortunately, the puzzlelike tomb is missing a few pieces; two of its kneeling angels are in the British Museum.

Taddeo di Bartolo's triptych for the main altar commands the spacious nave. Painted in 1401 it depicts the *Assumption of the Virgin with Saints,* the *Annunciation,* and the *Coronation of the Virgin.* Other works dedicated to the Madonna include a *Madonna and Child* by Sano di Pietro on a pillar along the north aisle and the same subject in a bas-relief by Benedetto da Maiano.

M

Michelozzo designed the church of SANT' AGOSTINO in 1427 and contributed the terra-cotta relief above the doorway depicting the *Madonna and Child with Saints John the Baptist and Augustine*. Inside the redesigned interior (1784–91) is Bronzino's *Raising of Lazarus*. Notice Donatello's wooden crucifix over the main altar and Pollauolo's wood crucifix in the earlier church.

The TORRE DEL PULCINELLA is a gift from a Neapolitan bishop exiled to Montepulciano for his amorous transgressions. The *Pulcinella* is the black-and-white clown that strikes the clock bells on the hour.

The MUSEO CIVICO AND PINACOTECA CROCIANI, housed in the Palazzo Neri-Orselli, contains a collection of Tuscan and Umbrian sacred images from the 15th–18th centuries. Bequest to the city in the 19th century, significant works include two altar-pieces by Andrea della Robbia: a *God the Father* and a *Madonna and Child with Saints Bartholomew and Longinus.*

While the city's most spectacular sanctuaries lie outside its walls, two Baroque churches in Montepulciano are worth a visit. Near the 17th-century Jesuit College is the CHIESA DI GESÙ (1689–1733) by Andrea Pozzo decorated with illusionist paintings by Antonio Colli and S. Cipriani. The elegant church of SANTA LUCIA (1633) houses a *Madonna* by Luca Signorelli.

Four churches beyond the city walls are jewels in an already rich landscape.

The CHIESA DELLA MADONNA DI SAN BIAGIO (1518–45), built by Antonio da Sangallo the Elder, stands atop the site of a former church dedicated solely to San Biagio. Sometimes called the Temple of San Biagio, it is a masterpiece of High Renaissance building, devoutly adhering to the architectural models of symmetry and rationality.

Constructed to house a 14th-century fresco, the venerated image of the *Madonna and Child with St. Francis,* the church attracts an equal number of devotees seeking the architectural purity of the structure as it does pious worshipers seeking the miraculous intercession of the Virgin.

The relics of native Sant' Agnese of Montepulciano can be visited in her titular church, SANT' AGNESE (14th century). The present church was built atop a church St. Agnes built with her own hands, Santa Maria Novella. This inexhaustible Dominican nun was born Agnese Segni in 1268; she died in 1317 and was canonized in 1726. Inside is a fresco of the *Madonna* by Simone Martini.

SANTA MARIE DEI SERVI is a 14th-century church with a Baroque interior by Andrea Pozzo. Inside is a *Virgin and Child* from the school of Duccio di Buoninsegna.

SANTA MARIA DELLE GRAZIE is graced with Giovanni della Robbia's *Mary of the Graces*. Its 16th-century cypress wood organ is unique to Italy and attracts musicians from around the world.

NAPOLI

(NAPLES)

While Vesuvius languorously sleeps above her head and the waters from the vibrant bay lap at her feet, Naples and her people erupt with exuberance and rapture. Legend claims the city was founded atop a siren's tomb, and there seems to be a bit of a siren in all Neapolitans, who enchant foreigners and beckon them to love Naples as deeply as its citizens do. The call is as irresistible now as it was to the ancients.

The *Campania Felix,* fertile or fortunate countryside, graces the region with both abundance and beauty. In return, Naples has graced Italy with the most widely known and widely loved foods; Naples is the homeland of pizza, spaghetti, and mozzarella. Theatre is also a particularly Neapolitan gift, and while opera draws throngs to its theatre, the greatest stage is Naples itself. Here daily life is as rich and dramatic as Naples's many festivals. It is a city where the sacred and profane are inextricably linked, where religion and superstition are faithful companions. Unfortunately industrialization and pollution are asphyxiating its glorious artistic and architectural past, gilding its history with a thin layer of smog. In his *Ode to Naples* (1820), Percy Bysshe Shelley called Naples a "Metropolis of a ruined paradise." The paradise, however, is not lost; it exists in the Neapolitans themselves, whose spirit and exuberance are indomitable.

Greek colonists settled in the area surrounding the Bay of Naples in the 8th century B.C., founding cities like Cumae and Parthenope, which would later become Neapolis, "new town," shortly thereafter in 474 B.C. Despite Etruscan efforts to control the abundant *campagna,* the Greek colonies flourished until the 4th century B.C., when it fell to the control of the increasingly mighty Roman Empire. The fertile and spectacular land and seascapes ripened into the Roman playground for the elite.

In the 5th century A.D., Naples, like the rest of Italy, fell. Throughout the Middle Ages it endured Italianic, Visigoth, and Longobard invasion. The Norman Conquest reached Naples in 1139 under Roger II; it and all of southern Italy were consolidated under Norman rule. Naples was named capital of the Norman Empire, and in 1224 Frederick II founded the city's university.

In 1268 Charles of Anjou gained control of the kingdom, ushering in two centuries of Angevin rule. Prosperity grew and continued with his successors and through to the succession of power of the House of Aragon. The Aragonese dynasty, inaugurated under Alphonso the Magnanimous in 1442, experienced economic, cultural, and population growth. The alliance between Louis of France and Ferdinand of Spain in 1503 began 200 years of Spanish rule in Naples. Spanish viceroys governed and embellished the city with lavish palaces, churches, and monasteries.

Economic and cultural decline and a brief period of Austrian occupation followed a devastating plague in 1656. In 1738 the Bourbon kings usurped control of Naples and Sicily. The enlightened dynasty established the national library and the theatre and encouraged excavations in Pompeii and Herculaneum. In 1799 the Bourbons fell to French revolutionaries. Seven years later, Joseph Bonaparte (Napoleon's brother) was crowned king of Naples. He was replaced in 1808 by Joachim Murat (Napoleon's brother-in-law). In 1815, the Bourbons regained control.

On September 7, 1860, the revolutionary, Giuseppe Garibaldi, entered Naples. A month later, on the 21st, the citizens voted to join the united Italy.

PLACES TO VISIT

Dedicated to the city's patron saint, SAN GENNARO (St. Januarius), the cathedral of Naples, physically and symbolically incorporates Neapolitan early Christian and pagan origins. The 13th-century structure, which was thoroughly rebuilt in the 15th, 17th, and 18th centuries, includes Naples's earliest surviving church, Santa Restituta (4th century), which itself was founded atop an earlier temple to Apollo. In 1294 Charles I of Anjou began construction. The massive site not only incorporates an early Christian church but also covers the space once occupied by the church of Santa Stefania (5th century) and four early Christian baptisteries. The church was completed in 1323. Despite ravaging earthquakes in 1349 and 1456 and facade rebuilding in 1407 and 1905, the structure retains its French Gothic appearance.

One hundred and ten antique columns that once gloriously adorned pagan temples now serve to support the interior of the massive edifice; here Christian architects turn even stone into a suppliant. Luca Giordano painted Naples's 46 patron saints that hover above the arches and the tondi. Notice the tombs of Charles I (d. 1285) and Charles Martel, king of Hapsburg, and his wife, Clementina, constructed by Domenico Fontana in 1599. They were moved from the choir and now sit above the interior central doorway.

The *Cappella Minutolo* (right transept) houses the tombs of Cardinal Arrigo Minutolo (1402–05) and Orso and Filippo Minutolo. The family chapel includes 13th-century frescoes by Montano d'Arezzo and cosmatesque majolica paving with animal motifs. The famed chapel is mentioned in Boccaccio's *Decameron*. Entombed within the *Cappella Tocco* (right transept) is its patron Giangiacomo Tocco. The frescoes from 1312 are attributed to Pietro Cavallini. In the *Cappella San Lorenzo* (left transept) a fresco of the *Jesse Tree* (c. 1315) by Lello da Orvieto illustrates the prophecy of Christ's coming and parentage from Isaiah 11:1–3. The sacristy contains portraits of Neapolitan bishops and Aniello Falcone's *Rest on the Flight into Egypt* (1641).

Below the main altar is the *Crypt of San Gennaro* (1497–1506) by Tommaso Malvito. Two bronze doors enclose the crypt altar, atop of which sits the saint's funerary urn, brought from Montevergine to the Duomo. Before the urn is a statue of Cardinal Oliverio Carafa, the church founder, shown kneeling in prayer before the sacred remains.

The 4th-century church of Santa Restituta forms a large chapel on the left side of the Duomo's nave. Rebuilt after the 14th-century earthquake, it retains few of its early Christian elements. Twenty-seven of its columns may be from the earlier temple to Apollo, and fragmentary floor pavement dates to the 4th century. Luca Giordano contributed the ceiling painting depicting *Sta. Restituta Arriving in Ischia*. Lello da Orvieto created a mosaic that unites the three most significant figures in the church; signed and dated 1322, his mosaic depicts the *Madonna with Saints Januarius and Restituta*. The original mosaics are preserved in the adjacent 4th-century baptistery of *San Giovanni in Fonte*.

The *Cappella del Tesoro di San Gennaro* (1608–37) is the Duomo's climax, its literal boiling point. Naples's patron saint, San Gennaro (250–305), was the bishop of Benvenuto, beheaded at Pozzuoli under Diocletian. According to legend, the stroke that chopped his head off also cut off San Gennaro's index finger. The faithful onlookers caught his blood in a sponge and preserved it in two phials. Popular belief holds that this sacred blood liquefies three times a year during public ceremonies: on the first Saturday in May at Santa Chiara (the Feast of the Translation of the Relics), in the duomo on September 19 (San Gennaro's Feast Day), and on December 16 (the anniversary of Vesuvius's threatened eruption in 1631). Quick liquefaction is auspicious, while a slow boil spells misfortune.

The chapel of San Gennaro was built to fulfill a vow made by the Neapolitans during the plague of 1526–29 seeking deliverance and saintly intervention. A Latin inscription within the chapel reads: "Naples, delivered from famine, war, plague, and the flames of Vesuvius, dedicates (this chapel) to San Gennaro, the citizen savior of the homeland." Domenichino (1631–38) and Lanfranco (1641–43) contributed to the chapel's frescoes. Before he was stormed out of the city, Domenichino painted a cycle, *San Gennaro with Scenes from His Life and Miracles*. Notice Giuseppe Ribera's oil painting, the *Miracle of San Gennaro Emerging Unharmed from the Fire*. San Gennaro's relics are preserved behind the altar in a silver gilt bust, which con-

N

105

tains the saint's skull and the two phials of his blood.

The CATACOMBS OF SAN GENNARO lie north of the duomo, on a hillside that once lay outside the city. Created in the 2nd century, the galleries were used through to the 11th century. Built around the tomb of an early Christian family, the catacombs hold the bishop-saint Agrippinus (3rd century); the martyr and Neapolitan patron San Gennaro (5th century); the dukes of Naples, Stephen I (d. 800) and Stephen III (d. 832); Bishop John IV (9th century); and St. Athanasius (d. 877). In 831 the prince of Benvenuto stole San Gennaro's relics for his own city, and the popularity of the site as a place of pilgrimage waned. The galleries contain numerous early Christian frescoes and mosaics, including an image of San Gennaro (5th century) in the pose of an Orant (a figure with hands raised in an attitude of prayer) with the inscription above it, "Sancto Martyri Ianuario"; mosaics (4th century) depicting bishop's busts, and frescoes (2nd–3rd centuries) of *Adam and Eve* and *David and Goliath.* On the lower level is the Basilica of Sant' Agrippinus with several sarcophagi and 9th-century paintings depicting Christ, the apostles, and saints.

The Seven Acts of Mercy literally and symbolically define the charitable institution of PIO MONTE DELLA MISERICORDIA (1658–78). Seven noblemen founded the organization in 1601, which continues to operate today under

seven governors. Its mandate is to carry out the seven acts of mercy—feeding the hungry, giving drink to the thirsty, welcoming the stranger, clothing the naked, visiting prisoners, administering to the sick and dying, and burying the dead. These works of corporal charity, described in Matthew 25:35–37, nurture an individual's love for their neighbor and love for God.

Inside the octagonal church are artworks that exalt the individual acts; notice Fabrizio Santafede's *Peter Rescuing Tabitha* (1612) and Battistello's *Liberation of St. Peter* (1615). The church masterpiece is Caravaggio's *Seven Acts of Mercy* (c. 1607), which features the seven acts in one composition. Within the shadowy scene, the Virgin Mary and Christ Child descend from the heavens to witness the undertaking of the charitable acts on earth. Ironically, Caravaggio (1571–1610)—who fled to Naples after killing a man and lived a life seemingly devoid of charity—imbues the works with unparalleled tenderness, emotion, drama, and sanctity.

Visit the adjacent *Pinacoteca* that houses 17th- and 18th-century Neapolitan artworks.

The Franciscan church of SAN LORENZO MAGGIORE (1270–75) was founded in the 6th century by Bishop John II and built atop a Greco-Roman *macellum,* the city's 1st-century B.C. marketplace. Charles I of Anjou commissioned the 13th-century reconstruction to commemorate his victory over Benvenuto. Baroque renovations added in the 17th and 18th centuries were removed in the 19th century, and the church's French Gothic appearance was restored.

Inside, notice the tomb of Catherine of Austria (c. 1320s) by Tino da Camaino. Atop the main altar are statues of *St. Laurence, St. Anthony,* and *St. Francis* (16th century) by Giovanni da Nola. They are set above bas-reliefs illustrating stories from the lives of the grilled martyr, the church doctor, and the stigmatized friar. Also notice the 17th-century decoration in the *Cappella Cacace* and the *Cappellone di Sant' Antonio.*

During Christmastime, along the street leading to the church of SAN GIROLAMO ARMENO, Neapolitans flock to buy carved and terra-cotta figurines to populate their Christmas cribs, or *presepi.* Among the traditional items are Holy Families, Magi, angels, shepherds, oxen, donkeys, sheep, architectural ruins, and lots of miniature food. The church that looms over the street is no miniature model. Founded in the 8th century by nuns who fled Constantinople and absconded with the head of Gregory, the bishop of Armenia, the church was built between 1574 and 1580. It is a majestic edifice suitable for its congregation, largely nuns from noble families.

The church houses numerous saintly relics, including the blood of St. John the Baptist and St. Patrizia and St. Laurence's forearm. Its carved wood ceiling was painted by Teodoro d'Errico (1580–82), while its walls and chapels contain Luca Giordano's *Nuns' Flight to Naples with St. Gregory's Relics* (1679) and works by Buono, Lama, De Rosa, and Francanzano. In the church cloisters among the orange trees lies a well (1730) carved by Matteo Bottiglieri that depicts *Christ and the Samaritan Woman* from John 4:7–9 in a life-size stone conversation.

The church of GIROLAMINI or San Filippo Neri was built for the order of the Oratoriani between 1592 and 1619. St. Philip Neri (1515–95) founded the Oratorians, a charitable brotherhood devoted to the Virgin Mary that derived its name from their meeting place, an oratory. Philip suffered from a heart condition mentioned in Psalm 118:32— "When thou didst enlarge my heart"— that he believed brought on a state of ecstasy and spiritual bliss. The Oratoriani ministered to the sick and supported arts and culture; their church reflects their aesthetic ministry.

Inside are Luca Giordano's *Christ Expelling the Money Lenders from the Temple* (1608), Guido Reni's *St. Francis* and his *St. John the Baptist,* and Pietro da Cortona's *St. Alexis.* In the adjacent convent is the *biblioteca* (library) with a sumptuous public reading room and a small painting gallery with works by notable 16th- to 18th-century artists.

The church of SAN PAOLO MAGGIORE was built atop a 1st-century A.D. Roman temple dedicated to the

N

Dioscuri, the sons of Zeus. The church stands in the Piazza San Gaetano, the city's ancient *agora*. The piazza takes its name from St. Cajetan, who founded the nearby monastery in 1538. Between 1583 and 1603, the Theatine confraternity member Francesco Grimaldi rebuilt the site's original medieval church, a structure which suffered earthquake and collapse in 1688. The immense interior is covered with opulent decoration. The ceiling nave frescoes by Massimo Stanzione illustrate the *Lives of Saints Peter and Paul* (1644). Notice four statues of the four cardinal virtues, *Prudence, Temperance, Justice, and Fortitude,* which govern acceptable behavior for churchmen. In the *Cappella Firraro* (1641) are the Firraro family tombs, with a stunning *Madonna and Child* atop the altar.

The delight of the Benedictines of the church and convent of **SANTI SEVERINO E SOSSIO** is a plane tree planted by St. Benedict himself. Though the tree was cut down in the mid-20th century, its trunk has sprouted two new limbs, a sure sign of the indomitable spirit of the Benedict's Order, which, ironically, was moved from the complex in 1835 when the *Archivo di Stato* (state archives) took occupancy. Unfortunately, the Italians destroyed most of the documents in 1943.

The church, founded in 902, was rebuilt between 1494 and 1537. Francesco de Mura contributed the ceiling frescoes illustrating the *Life of St. Benedict* (1740). Within the numerous chapels are scenes of the *Nativity, Epiphany, Annunciation,* and the *Deposition* by Pino, Criscuolo, Salerno, and Tenerello. Numerous funerary slabs in the church flooring include the tomb of one of the church's artists, Belisario Corenzio, who died on the church pavement after plummeting to his death while working on the ceiling. Dramatic deaths befell numerous souls entombed within the church. The *Cappella Sanseverino* entombs three brothers—Ascanio, Jacopo, and Sigismondo—each poisoned by their uncle in 1516 so he might gain the family wealth in one fell swoop. Giovanni da Nola executed the tombs between 1539 and 1545. Also notice the beautifully carved choir stalls (1560–73) by Benvenuto Tortelli.

The enchantingly morbid and curiously enthralling **CAPPELLA SANSEVERO,** or Cappella di Santa Maria della Pietà dei Sangro, houses the tombs of the princely family of Sangro di Sansevero. Built in 1590 by a vigorous Francesco di Sangro to fulfill a vow he made while deathly ill, the chapel was entirely redesigned by Raimondo di Sangro between 1749 and 1770.

The latter prince and alchemist decorated the chapel with marble and frescoed allegories in an iconographic scheme he conceived himself. Records also suggest Raimondo designed the pavement's labyrinth design. The ceiling painting depicts the *Glory of Paradise* (1749) by Francesco Maria Russo; beneath the windows are paintings of canonized family members and sculptures representing *Liberality, Sincerity, and Disillusionment* by Francesco Quierolo. The chapel's two most celebrated sculptures are cloaked enigmas: *Veiled Modesty* (1751) carved by Antonio Corradini seems to blush under her stone veil; and a *Veiled Christ* (1753) by Giuseppe Sammartino does not hide, but subtly reveals Christ's wounds.

The church and monastery of SAN DOMENICO MAGGIORE once accommodated St. Thomas Aquinas and Giordano Bruno; the former taught theology for the university of Naples and the latter was a philosopher and student of theology whom the Church burnt as a heretic. Built by Charles II of Anjou between 1283 and 1324, the structure incorporated the nearby church of San Michele Archangelo a Morfisa. The church suffered earthquake damage and was reconstructed in the 15th, 16th, and 19th centuries.

The church houses numerous famed Renaissance monuments. The *Cappella Brancaccio* contains frescoes (1308–09) by Pietro Cavallini depicting the lives of the saints; the *Cappellone del Crocefisso* is named for its venerated 13th-century *Crucifix,* which spoke to St. Thomas; and the *Cappella Carafa di Ruvo* (1511) is by Balsimelli. Visit the sacristy to see the *Triumph of the Dominican Order* (1709) by Francesco Solimena.

The Franciscan church and convent of SANTA CHIARA (St. Clare) is a majestic structure built to house Naples's

monarchs; its majesty would shock St. Clare (1194–1253), founder of the Order of the Poor Clares and venerated for zealously observing the mendicant lifestyle. Built from 1310–28, its patron, Queen Sancia di Maiorca, wife of Robert of Anjou (the Wise), supposedly died in the complex, having taken her vows after her husband's death. Opulent Baroque additions altered the church (1742–69); unfortunately, a bombing raid in 1943 destroyed both the French Gothic and Baroque elements. A mid-20th-century restoration reintroduced the Gothic structure but could not recover the many decorative contributions.

Among the royal tombs in the large interior are the tomb of Robert the Wise (1343–45) by Giovanni and Pacio Bertini and Tino di Camaino's three sepulchres: the tomb of Charles of Calabria (1330–33), the tomb of Charles's wife Mary of Valois (1333–38), and the tomb of their daughter Mary of Durazzo. Peruse the church for a glimpse at the tombs of more of Naples's sovereigns, who sought eternal rest among their royal predecessors.

The colorful *Chiostro delle Clarisse* (Cloister of the Clarissans) is an 18th-century enclosed rustic garden by Domenico Antonio Vaccaro. When the grapevines and wisteria are not in bloom, the delightful majolica tiles (1742) by Donato and Giuseppe Massa that decorate the walkways and benches and depict pastoral and garden scenes

N

with gaiety and cheer are enough to enliven the garden during its dormant season.

The seat of the Spanish Crown was transformed into the seat of the Jesuit Order in 1584 when the former palace of the Sansverino princes was turned into the church of GESÙ NUOVO (1584–1631) after the royal expulsion. The church's immense dome has been rebuilt twice, once after the earthquake of 1688 and again in 1744.

Inside, Francesco Solimena's *Heliodorus Driven from the Temple* (1725) is a fitting subject to hang above the entrance. Heliodorus, in an attempt to rob Solomon's temple, was driven back by a rider accompanied by angels—the scene reminds those contemplating robbing the richly decorated Gesù Nuovo to beware. Also notice Stanzione's *Life of the Virgin,* Corenzio's *St. Ignatius and St. Francis Saverio,* and statues of *David and Jeremiah* by Fanzago.

The endless votive offerings lining the walls of the *Chapel of the Visitation* commemorate and give thanks to San Giuseppe Moscati (1880–1927). His work as a doctor and chemist earned him the devotion of many and canonization in 1987.

In the piazza before the church is the *Guglia dell'Immacolata,* an 18th-century Jesuit spire that depicts Jesuit saints and stories from the life of the Virgin. The work boasts the Jesuit belief in the doctrine of the Virgin's immaculacy. While the idea was hotly debated

since the Middle Ages (the Dominicans denied it while the Franciscans upheld it), Pius IX defined the doctrine of the Immaculate Conception as an article of Roman Catholic faith in 1854.

Famed for its Renaissance sculpture and painting, the church of SANT' ANNA DEI LOMBARDI or MONTEOLIVETO was founded in 1411 atop a hillside garden outside the city. A favorite Aragonese church, Monteoliveto contains numerous masterful Renaissance sculptures. A bombing raid in 1944 destroyed the 17th-century facade, which was replaced by a reconstruction imitating its 15th-century appearance.

The papal architect Domenico Fontana is buried within a sepulchre (1627) in the church vestibule. Immediately upon entering the church are two noteworthy Renaissance tombs: the Ligorio family tomb (1524) by Giovanni da Nola (left) and the Pozzo family tomb (1532) by Giuseppe Santacroce. Within the *Piccolomini Chapel* is Antonello Rossellino's bas-relief *Nativity* (c. 1475), the *Tomb of Mary of Aragon* (d. 1470) begun by Rossellino and completed by Benedetto da Maiano, and a *Crucifixion* (1550) by Giulio Mazzoni. In the *Terranova or Correale Chapel* is the stunning bas-relief of the *Annunciation* and the *Life of Jesus* (1489) by Benedetto da Maiano. The *Chapel of the Holy Sepulchre* contains Guido Mazzoni's emotive terra-cotta *Pietà* (1492), featuring contemporary Neapolitan portraits. Giorgio Vasari contributed ceiling frescoes (1544) to the

Old Sacristy with wooden-inlay Neapolitan vistas (1506–10) by Fra Giovanni da Verona.

SAN GIOVANNI A CARBONARA was built in 1343 and dedicated to St. John the Baptist. The church derives its name from the street atop which it was built. Lying outside the city during the Middle Ages, the area was used as a garbage dump where refuse was burned or carbonized, *ad carbonarum.* The land was donated to Augustinian monks in 1339, and King Ladislas enlarged the church in the 15th century. The newly upgraded and embellished church was both suitable and worthy to house a royal tomb.

Climb the curving monumental staircase (1707) where the Neapolitans staged a revolt against the Nazis in the fall of 1943. Dominating the structure's numerous funerary monuments is the monumental tomb of King Ladislas (d. 1414). In 1428 the king's sister Joan II commissioned a 59-foot equestrian statue of a sword-wielding Ladislas being blessed by a bishop, despite his having been excommunicated before his death. Built by Marco and Andrea da Firenze, the sculptural group includes the king and his sister enthroned and the monarch's tombs being held aloft by representations of the virtues. The *Cappella Caracciolo del Sole* (1427) entombs Joan II's lover, Sergianni Caracciolo, a powerful Neapolitan dignitary who was murdered nearby in 1432, possibly under the orders of Joan II. The circular chapel contains Caracciolo's tomb (1441), stunning majolica flooring (1440), and 15th-century frescoed walls depicting the *Monastic Life* and the *Life of the Virgin Mary.* Tommaso Malvito's circular marble-lined *Cappella Caracciolo di Vico* (1517–57) rivals and may precede Bramante's Tempieto in Rome. Giorgio Vasari contributed Old and New Testament frescoed scenes in the *sacristy* and a *Crucifix* (1545) in a chapel in the church courtyard.

The CERTOSA DI SAN MARTINO is a Carthusian charterhouse set atop the Vomero, a Neapolitan hilltop over 800 meters above the city. Labyrinthlike steps and roads ascend to the site, which until the 19th century was sparsely occupied farmland. The magnificent monastery and its treasures compete with the spectacular view of the Neapolitan Gulf.

Its patron, Charles of Anjou, began construction on the monastery in 1325. The complex was completed in 1368 and renovated in the 17th and 18th centuries. A visit to the prestigious and wealthy complex begins outside the entrance at the WOMEN'S CHURCH, where women, prohibited to enter the Certosa, could congregate and pray. Immediately inside the monastery is the courtyard and Gothic church. A storehouse of sumptuous 17th- and 18th-century artwork, the church contains a *Crucifixion* by Lanfranco, a *Nativity* by Guido Reni, a *Pietà* and *Last Supper* by Stanzione, the *Institution of the Eucharist*

N

and the *Twelve Prophets* by Ribera, and the *Triumph of Judith* by Luca Giordano. A highlight is Ribera's masterpiece, the *Descent from the Cross,* atop the main altar.

Cosimo Fanzago designed the adjacent large cloister in 1623. He contributed five busts of Carthusian saints depicting *St. Martin of Tours, Bishop Nicola Albergati, St. Bruno, St. Hugh,* and *St. Dionysius.* The sixth bust depicting *St. Januarius* is by Domenico Antonio Vaccaro. Fanzago, who worked in the complex for over 25 years, also designed the monk's cemetery in the central courtyard of the monk's cells.

The charterhouse also boasts the greatest collection of Nativity scenes. The creation of *presepi* or crèches is a proud Neapolitan tradition that links to St. Francis, who, with papal permission, recreated the first live Nativity scene, and to the Neapolitan love of theatre. In the *Sezione Presepiale* (Crèche Section) is the famed *Presepe Cuciniello,* with over 200 hundred figures. The figures range from priests to beggars, kitchen wives to prostitutes, nobles to vagabonds, locals to foreigners, and dogs to horses, and their surroundings include all imaginable implements from daily life. The exceptional nativity collection includes various detailed works from miniature to life-size.

The MUSEO NAZIONALE DI SAN MARTINO documents the history of Naples, its art and life, in meticulous detail.

It is impossible to visit all of Naples's churches. The following provides a glimpse at the most significant elements of commonly visited Neapolitan edifices. SANT' ANGELO A NILO (founded 1385) contains the funerary monument (1426–28) of the church founder, Cardinal Rinaldo Brancaccio, by Donatello and Michelozzo. Notice the bas-relief on the front of the sarcophagus beautifully depicting the *Assumption of the Virgin.* Dedicated to Pope Celestine V (1294), SAN PIETRO A MAIELLA (13th century) honors the life of a pope who renounced his position and lived as a hermit in the Maiella mountains. The life of the hermit, pope, and saint San Pietro Angeleri is commemorated by stunning ceiling paintings in the nave by Mattia Preti (1656–61). The nearby convent houses a conservatory (1828) where male orphans studied music and history. Many of the conservatory's sopranos were castrated *(I castrati)* to maintain their stunning voices. The school's most famous *castrato* was Farinelli (1705–82). The PURGA-TORIO AD ARCO is a 17th-century monument dedicated to the cult of the dead. Decorated inside and out with skulls and crossbones, atop the main altar is the *Virgin Mary with the Souls of Purgatory* (c. 1630) by Stanzione. SAN GIORGIO MAGGIORE (renovated 17th century) was founded between the 4th and 5th century by Bishop Severus and still retains its early Christian apse. A relic from the crown of thorns is housed in the church of **SANTA MARIA INCORONATA** (St. Mary Crowned). All that remains of the now stripped interior are frescoes depicting *Biblical Events* and the *Triumph of Religion and the Seven Sacraments* by Roberto d'Oderisio. Yearly on the 16th of July the church of **SANTA MARIA DEL CARMINE** (13th century) hosts the famous Neapolitan festival of the *Madonna del Carmine,* when fireworks commemorate the burning of the church's original bell tower. The venerated 15th-century painting of the *Madonna della Bruna* (Brown Madonna) is a greatly revered church highlight.

The decoration within the **PALAZZO REALE,** the Royal Palace, incorporates secular and sacred imagery. Begun in 1600 by Domenico Fontana and completed in 1837 after a devastating fire by Gaetano Genovese, the palace was originally built in anticipation of an unrealized visit by Philip III of Spain. The palace includes various state offices, royal apartments, a chapel, and Naples's national library.

Housed in the sumptuous *Museo dell'Appartamento Storico di Palazzo Reale* is an *Annunciation* by Artemisia Gentilleschi, the cycle of the *Virtues of Charles of Bourbon and his wife Maria Amalia* by Francesco de Mura, various frescoes depicting the *Military Triumphs of the House of Aragon* by Belisario Corenzio, a series of the *12 Proverbs* by Federico Zuccari, *The Prodigal Son* by Mattia Preti, and a tapestry depicting the *Allegory of Modesty.*

The *Biblioteca Nazionale Vittorio Emmanuele III* was founded in 1734 and supported by the Minister of Education, Neapolitan historian and philosopher Benedetto Croce (1866–1952). The library contains important manuscripts and papyri discovered in nearby ancient excavations. The collection includes almost 2,000,000 works.

The **MUSEO E GALLERIE NAZIONALE DI CAPODIMONTE** was opened in May 1957. Its palatial home was constructed between 1738 and 1838 for the Bourbons. The surrounding park provided a royal hunting ground, a perfect retreat from the city congestion. The collection houses among the finest artworks in Italy. The majority of the collection comes from the inheritance of Charles III of Bourbon from his mother, Elisabetta Farnese. Additional contributions include the Borgio Collection and the De Ciccio collection.

Among the museum's many masterpieces are numerous portraits, including Raphael's *Portrait of Cardinal Alessandro Farnese* (1509–11); Titian's three portraits, *Cardinal Ranuccio Farnese* (1542), *Pope Paul III* (1545–46), and *Cardinal Alessandro Farnese* (1545–46); Lotto's *Portrait of the Bishop of Treviso* (1505); Mantegna's *Portrait of Francesco Gonzaga* (1462); and Sarto's *Portrait of Leo X with Cardinal Giulio Medici* (1525). Numerous masterful works depict sacred and secular themes. Do not miss Raphael's *Moses Before the Burn-*

N

113

ing Bush (1514), Botticelli's *Madonna and Child with Angels* (1468–69), Masolino's *Assumption of the Virgin* (1428), Bellini's *Transfiguration* (1478–79), Lotto's *Madonna and Child with St. Peter Martyr*, Romano's *Madonna della Gatta* (1523), Titian's *Danae* (1544–46), Giambologna's *Rape of the Sabines* (1578), Bruegel's *The Blind Leading the Blind* (1568), Corregio's *Marriage of St. Catherine* (1585), A. Carracci's *Pietà* (1599–1600), Gentileschi's *Judith and Holofernes* (1630), Giordano's *Madonna of the Baldachin* (1686), Preti's *St. Sebastian* (1657), Raphael's *Eternal Father*, Masaccio's *Crucifixion* (1426), F. Lippi's *Annunciation*, Mantegna's *St. Eufemia*, and Caravaggio's *Flagellation*.

ORVIETO

Crowning a summit of volcanic rock, Orvieto boasts a spectacular view of the Umbrian countryside. It stands 1,035 feet above sea level. Naturally fortified by its tall cliffs, Orvieto's defensive potential appealed to the Etruscans, the Romans, and the Longobards but also to the medieval and Renaissance papacy. Thomas Aquinas made it famous as a place of spiritual pilgrimage, and Pope Clement VII turned it into a papal refuge. Today this natural fortress is not an obstacle to pilgrims seeking the divine solace of its cathedral or to those in search of a glass of Orvieto's famed white wine.

Orvieto's fame is linked to the Miracle of Bolsena. In 1263 a Bohemian priest, returning from a pilgrimage to Rome, stopped at a church at Lago di Bolsena to celebrate Mass. Skeptical of the truth of transubstantiation, the priest became a believer when, during the celebration of Eucharist, the consecrated host shed drops of real blood, leaving a cross-shaped stain on the corporal (the altar cloth used in the sacrament of Eucharist). The bloodstained corporal was presented to Pope Urban IV, temporarily residing in Orvieto. To commemorate the miracle, Pope Urban proclaimed the Feast of Corpus Christi. The Cathedral of Orvieto was built to enshrine the relic, promote the doctrine of transubstantiation (the transformation of the bread and wine of the Eucharist into the substance of the body and blood of Christ), and reveal the Eucharist as the only means of attaining salvation. The bloodstained corporal has attracted many pilgrims, including Pope Julius II, who in 1506 came to Orvieto to adore the relic before his first campaign north. According to tradition, he attributed his immediate victories and eventual triumph over the French to the intervention of the relic.

PLACES TO VISIT

The **CATHEDRAL OF ORVIETO**, begun in 1290, built on the site of two older churches, and dedicated to the Virgin, is a miracle of art dedicated to a miracle of faith. The church was likely planned by Arnolfo di Cambio, although some believe an obscure monk, Fra Bevignata da Perugia, was responsible for the design. The facade's famed sculpture, reliefs, and mosaics illustrate the way of salvation for the faithful. Lorenzo Maitani was responsible for the meticulously detailed carving of four enormous panels on the facade. Begun in 1320, the four piers represent, from left to right, the story of Genesis, Old Testament prophecies of the coming of the Messiah, the life of Christ, and the Last Judgment. Christ is portrayed throughout as Creator, Messiah, Teacher, Redeemer, Church Founder, and Judge. The Last Judgment scenes are certainly the most moving; Maitani's visions of those condemned to the Inferno are sure to cause even the most virtuous viewers to tremble.

Above each pier is a symbol of the four evangelists: the angel for St. Matthew, the lion for St. Mark, the eagle for St. John, and the ox for St. Luke. At the apex of each of the pointed arches are bronzes of St. Michael on the left, the Agnus Dei in the center, and an angel on the right.

Marble angels pull back a stone curtain to reveal the Madonna and Child enthroned in the lunette above the central portal. Above them, the stunning rose window reveals the Head of the Redeemer at its core. The mosaics throughout reveal stories from the life of the Virgin.

The modern bronze doors provide a great contrast to the medieval decoration. Built in 1970 by the sculptor Emilio Greco, the door decoration represents Misericordia and the seven acts of corporal charity. Pope John XXIII once proclaimed that on Judgment Day, the cathedral's facade would be assumed into heaven.

Inside the church, within the Cappella dei Corporale (1350–61), is the reliquary containing the corporal from the Miracle of Bolsena. The jeweled reliquary that houses the sacred cloth was designed by Ugolino di Vieri in 1338 and decorated with scenes relating to the Eucharist: the Last Supper, Christ's entry into Jerusalem, the Crucifixion, and the Entombment. The mural cycle on the walls, by Ugolino di Prete (1357–64), depicts similar Eucharistic scenes and the events of the miracle.

Luca Signorelli's San Brizio Chapel (1499–1504), dedicated to the Assumption of Mary, is the most celebrated work in the cathedral. Directly opposite the Cappella del Corporal, Signorelli's murals proclaim a similar message: salvation can only come from the church and through union with Christ, therefore, only through the Eucharist. The ceiling vaults, begun in 1447 by Fra Angelico, represent Christ in majesty

O

with the apostles. The commission passed to two other artists before Signorelli, who took up the brother's work.

Scenes on the wall vaults deal with the doctrine of last things (death, judgment, heaven, and hell). The cycle includes the rule of Antichrist, the end of the world, the resurrection of the dead, the damned entering hell, the coronation of the elect, and the elect entering heaven. Notice the two figures in black in the rule of Antichrist; the full figure is Signorelli, with Fra Angelico standing behind him. Surely, they recognize the true path to salvation. Signorelli's vision of the Last Judgment, especially of those without hope of salvation, looks back to Maitani's facade and influences Michelangelo's treatment of the subject in the Sistine Chapel.

Below the murals are portraits of six authors framed in grotesque panels. They are identified as Dante, Statius, Virgil, Lucan, Ovid, and Cicero. Excluding Dante, they are pagan predecessors to Christian ideas of the end of life and the afterworld. Overall, the chapel decoration reveals the power of the Eucharist as the means of attaining heavenly glory.

The MUSEO DELL'OPERA DEL DUOMO in the Piazza del Duomo houses paintings by Martini, Signorelli and his studio, and Lanfranco, among others from the 13th to 16th centuries. Several sculptures by Arnolfo di Cambio, Andrea Pisano, and della Robbia are of interest, as is the museum's collection of priests' vestments.

The POZZO DI SAN PATRIZIO (St. Patrick's Well) is a deep, dank chamber named for its fabled similarity to the Irish cave where the saint died. It was commissioned by Pope Clement VII to ensure the town's water supply during an expected siege after he fled Rome after the Sack (1527). The well is a feat of engineering and architecture designed by Antonio da Sangallo the Younger. It is 200 feet deep and 42 feet in diameter, illuminated by 72 arched windows, with two spiral staircases leading down into the well. Halfway down the well's 248 steps is a small Etruscan tomb, a reward for those brave enough to venture into the well.

PADOVA

(PADUA)

St. Anthony of Padua attracts pilgrims and tourists alike to his beloved city. A Christian saint and Doctor of the Church (1946) praised for his learning, his preaching, his miracles, and his visions, Anthony draws pilgrims seeking his intercession. As the patron saint of travelers and finder of lost articles, St. Anthony's shrine receives travelers grateful for his protection and the odd tourist desperately seeking a lost passport.

Padua's rich artistic treasures and intellectual atmosphere match its spiritual legacy. The city's elite patronized masterful artists, including Giotto, Guariento, Menabuoi, Donatello, and Mantegna, and its famed university (the second oldest in Italy) attracted Dante, Petrarch, Vergerius (a Latin lecturer), Galileo, William Harvey (developed the theory of blood circulation), and the lesser known Elena Lucrezia Corner Piscopia (the first woman to earn a university degree, 1678).

The 4th-century B.C. fishing village Patavium claimed its unfounded legendary origins after Virgil, who asserted that the Greek hero Antenor settled here in the 12th century B.C. Perhaps, had the villagers truly descended from a Trojan War hero, they would have suppressed the Longobards in 602; unfortunately, the thriving Roman municipium fell.

In the 12th century Padua emerged from a 6th-century convalescence as a free commune. The independent city, administered by the Da Carrara family from 1337 to 1405, fostered an enlightened cultural and learned environment. Though Carrarese control ended in the 15th century with Venetian conquest and domination, the newly acquired member of the republic continued to pursue its enlightened path. By the 16th century Padua's unending cultural progress earned the city the reputation of a dynamic center with Europe's most promising medical school. In the 18th century Napoleon defeated the Venetian Republic and Padua fell to the Austrians. In 1866 Padua was annexed to Italy.

PLACES TO VISIT

Giotto's famed fresco in the CAPPELLA DEGLI SCROVEGNI (Scrovegni Chapel) attracts endless visitors to a small unassuming brick building that commemorates a sinful money-lending Paduan and his son. Built atop Patavium's ruined ancient Roman amphitheatre, the 14th-century structure is also known as the Arena Chapel or the Madonna dell'Arena.

In 1300, Padua's wealthiest citizen, Enrico Scrovegni, purchased the land to build a funerary chapel dedicated to the Virgin which he hoped would atone for his father's usury, glorify the Scrovegni family, and ensure Enrico a seat in heaven. Enrico inherited his fortune from his father, Reginaldo. Reginaldo's transgressions were so offensive to the Church that he was denied a Christian burial. Dante assigned the sinner to the seventh circle of hell in his *Inferno* (Canto XVII); there Reginaldo sits among other usurers and stares at the ground, his punishment for "making money breed."

Between 1304 and 1307 Giotto frescoed the interior with a New Testament cycle depicting the lives of the Virgin and Christ, the Last Judgment, the Seven Virtues, and the Seven Capital Sins. The 38 panels of the New Testament cycle depict *St. Joachim Chased from the Temple, St. Joachim Taking Refuge*

Among the Shepherds, The Angel Appears to St. Anne, The Angel Appears to Joachim, Saints Joachim and Anne Meet at Jerusalem's Golden Gate, The Birth of the Virgin, The Presentation of the Virgin, St. Simeon Receives the Rod, The Prayer for the Rods, Mary and Joseph's Marriage, The Wedding Procession, The Angel Gabriel Receives His Orders, The Annunciation, The Visitation, The Nativity, The Adoration of the Magi, The Presentation, The Flight into Egypt, The Massacre of the Innocents, Jesus and the Doctors, Jesus' Baptism, The Marriage at Cana, The Resurrection of Lazarus, The Entry into Jerusalem, Chasing the Merchants from the Temple, Judas Receives 30 Pieces of Silver, The Last Supper, The Washing of the Feet, The Kiss of Judas, Jesus Before Caiaphas, The Crown of Thorns, Calvary, The Crucifixion, The Deposition, The Resurrection, The Ascension, and *Pentecost.*

Notice both the chapel's patron and its artist depicted among the saved in the *Last Judgment.* Enrico proudly presents a model of the chapel to the Virgin Mary while Giotto stands among a crowd of blessed onlookers. Though Enrico fled Padua in 1320 and died in Venice in 1336, his remains were returned to his native city and entombed in his chapel. Before his tomb, above the altar, are statues by Giovanni Pisano.

The MUSEO CIVICO, housed in the former convent of the Eremitani, contains an archaeological collection, a painting gallery, and the Museo Bottacin with its precious coin, medal, and seal collection. Highlights in the painting gallery include Giotto's *Crucifixion* (originally made for the Scrovegni Chapel altar), Jacopo Bellini's *Christ in Limbo*, Guarentino's *Armed Angels*, Andrea Previtali's *Madonna*, Palma il Giovane's *Santa Cristina*, Il Romanino of Brescia's *Virgin and Saints*, Tintoretto's *Crucifixion* and *Martyrdom of Saints Primo and Feliciano*, Veronese's *Crucifixion*, Giambattista Tiepolo's *St. Patrick Bishop of Ireland*, Giorgione's *Leda and the Swan*, and Giovanni Bellini's *Deposition*.

Allied bombing devastated the church of the EREMITANI (1276–1306) in 1944. Many precious frescoes were lost. Fortunately, the few salvageable and incomplete remains were diligently restored; notice the fragile frescoes by Guarentino depicting *Saints Augustine, Philip, and James.* Unfortunately, Andrea Mantegna's frescoed cycle of the lives of Saints James and Christopher in the Ovetari Chapel (1454) did not escape destruction. The two miraculously surviving frescoes depict the *Martyrdom of St. James* and the *Martyrdom of St. Christopher.* Faded photographs capture the chapel before the 1944 destruction; however, they merely hint at its original beauty.

Padua's Duomo, the CATTEDRAL DI SANTA MARIA ASSUNTA, suffered endless reconstructions by numerous artists, including Michelangelo. Despite frequent efforts at completion, the church facade remains unfinished and its somber interior attracts little attention. However, the adjacent BAPTISTERY (1260) is a frescoed

ANTHONY OF PADUA (1195–1231).

Born to a wealthy Portuguese military family in 1195, Anthony's wealth and station were secured. At 15 Anthony abandoned his privileged life and luxurious inheritance to join the Congregation of Canons Regular of St. Augustine and devoted his days to study and prayer.

Visitors to Anthony's monastery altered the young monk's life. A group of Franciscan friars sojourned at the Monastery of Coimbra before embarking on an evangelizing mission in Morocco. There, friars were brutally martyred for their faith and their mutilated bodies returned to the Portuguese monastery. Moved by the friars' sacrifice for faith, Anthony wished to suffer martyrdom. He immediately joined the Franciscan Order and accompanied a group of evangelists to Africa with the hopes of an imminent martyrdom in a hostile environment.

In Africa, Anthony succumbed to illness, not to the infidel. Instead of being martyred, Anthony was sent home. A fortuitous storm cast his ship off course to Sicily, where local Franciscans welcomed the castaway. In May 1221 Anthony accompanied the Sicilian friars to Assisi for a meeting of the General Chapter of the Order of St. Francis.

Anthony did not return to Sicily; he instead journeyed north to Fiorli. There, sickly and humble, Anthony led a hermetic existence fulfilling kitchen duties and practicing mortification of the flesh.

At an ordination ceremony, Anthony's superior asked the friars to volunteer to replace an ill priest who was to give a sermon. When all the friars shrank back, unwilling, the superior ordered Anthony to speak. Seized by divine inspiration, Anthony's initial hesitant words were transformed into rousing song, and he spoke with scholarly insight and stirring emotion.

News of Anthony's eloquence and ability spread quickly, and St. Francis instructed him to preach throughout Italy. Anthony's electrifying sermons drew great crowds. However, on one occasion when the crowd seemed uninterested, the preacher turned his attention to an attentive audience—the fish in a nearby stream! Able to rouse devotion and reverence from all nature, Anthony once converted a Jew who doubted Christ's presence in the Eucharist by leading an ass before the Host, whereupon the beast kneeled before the Sacrament. Anthony's human touch enabled him to reattach a man's leg after the sinner had severed it in penance for kicking his own mother. Il Santo even received a vision of the Virgin and Child and was seen one evening holding the Infant Jesus on his lap.

In 1227 St. Anthony was elected the Minister Provincial of friars in Northern Italy. He continued preaching and teaching theology until he retired to Padua in 1230, exhausted and ailing. He fell ill and died at a convent of the Poor Clares on June 13, 1231. Il Santo's speedy canonization soon followed on May 30, 1232.

P

jewel. The baptistery was frescoed by Giusto de' Menabuoi (1370) and built by the da Carraras, who hoped the edifice would rival the Scrovegni Chapel as a gift of devotion and secure the da Carrara family a heavenly post above the Scrovegni's.

Menabuoi's fresco depicts Christ Pantocrator flanked by angels and saints above Old and New Testament scenes with the Holy Ghost descending from the dome. Atop the altar is Menabuoi's *Virgin Enthroned with St. John the Baptist.*

The BASILICA DI SANT'ANTONIO, begun one year after Anthony's death, rose to accommodate the multitudinous pilgrims gathering to visit Anthony's mortal remains. The grand edifice reflects the ardor with which Anthony's devotees sought to honor their beloved saint. Anthony repays their gratitude and devotion; eight centuries after his death the "Wonder Worker" continues to produce miracles and intercede for the faithful. Locals refer lovingly to Anthony as "Il Santo" (the Saint) and undoubtedly, though he was born in Portugal, Anthony of Padua was a local wonder.

Il Santo's church was built atop the small church where he was buried, the Santa Maria Mater Domini. The new church built between 1232 and 1307 combines Romanesque, Gothic, and Byzantine architecture; the various styles unified in one structure reflect Anthony's multitudinous appeal and diverse pilgrims unified in their devotion to him.

Within, the Cappella dell'Arco del Santo (1500–46) houses Anthony's tomb. Sixteenth-century marble reliefs lining the chapel walls executed by Jacopo Sansovino and Tullio and Antonio Lombardo depict the Life of St. Anthony. The stunning Venetian reliefs compete with votive photographs and offerings deposited by thankful pilgrims from around the world.

The Cappella del Beato Luca Belludi contains vibrant frescoes of Saints James and Philip by Giusto de' Menabuoi (1382), and the Cappella di San Felice houses Altichiero's marvelous 14th-century Crucifix.

A bronze sculpted Madonna, six Paduan saints, and a relief cycle of the Life of St. Anthony by Donatello (1443–50) decorate the high altar, and a stone Deposition, also by Donatello, crowns the altar. To the left, delicate mythological figures and decorative motifs are woven into a stunning bronze Easter candelabrum by Briosco (1519). Twelve bronze relief Old Testament scenes decorate the choir walls.

The Cappella del Tesoro houses one of Christendom's more unique sacred relics. Known for his power to preach, St. Anthony's head-shaped reliquary fittingly contains his tongue and larynx. Anthony's life of pious deeds and sacred speech reflect his motto, "The only ones who preach correctly are those who confirm by their actions what they announce with their mouths." Through thousands of Masses yearly at the basilica and St. Anthony's continued intercession, his words and deeds are alive today.

Noble and serene, the equestrian monument of Gattamelata—"the Honeyed Cat"—stands in the piazza before Anthony's basilica, a testament to the efficacy of military glory achieved by defending the Christian faith as a means to gain a seat in Paradise. Executed by Donatello between 1447 and 1453, the statue is the first large-scale Renaissance equestrian monument. The condottiere Erasmo da Narni, depicted here dignified and peaceful, marches towards heavenly glory, the epitome of the Christian active and contemplative life.

Other Paduan churches shouldn't be missed. A few notable treasures are the following: The ORATORIO DI SAN GIORGIO (1377) is a mortuary chapel beautifully frescoed by Altichiero and Jacopo Avanzi. The nearby SCUOLA DEL SANTO contains 16th-century Venetian frescoes, including some early works by Titian (1511). Inside the massive church of SAN GIUSTINA, the eleventh largest Christian church, notice Paolo Veronese's *Painting of the Martyrdom of St. Justine* (1575), a 16th-century carved choir stall depicting the Old and New Testament, and the Arca di San Luca (the tomb of St. Luke, 1316), which once housed the evangelist's relics.

PALERMO

P

Palermo's reverence for its two patron saints, Santa Rosalia and San Benedetto, are modern reminders of the city's history of ethnic tolerance and diversity. Rosalia, the niece of the Norman king William II of Sicily, and Benedetto, the son of Ethiopian slaves, recall Palermo's golden age. In the 12th century, peace, prosperity, and tolerance flourished under enlightened Norman monarchs who cultivated a multicultural and multifaceted environment.

According to legend, native-born Rosalia retired to the nearby Monte Pellegrino (Mount Pilgrim) in 1159 to live a hermetic existence in prayer. In 1624, while the plague devastated Palermo, Rosalia appeared to a hunter on the mountainside. She revealed the site of her cave and bodily remains, and the hunter returned to the city with the newly discovered relics. Three days later, the city was freed from the plague. Benedetto, born near Messina in 1526, also retired to the hermetic solitude of Monte Pellegrino. At age 20 he was invited to join a group of Franciscan hermits after being ridiculed for being black. He soon became their leader, and the group moved to Palermo, where he lived a life of poverty and service. He died in Palermo in 1589.

A white saint and a black saint jointly protect Palermo. They are invoked against the plague, racial prejudice, and religious persecution, and are called to

121.

protect immigrants and exiles. Unfortunately, Rosalia and Benedetto do not intercede to protect against Palermo's modern plagues: poverty and the Mafia. However, the pestilence that sent much of the city's cultural and architectural past into decay can be remedied. Palermo is not a paradise forever lost, but an Eden awaiting reclamation.

Paleolithic man settled in the hillside caves of Monte Pellegrino (606 meters) overlooking the spectacular bay of Palermo, known as the Conca d'Oro (the golden shell). Thousands of years later in 858 B.C. the Phoenicians settled the same site and established trade routes, thus capitalizing on its strategic location. The Phoenician colony is known only by its Greek name, *Panormus* (all-haven). This "haven" brought security and prosperity, necessitating the 4th-century construction of fortification walls that divided the settlement into *Paleapolis*, the earlier upper city, and *Neapolis*, the new lower city that extended towards the harbor.

Rome conquered Palermo in 254 B.C., ending six centuries of Carthaginian rule. Though it continued to be an important trade route, prosperity declined under the Romans. In A.D. 491, Sicily was conquered by the Vandals, followed by the Ostrogoths. In 535, Christian Byzantium subjugated Sicily. However, prosperity and stability continued to wane until Arab domination in 831. Under Arab rule agricultural, artistic, and intellectual pursuits burgeoned. The productive climate flourished under the succeeding Norman rule.

In 1072 Christendom reclaimed Palermo. The Normans, however, tolerated and even encouraged a multicultural climate. King Roger II (1130–54) cultivated ethnic diversity and exchange, recognizing among his multiethnic subjects—Arabs, Greeks, Lombards, Jews, Persians, Turks, and Africans—the opportunity for political, scientific, scholarly, and artistic growth. A visitor to the city would be struck by the numerous languages spoken—Greek, Arabic, Latin, and French—and surely feel at home in the liberal environment. Peace and prosperity lasted through Frederic II's rule. The revolt of the Sicilian Vespers (1282–1303) ended French rule and inaugurated Palermo's Spanish domination. During the 16th century the Spaniards renovated and embellished the declining city, adding churches and palaces and reorganizing the city layout. The Bourbons acquired power in 1734 following brief rules by the House of Savoy and Austria. Despite efforts at urban and cultural renewal, the city continued to decline through to the unification of Italy. On May 27, 1860, Garibaldi entered Palermo. However, in the 20th century, cultural renewal and a return to prosperity remain elusive. While poverty flourishes and the Mafia reign, intervention by the Italian government offers little hope. Optimistic, Palermo's citizens wait in anticipation of returning their neglected city into a prosperous haven.

PLACES TO VISIT

Palermo's hybrid CATHEDRAL has served as both a Christian church and a mosque. Dedicated to Santa Maria dell'Assunta, St. Mary of the Assumption, the cathedral was built upon a preexisting basilica that was transformed into a mosque in the 9th century. In 1185, Walter of the Mill (Gualtierio Offamimio), archbishop of Palermo, founded the present cathedral. Construction continued throughout the following centuries, and the structure was significantly altered in the 15th and 18th centuries.

Walking around the massive edifice you will see that the various phases of construction are still visible. Remains from the original exterior include two massive Gothic arches, two intricately carved original 12th-century towers, and a Gothic doorway (1352). The 15th-century central portal frames bronze doors depicting *Old and New Testament Stories* (1961) that replaced earlier 18th-century wooden doors. The south facade, the most commonly used entrance, reveals 15th-century additions. The Catalan porch (1453) includes numerous fragments from earlier buildings and a column (left) from the previous mosque with an inscription from the Koran.

The structure's original interior splendor was completely transformed between 1781 and 1801 by the Neapolitan architect Ferdinando Fuga.

The addition of side aisles and a transept transformed the basilican floor plan into a Latin cross design, and a massive cupola crowned the renovation. Six medieval royal sepulchres reveal clues to what must have been a sumptuously decorated Norman church. The classically inspired porphyry sepulchres entomb Frederick II (d. 1250); his father, Henry VI (d. 1197); Roger II (d. 1145); his daughter, wife of Henry VI, Constance (d. 1198); Frederick II's son, Duke William of Athens (d. 1338); and Frederick II's wife, Constance of Aragon (d. 1222).

Dispersed throughout the nave are statues depicting saints by Francesco Laurana and Antonello Gagini that once stood upon the high altar alongside the *Resurrection* altarpiece. To the right of the main altar is the Chapel of Santa Rosalia, her sacred relics encased in a silver urn within. The church also houses various saintly appendages including Santa Rosalia's tooth, St. Agatha's arm, and St. Mary Magdalene's foot.

The church treasury houses a jeweled crown (12th century) taken from the tomb of Constance of Aragon in the 18th century alongside numerous royal bobbles from the host of royal tombs.

Do not confuse the now deconsecrated church of SAN GIOVANNI DEGLI EREMITI (St. John of the Hermit's) for a mosque; the Arab architecture is certainly the work of Islamic craftsmen, but its patron was a Christian, Roger II, the Norman king who preached ethnic

P

tolerance. Many suspected this enlightened ruler was actually a crypto-Muslim. Despite suspicions, accommodating the pope's wishes, Roger II converted over 300 mosques into Christian churches during his rule.

The hermit's church built between 1132–48 stands atop an area once consecrated to a mosque. Inside notice the 10th-century remains of the original mosque and a fragmentary 12th-century fresco of the *Madonna and Christ*. Beyond the church is an elegant cloister and garden belonging to a former Benedictine monastery.

Originally named Santa Maria dell' Ammiraglio (1143) in honor of its patron George of Antioch, admiral of the Norman kingdom's fleet, the church of the **MARTORANA** took on the name of the adjacent convent's founder, Eloisa Martorana. The convent was established in the 12th century and was given the church in 1433. Today it shares cathedral status with the church of San Demetrio in Piana degli Albanesi and conducts Greco-Byzantine rites. The church's new status reflects the importance of its founder, George of Antioch, who was an Orthodox Greek Christian.

Although the convent no longer exists, the nuns' memory lives on in the making of the traditional marzipan fruit, *frutta di Martorana*. The Martorana nuns were unsurpassed marzipan makers. So real were their fruits that when hung from orchard trees they were mistaken for the real thing.

While the church facade is a 16th-century addition, the adjacent campanile is a 12th-century original, which collapsed in the earthquake of 1726 and was restored in the 19th century. Inside the church are among Palermo's most stunning 12th-century mosaics commissioned by the Greek admiral. A golden *Christ* looks down from the dome surrounded by *Prophets, Evangelists,* and a Byzantine hymn in Arabic lettering. The *Annunciation* and the *Presentation in the Temple* decorate the altar, and throughout the church are *St. Anne and St. Joachim, The Nativity, The Dormition of the Virgin,* and *George of Antioch Presenting the Church to the Virgin.* Notice the mosaic depicting *Roger II Crowned by Christ.* Customarily, the pope crowned Christian kings; however, Roger, resplendent in Byzantine dress and an apostolic stole, clearly indicates that God himself institutes his royal authority.

Maio of Bari founded the church of **SAN CATALDO** in the 12th century, now headquarters of the order of the Knights of the Holy Sepulchre. The simple red-domed structure and incomplete interior remains as it was when its founder died in 1160. The small rectangular structure served as a post office from 1787 until it was reconsecrated in 1885.

The Jesuits erected their first Sicilian church between 1564 and 1633, named, of course, **IL GESÙ** (Jesus). The Jesuit zeal soon gained popular favor; however, their time on Sicilian soil was brief, and in 1768 the order was expelled. The stunning Baroque interior once overflowed with sculptures and paintings from the 17th and 18th centuries. Notice a depiction of *Two Saints* by Pietro Novelli and sculptures by Gioacchino Vitaliano.

Adjacent to the church is the Baroque *Casa Professa,* a communal library founded in 1760.

A delicate rose window and an ornamental portal covered with zigzag designs define the 13th-century facade of the church of SAN FRANCESCO D'ASSISI. A treasury of paintings and statues from the 15th to 18th centuries, the church also claims the first major Renaissance work in Sicily, the portal (1468) framing the *Cappella Mastrantonio* sculpted by Francesco Laurana and Pietro da Bonitate. Inside the chapel is a *Madonna and Saints* by Vincenzo da Pavia. Giacomo Serpotta's allegorical statues (1723) decorate the presbytery and nave; four of the eight statues depict *Victory, Chastity, Theology,* and *Modesty.* Giovanni Battista Ragusa contributed eight statues (1717) depicting *Sicilian Saints.* The church also houses numerous sculpted works by Antonello Gagini and his son Domenico.

Giacomo Serpotta contributed masterful works to three of Palermo's most prestigious 16th-century oratories. Born in Palermo in 1656, he was known as the master artist of the city's oratories for his contribution of molded ornamental frames. The ORATORIO DEL ROSARIO DI SAN DOMENICO (the Oratory of the Rosary of St. Dominic) contains numerous of the native son's stucco allegorical statues (1720), the most famed among them *Justice* and *Strength.* Atop the altar is Van Dyck's *Madonna of the Rosary* (1624–28), commissioned in Palermo and completed in Genoa after the artist fled the plague-ridden city. The scene depicts the Virgin, St. Dominic, and the city's patron, St. Rosalia. St. Dominic is credited with inventing the rosary when the Virgin gave him a string of beads in a vision. He called the beads "Our Lady's Crown of Roses." Also notice Luca Giordano's *Agony in the Garden* and Pietro Novelli's *Coronation of the Virgin.* The ORATORIO DEL ROSARIO DI SANTA ZITA contains Serpotta's reliefs of the *Stories of the New Testament* and the *Battle of Lepanto* (1685–1717). Dedicated to the Virgin of the Rosary, the oratory commemorates the Virgin's intercession and the victory of the Christians over the Turks at the Battle of Lepanto (1571). The ORATORIO DI SAN LORENZO (1569), built by the Company of St. Francis, commissioned Serpotta to execute scenes from the lives of St. Lawrence and St. Francis (1699–1707). Most notable is his *Martyrdom of St. Lawrence.* A *Nativity* by Caravaggio (1609) stood atop the altar until 1969; the stolen painting is yet to be recovered.

Standing high atop the medieval city, the PALAZZO DEI NORMANNI or Palazzo Reale is a physical reminder of Palermo's varied history. Begun in the

P

9th century by the Saracens, the palace was enlarged and embellished by the Normans and renovated by the Spanish in the 17th century.

The palace highlight is the *Cappella Palatina*, a private chapel built by Roger II between 1132 and 1140. Every surface, from the floor to the ceiling, is sumptuously decorated. The basilican-plan chapel is topped with a cupola and contains the most spectacular mosaics in Sicily. Created by Byzantine craftsmen (c. 1140–50), the golden mosaics depict *Christ Surrounded by Angels, David, Solomon, Zechariah, St. John the Baptist and the Evangelists, The Annunciation, The Nativity, The Flight into Egypt, The Presentation in the Temple, The Baptism, The Transfiguration,* *The Raising of Lazarus,* and *The Entry into Jerusalem.* A stunning vision of *Christ Pantocrator* crowns the apse.

The nave's mosaics depict stories from the Old Testament while the aisle mosaics depict scenes from the lives of St. Peter and St. Paul.

The **PALAZZO ABATELLIS** houses the Galleria Regionale della Sicilia (the regional art gallery of Sicily). The collection contains the following masterpieces: Francesco Laurana's *Bust of Eleonora of Aragon* (c. 1471); Antonello da Messina's *Annunciation, St. Jerome, St. Augustine,* and *St. Gregory,* and a dramatic 15th-century fresco of the *Triumph of Death;* and Malvagna's *Virgin and Child with Saints Catherine and Barbara.*

PERUGIA

Second only perhaps to Perugian renown for producing rich chocolate is the Perugian identity as both the most bellicose populous and the most devout. According to an old proverb, Perugians are either devils or angels. Their power and piety might be linked to the city's topography; perched atop one of the many Umbrian hills, Perugia is a strategic military site and at the same time is physically close to the heavens.

As they did with most Umbrian cities, the Etruscans were the first to dominate Perugia. Local tradition holds the Etruscans to be the sons of Noah, and a native monk in the Middle Ages wrote that Noah himself chose the hill of the present city to call his home. Noah's so-called "sons" inevitably fell to Roman control. While Rome occupied the area for nearly 1,000 years, little trace of their presence remains. Perugia was not untouched by the barbarian and pontifical wars that followed; however, it fought fiercely to assert its independence. There are few cities in Umbria that did not face the wrath of Perugia, and even today it retains its dominance, much more peaceably, as the capital of the region. While history dictated that the city be constructed for defense and not beauty, its Gothic and Renaissance constructions recall times of prosperity and peace. The city's credo *Processione, Persecuzione, Protezione* (procession, persecution, protection) reveals the reality that sacred pursuits were overshadowed by secular ones, as such, religious edifices suffer from their inferior status.

PLACES TO VISIT

Supplying water to hilltowns always poses problems, and at the heart of Perugia's principle square is a fountain that attests to this difficulty. The FONTANA MAGGIORE (Grand Fountain, c. 1277), is always running dry. Fortunately, its artistic value far surpasses its practical use. Designed by Fra Bevignate, a local monk and architect, the fountain marries sacred and secular images. It was realized through the sculptural talents of Nicola and Giovanni Pisano. The sculptured lower basin (the last major work of Nicola Pisano) combines symbols of the months of the year, scenes of domestic life, Roman legends, Old Testament stories, and the arts and sciences. The middle basin (largely the work of Giovanni Pisano) shows allegorical symbols of Perugia, saints, biblical figures, and 13th-century city officials. Three bronze Nereids rise from the basin bearing a griffin (symbol of the city) on their heads to crown the fountain.

A flight of steps behind the fountain leads into the city's Duomo. As you approach, a bronze statue of Pope Julius III gives his eternal blessing. The CATHEDRAL OF SAN LORENZO is an architectural casualty of Perugia's many wars. The Gothic church was planned in 1300 and begun in 1315, but work soon halted when its funds were reallocated to war efforts. In 1345 the bishop of Perugia resurrected the plans to build the church. He laid a foundation stone that sat untouched for nearly a century until work resumed. Even today, the exterior remains unfinished.

The checkered facade's pink marble is native to the region. On the right is a sculpted pulpit (1425) in honor of San Bernardino that marks the spot where he preached to the citizens. A crucifix above the door is the gift of a penitent soldier who mistakenly shot his cannon into the facade and used the cross to patch the hole.

Inside the church, to the right of the entrance, is the CAPPELLA DI SAN BERNARDINO with Federico Baroccio's *Descent from the Cross* (1567–68). Directly opposite, to the left of the entrance, is the CAPPELLA DEL SANT' ANELLO (Holy Ring). Here, an ornate silver casket holds the Virgin Mary's wedding ring. It can be seen five times a year on various feast days. In 1472 Winterio di Magonza "piously" stole the ring from nearby Chiusi.

A porphyry urn in the wall of the left transept holds the remains of Popes Innocent III, Urban IV, and Martin IV. The three popes died in Perugia. Only the triple-tiered papal tiara that crowns the urn betrays their tie to Rome.

P

Do not miss the **MUSEO DELL' OPERA DEL DUOMO,** accessed through a door in the right transept, that houses works by Perugino's school and Luca Signorelli and includes important manuscripts and church records.

The **GALLERIA NAZIONALE DELL' UMBRIA** houses the most complete collection of Umbrian art. Its treasures span the 13th century through 19th century, with works by Duccio, Fra Angelico, Piero della Francesca, Benozzo Gozzoli, Simone Martini, Nicola and Giovanni Pisano, Taddeo di Bartolo, Perugino, and Pinturrichio.

Perugia's many churches suffered a fate similar to that of its Duomo; they were plagued with neglect, pillage, destruction, and redecoration. **SAN ERCOLANO** houses the remains of a local martyr saint who was decapitated by Totila while defending the besieged city. It is constructed on the supposed spot of his death, near the city's first Etruscan walls.

SAN DOMENICO is a massive, unfinished Gothic church based on Giovanni Pisano's designs. It suffered successive collapse and rebuilding, and its Gothic window, while the largest in Italy, is not decorated with its original glass. Inside is Pisano's tomb of Pope Benedict XI, who died in Perugia after seeking solace from Rome. He was supposedly poisoned.

Visit **SAN PIETRO** simply to see the only church whose treasures weren't looted. The Benedictine abbot Pietro Vincoli built it in the 10th century.

Inside the dark church is a "miraculous column" (second on the left). According to tradition, the column began to fall during construction, and it was immediately steadied when the abbot built it. Paintings within the church include a *Pietà* by Perugino, three Vasari canvases, and a *Garden of Gethsemane* by Guido Reni that was struck by lightning.

If you are traveling with your true love, visit **SAN COSTANZO,** the local patron saint of lovers. Lovers come to the shrine on his feast day for blessing. If the saint blinks at a couple, their love is certain to flourish and end in a happy marriage.

The **ORATORIO DI SAN BERNARDINO** (1450) stands in what was once a field where Franciscans preached. The choir (1524–35) is renowned for its fantastically carved vision of mythical beasts and tender scenes of mother and child. The doors of the choir open onto a small balcony that commands a vista of Assisi, the heart of Franciscan life.

SAN AGOSTINO boasts a choir designed by Perugino (1502). Its wooden beasts were carved by the Florentine Baccio d'Agnolo.

SAN SEVERO is a must for Raphael followers. A fresco, signed and dated (1505) by Raphael, proves to be his first complete work. Only the upper half is by his hand. Perugino, Raphael's teacher, completed the lower half in 1520 after Raphael's death.

The **UNIVERSITY OF PERUGIA'S** three main branches of study (jurisprudence, science, and theology) has attracted many lawyers, scientists, and religious scholars since its founding in 1400. Many popes studied in Perugia, and St. Thomas Aquinas lectured here.

As you stroll along Perugia's streets notice the carved garlands and decorative friezes above residential doorways. Many reveal religious sentiment. Surely these are the houses of the angelic citizens. Some of the inscriptions read *Juanna coeli* (door of heaven), *A Deo cuncta—a domino omina* (all things from God), *Orant vivas et Doe vives* (pray to live and thou shalt live to God) and *Ecce spes I.H.S. mea semper* (Christ always my hope).

PIENZA

Pienza is the ideal Renaissance city with an urban plan modeled on the principles of order, harmony, and clarity. It is the gift of one man, Pope Pius II, humanist scholar and art patron, to his native birthplace. Pienza is defined by Pius's six-year rule.

The ancient village of *Corsignano* (modern Pienza) became the property of the nearby abbey of Monte Amiata in the 9th century. It later passed into Sienese possession and finally into the hands of the Piccolomini family, whose illustrious son, Enea Silvio Piccolomini, secured its fame. Born in 1405, this diplomat, geographer, poet, and historian was elected pope in 1458. He chose the name Pius II and rechristened his birthplace, the place of piety, Pienza. Pope Pius approved papal funds to glorify his city and commissioned the architect Bernardo Rossellino (Leon Battista Alberti's pupil) to redesign the town on an organized grid centered around a piazza which included the cathedral and papal, episcopal, and municipal

palaces. By August 13, 1462, construction progressed sufficiently to approve a bull elevating his native home to an episcopal see and officially sanctioning the new name. However, his papal privilege was interrupted by duties in the Holy Land. In hopes that his hometown project not be adulterated by the visions of another, he issued a papal bill ordering nothing to be touched until his return.

Pienzans remain faithful to those orders. Pope Pius never returned, yet his dream, while only partially realized, remains as pure today as when he last looked upon it.

PLACES TO VISIT

Piazza Pio II is the heart of both Pienza and Pio's vision—a dream begun. It is flanked by four structures: the cathedral, Palazzo Piccolomini, Palazzo Vescovile (Bishop's Palace), and the Palazzo Comunale.

Pius II oversaw all aspects of the transformation of the CATTEDRALE DI SANTA MARIA ASSUNTA from a Gothic into a Renaissance structure. Testament to his pride and magnanimous patronage is the Piccolomini coat of arms (five moons surmounted by a tiara and the keys of Peter) prominently displayed above the church entrance and throughout the interior. Reconstructed between 1459 and 1462, the Renaissance facade masks the original Gothic interior. Perched dramatically on a cliff edge, the apse offers spectacular views and abundant light through its slender windows. However, its precarious position resulted in structural weakness and potential collapse. Cracks are visible in the crypt of San Giovanni, which also houses Rossellino's travertine baptismal font.

Pius's personal devotion to the Virgin is evidenced in his commission of decorative altarpieces dedicated to Mary. Painted by Sienese artists between 1461 and 1463, they represent the *Madonna and Child with Saints Bernardine, Anthony Abbot, Francis and Sabina* by Giovanni di Paolo; the *Madonna and Child with Saints Catherine of Alexandria, Matthew, Bartholomew and Lucy* by Matteo di Giovanni; the *Assumption with Saints Agatha, Callistus, Pius I, and Catherine of Siena* by Vecchietta; the *Madonna and Child with Saints Mary Magdalene, Philip, James, and Anne* by Sano di Pietro; and the *Madonna and Child and Saints Jerome, Martin, Nicholas, and Augustine* by Matteo di Giovanni.

Pope Pius's personal residence, **PALAZZO PICCOLOMINI,** is modeled on the Palazzo Rucellai in Florence. Begun by Pius II and completed by his nephew Pius III, the palace was the family residence until 1962. The linear harmony and proportion is contrasted by a hanging garden in the inner courtyard that overlooks the Orcia Valley. Tours of the papal chambers, dining room, music room, library, and armory offer a glimpse of Pius's private world.

The **PALAZZO VESCOVILE** was built for Pius's friend, Cardinal Rodrigo Borgia, later pope. It houses the Museo della Cattedrale, a collection of Sienese and local works. Pius's liturgical vestments, including a luxurious silk embroidered cape with scenes of the life of the Virgin and a stunning silver crosier are seen here as well. Significant works include Bartolo di Fredi's *Madonna of the Misericordia* (1364), Vecchietta's *Madonna and Child with Saints* and *Annunciation,* and Fra Bartolomeo's *Rest on the Flight into Egypt.*

Venture beyond the city center to experience Pienza's Etruscan, Roman, and medieval past, one untouched by Pius's Renaissance zeal. About a half mile outside Pienza is 11th-century Corsignano's parish church, the **PIEVE SANTI VITO E MODESTO.** Inside, at the simple font, Aeneas Silvius Piccolomini, the future Pius II (1458–64) received baptism. Archaeological remains suggest the site served early Christian baptismal practice (total immersion) and a possible earlier Dionysian cult practice involving water and fertility rites. A nearby natural spring and Etruscan carved caverns known as the Rimitorio offer evidence of pagan practice.

PISA

An ancient maritime port, a medieval university, and a leaning tower define Pisa. They act as physical references to its rich, multifaceted past. In the 12th century, Pisa, the "city of marvels," reached its cultural and economic zenith. Naval might and prosperous maritime trade with the Middle East encouraged a stable and open atmosphere for the exchange of ideas. Science, philosophy, and art flourished as a result. The characteristic Pisan-Romanesque architecture, incorporating Italian building principles with Oriental and Islamic influences, spread throughout Italy. The mathematical discoveries of Leonardo Fibonacci (1165–1235), among them the rediscovery of the principle of the Golden Section, spread throughout Europe. While artistic growth dwindled with Pisa's decline in the 14th century, intellectual endeavors flourished. Pisa's native son, Galileo Galilei (1564–1642), famed physicist and astronomist, developed the principle of the pendulum to measure time, built one of the earliest microscopes, and invented the telescope. In 1633 he was interrogated by the Inquisition for supporting Copernicus's theory for planetary motion. He died at age 78, under house arrest, blind and chastised for his beliefs. Galileo's research is now a source of pride for the city. Today, the university established by Pope Clement VI in 1343 continues to produce renowned scholars.

The celebratory atmosphere during the Festa di San Ranieri, June 16 and 17, is a particularly pleasurable time to visit Pisa. The city's patron saint, St. Ranieri (1117–60), is commemorated with the Luminara. On June 16, the eve of his feast day, during a candlelit celebration, a flotilla of lit lanterns is launched down the Arno. On his feast day, June 17th, a regatta with historic boats from the four historic districts compete in a two kilometer race on the Arno.

Pisa is one of the few Tuscan towns whose Roman period outshines its Etruscan origins. Settled along the mouth of the Arno in the 7th century B.C., it prospered as a Roman naval and commercial port between 180 B.C. and A.D. 476. In A.D. 888 the city became an independent republic. Led by the city's archbishop, the Pisan fleets participated in the First Crusade. Pisa's greatest conquests, however, were for secular gain. By the early 12th century it controlled Corsica, Sardinia, Sicily, North Africa, and the Balearic Islands. The Pisan Empire was expanded and secured in 1135 when it sacked its greatest rival, Amalfi. This victory inaugurated Pisa's most prosperous and productive century. Trade encouraged a cosmopolitan atmosphere; ships transported wool, iron, fur, leather, and timber to the Orient and returned

P

GALILEO GALILEI (1564–1642) was the first modern scientist. His interest in mathematics, mechanics, logic, and experimentation provided the foundation for all future scientific inquiry. Galileo arrived at his first extraordinary discovery, the principle of the pendulum, when he was only 17. This set his scientific career in motion, and he continued to experiment in the fields of mathematics and magnetism while holding the chair in mathematics at the University of Pisa (1589–92) and the University of Padua (1592–1610). During his university postings Galileo built a thermoscope (designed to measure heat) which eventually led to the birth of the thermometer, devised and built a geometrical and military compass, and patented a hydrostatic balance (a machine to raise water).

Shortly after 1594, Galileo turned his interest toward studying the behavior of falling bodies. Until this time, scientists accepted Aristotle's assertion that the rate of fall was proportional to the weight of the body: the heavier the object, the faster it falls to the earth. However, Galileo posited that in a vacuum, all objects would fall at the same rate. Legend claims that Galileo dropped two cannonballs, one ten pounds heavier than the other, from the Tower of Pisa. Both hit the ground simultaneously, thus disproving Aristotelian physics with one simple experiment.

Galileo soon turned his attention to astronomy. The discovery of a new star (1572) by the Danish astronomer Tycho Brahe challenged the Aristotelian belief that the heavens were perfect and unchanging. When in 1604 another star was discovered, Galileo was asked to lecture on their significance at three public lectures in Padua. Galileo constructed his first telescope in 1609. With it he explored the heavens and made numerous observations; new stars, mountains on the moon, spots on the sun, and the four moons of Jupiter were soon described in his book the *Siderius Nuncius* (The Starry Messenger).

Galileo also observed and confirmed that the Copernican system was accurate; the earth is not the center of the universe and it revolves around the sun. However, by 1612 Galileo encountered serious opposition from Aristotelian astronomers. In 1614, Father Tommaso Caccini denounced Galileo's ideas from the pulpit of Santa Maria Novella in Florence. Matters worsened when Pope Paul V declared Copernicanism heretical, leading to Galileo being admonished in 1616.

In 1632, convinced that the new pope, Pope Urban VIII, would be more sympathetic, Galileo published his *Dialogo sopra I due massimi sistemi del mondo* (Discourses on the Two Chief World Systems). The book defended Copernicanism and presented the true laws of accelerated motion and the application of mathematics to a variety of physics problems. For this "crime" Galileo was brought before the Inquisition on the charge of heresy. He was condemned, and on June 22, 1633, he was forced to recant any views which denied the Ptolemaic theory that the earth was the center of the universe. Upon failing to do so, Galileo was sentenced to life imprisonment, which he spent in large part at his villa in Arceti near Florence. He died there in 1642, blind and dishonored.

with silk and spices. However, the most important exchange was the exchange of ideas, both scientific and philosophical.

On August 5, 1284, Genoa defeated Pisa in the naval Battle of Meloria. Soon, its territorial and commercial empire fell and was redistributed among its conquerors. In 1406, Florence gained control. The Medici supported engineering projects, scientific inquiry, and scholarship in Pisa. Lorenzo de' Medici even transferred the Florence University to Pisa. In 1562, Pisa briefly revisited its period of naval might when Cosimo I founded the Order of the Knights of St. Stephen to fight piracy. Pisa soon resumed its quiet scholarly existence and remained under Florentine control until Italian Unification.

PLACES TO VISIT

The **CAMPO DEI MIRACOLI** (Field of Miracles) encloses Pisa's spiritual complex, on which stands its famous Leaning Tower, Duomo, baptistery, and cemetery.

The origins of the field's name are uncertain, but the survival of its art and splendor for 800 years, especially through the bombing raid in 1944, attest to its miraculous nature.

In 1063, the Greek architect Busketos (Boschetto in Italian) began construction on the city's Duomo, the **CATHEDRAL OF SANTA MARIA ASSUNTA**. The massive Romanesque church (325 x 104 feet), a model Pisan-Romanesque building, was completed in the mid-12th century by Boschetto's successor, Rainaldo. Not surprisingly, the funds for the immense sacred project came from secular pursuits; booty from a victory over Sicily provided the revenue.

A fitting tribute, Boschetto's tomb is incorporated into the richly decorated facade (left arch). Fortunately, he did not live to see the cathedral ravaged by fire in 1595. In 1602 the bronze doors depicting the *Life of Christ* and the *Life of the Virgin,* designed by Gianbologna, replaced the burned originals. Miraculously, the *Portale di San Ranieri,* an original door cast in 1180 by Bonanno Pisano, still survives. The original portal covers the common entrance to the church on the south transept. Its decoration depicts the *Life of Christ.*

The interior was thoroughly reconstructed after the 16th-century fire, yet it retains its earlier splendor and treasures. The tomb of the Holy Roman Emperor Henry VII (1308–13), by Tino di Camaino (south transept), was especially revered by the Ghibelline Pisans and is mentioned by Dante in the Divine Comedy. On the floor below the dome are a few colored remains of the original 13th-century mosaic pavement. The golden mosaic *Christ Pantocrator,* completed by Cimabue in 1302, looks down from the apse vault onto Giambologna's *Crucified Christ.* Giambologna's two bronze angel candlesticks (1602) flank the choir and two 16th-century paintings, Andrea del Sarto's *St. Agnes* and Antonio Sogliani's *Madonna and Child.*

The "Lamp of Galileo" hangs above the nave, marking Galileo's balance of science and faith. Legend claims that Galileo, bored by the Mass, watched the lamp swing back and forth and was inspired to develop his theory of the pendulum. Unfortunately, this tale of Divine Providence is discredited by the fact that the bronze lamp was cast by Battista Lorenzi and hung in 1587, a few years after Galileo's discovery.

Ironically, the cathedral's most celebrated masterpiece, Giovanni Pisano's pulpit (1302–11), was long neglected in a church storeroom. After the fire, the pulpit was dismantled, placed in storage, and forgotten until 1926, when it was rediscovered and reassembled. Porphyry columns borne by carved lions support the pulpit. Its carved representations include the Theological Virtues, *Faith, Hope,* and *Charity* and the Cardinal Virtues, *Fortitude, Justice, Prudence,* and *Temperance.* The most dynamic relief panels depict the *Annunciation,* the *Visitation,* the *Nativity,* the *Adoration of the Magi,* the *Presentation in the Temple,* the *Flight into Egypt,* the *Massacre of the Innocents,* the *Crucifixion,* and the *Last Judgment.*

The BAPTISTERY is famed throughout Italy for its monumental size (361 x 180 feet) and the resulting acoustic clarity. Construction began in 1153, and its architect, Diotisalvi, modeled it on the cathedral's Romanesque decoration. Nicola Pisano and his son Giovanni Gothicized the upper drum when they took up work on the structure between 1277 and 1279. Cellino di Nese finally capped the structure with a Gothic dome in 1358. The ornate portals on the hybrid baptistery are worthy of attention, particularly the door opposite the cathedral.

Inside, the light and austere structure is Guido Bigarelli's octagonal baptismal font (1246). Following local practice, it was used for baptism by total immersion; notice the smaller surrounding basins for infant baptisms.

Nicola Pisano's pulpit, signed and dated 1260, stands on tall pillars carved with figures representing the Virtues. Classically inspired panels depict the *Life of Christ* and introduce a new dynamic artistic expression that lays the foundation for Renaissance sculpture.

Famed for its planned delicate beauty and its unintended slant, the TORRE PENDENTE (Leaning Tower) is not the sole leaning structure in Pisa. San Michele dei Scalzi and San Nicola are lesser-known leaners. Unobserved by most visitors, buildings in the Field of Miracles, including the baptistery and duomo, also lean.

Pisan architects, past and present, faced and face the almost impossible task of finding an area to build where the unstable alluvial soil can sustain the weight of a building. In 1173 when Bonanno Pisano began constructing the campanile, all seemed well, but by 1178 the obvious southeast slant could not be ignored. The tower was abandoned at the third level until Giovanni di Simone resumed construction 100 years later. He sought to straighten the tower by lightening the weight on its sinking side and curving the tower walls to oppose the lean. Careful observation reveals a slight curve visible to the eye. In 1360, Tomasso di Andrea da Pontedera completed the belfry and capped the tower.

Almost 300 steps must be scaled to reach the tower's 180-foot summit. In 1590, Galileo conducted experiments from the tower's peak to determine the effect of gravity on falling objects. However, a local curse keeps university students from wishing to follow in the famed scientist's footsteps. Any Pisan knows, "A student hoping to graduate should never chance a climb to the top."

The CAMPOSANTO is Pisa's celebrity cemetery. Legend claims that its sacred soil comes from Golgotha and arrived by the boatload when the local archbishop, Ubaldo dei Lanfranchi (1108–78), returned from a crusade to the Holy Land. This miraculous soil allegedly turns corpses to bones in a matter of days.

The campo is enclosed by a rectangular arcaded structure. Begun in 1277 by Giovanni di Simone, it was not completed until the 15th century. Taddeo Gaddi, Andrea di Buonaiuto, Antonio Veneziano, Spinello Aretino, Piero di Puccio, and Benozzo Gozzoli decorated its walls. In July 1944, a fire caused by Allied artillery bombardment consumed many of these works. Fortunately, a few survived and have been restored.

A walk along the arcaded galleries provide a glimpse of Pisa's past, its most famed citizens, and its spectacular art. Along the west arm hang chains once used to close the Pisan harbor. Nearby are numerous Roman sarcophagi and the notable family wall tomb of the Conti della Gherardesca (1315–30).

Tombs of the Pisan nobility are also located in the east arm, including the tomb of the scientist O. Mossotti (d. 1863), decorated with a female figure by G. Duprè. Note the statue of the "Inconsolable Woman" by L. Bartolini (1842).

P

The Cappella Ammannati, in the north arm, houses the tomb of another notable local, Pisan doctor L. Ammannati (d. 1359). The nearby Hall of Frescoes was constructed in 1952 to house the surviving war casualties. The *Triumph of Death* (1360–80), by an unknown master called the Maestro del Trionfo della Morte, has been arguably identified as the work of Orcagna, Traini, and Buffalmacco, to name a few. Painted after a plague ravaged the city in 1348, its subject is the transience of the earthly world and the certainty of death. Works by the same mystery artist include the *Last Judgment and Hell* and the *Slaughter of the Anchorites*. Also preserved is Taddeo Gaddi's *Patience of Job*.

Fortunately, photographic documentation of the destroyed frescoes exists and provides a glimpse of the lost work of Buffalmacco, Traini, and Gozzoli's remarkable *Tower of Babylon*. The south arm is a storehouse of Roman remains and medieval sarcophagi.

In the former 13th-century Ospedale Nuovo di Misericordia (New Hospital of Mercy) is the MUSEO DELLE SINOPIE DEL CAMPOSANTO MONUMENTALE, opened in 1979. It houses a collection of sinopia fragments mercifully recovered after the war. A sinopia is a preparatory sketch for a fresco drawn directly on the prepared plaster wall. This underdrawing is made with a red-brown pigment called sinopia that came from Sinopie on the Black Sea. Frescoes are painted on a wet base that dries quickly and permanently; sinopia drawings provide a necessary outline and guide the painter during the speedy painting process.

The Camposanto's sinopia drawings were revealed when frescoes fell from the walls during bombing raids. They were subsequently cleaned and restored. Seen together in the museum, they provide insight into the various ways artists used these underdrawing in their work, from rough outlines to detailed drawings. Can you recognize sinopie that correspond to surviving frescoes?

The MUSEO DEL DUOMO is a treasury for the buildings in the Field of Miracles, offering a historical survey of the Duomo, baptistery, tower, and cemetery and housing precious art too delicate, too important, or too insignificant to remain in the miraculous buildings. Works include the Duomo's first pulpit (1158–62) by Guglielmo, which was later replaced by Pisano's masterpiece. Removed from its perch atop the cathedral, an Islamic 11th-century bronze griffin brought to Pisa after the Crusades is housed in the museum, far from its original home. Among the nine busts by the Pisanos from atop the baptistery (1269–79) is Nino Pisano's grouping of *Christ Blessing Between the Virgin Mary and St. John the Evangelist*. Notice Giovanni Pisano's allegorical group of *Pisa Kneeling Before the Virgin Mary and Christ Child,* part of Emperor Henry VII's tomb monument (1312). The "Croce dei Pisani" (the Pisan's Cross) is a 12th-century bronze and silver gilt crucifix carried into battle by Pisan crusaders.

The second floor houses 14th–18th-century paintings by Battista Franco, Aurelio Lomi, and Guido da Seravallino. Illuminated choir books and Exultets (parchment scrolls with the liturgy printed on one side for the priest to read and pictures on the opposite side for the congregation to follow along) are among the beautiful and delicate liturgical accessories. Several rooms are devoted to the display of ecclesiastical vestments. The final rooms are dedicated to Carlo Lasinio, the man who restored the Camposanto frescoes in the 19th century and who fortunately recorded them in a series of etchings.

The Baroque church of SANTO STEFANO DEI CAVALIERI (1565–69) housed the military order of the Knights of St. Stephen. Founded in 1561 by Cosimo I, the brotherhood, whose duty it was to defend the faithful from the Muslims, came to an end in 1860.

The Knights of St. Stephen wore ceremonial costumes during each mass. Vasari originally designed change rooms for the knights in the two side aisles of the church; when the brotherhood ceased, the space was transformed for the congregation.

The ceiling paintings (1604–13) include works by Cigoli, Cristofano Allori, and Empoli, and among the painted coffers, a cycle depicts the history of the Order of St. Stephen. Empoli, Vasari, and Allori also contributed the wall decoration. Notice the trophies and banners hanging throughout the church; they are part of the booty knights took from the defeated infidels. They are a declaration of Pisa's independence and might.

Commanding the high altar (1709) is a statue of the order's patron, martyr, and pope, Stephen I (254–57).

Across the square is the PALAZZO DELLA CAROVANA (Palace of the Caravan), where the knights were trained in horsemanship and warfare. The Medici coat of arms decorates the facade, and a statue of Cosimo I stands before the palace. In 1810, 60 years before the order was inactive, the palace became the site of an elite university founded by Napoleon, the Scuola Normale Superiore.

The PALAZZO DEL' OROLOGIO (Clock Palace), rebuilt in 1607 by Vasari, incorporates the adjacent TORRE DELLA FAME (Tower of Hunger) made famous by Dante in his *Inferno (Canto XXXII)*. In 1288 Count Ugolino della Gherardesca and his sons were starved to death after the commander of the Pisan fleets, Ruggieri, charged him with treason in the Battle of Meloria (1284). Delegated to Dante's circle of hell for traitors to kin and to country, the count gnaws on his accuser's head for eternity.

The large Dominican church, SANTA CATERINA (1251–1300), has a typically Dominican sparse interior. Notable works include Nino Pisano's *Tomb of the Archbishop Simone Saltarelli*, Fra Bartolomeo's *Madonna with Saints* (1511), and Francesco Traini's *Apotheosis of St. Thomas*.

P

SAN ZENO is among the oldest Pisan churches, with Roman fragments incorporated into the structure. It was founded before A.D. 1000, rebuilt by the Benedictines between 1100 and 1180, and deconsecrated in 1809. Until 1972 it was used for storage and is now the site for art exhibitions and musical concerts.

Founded in 1211 during the time of St. Francis, the church of SAN FRANCESCO was mainly constructed by Giovanni di Simone between 1265 and 1270. Construction was completed in the 14th century and the facade finished in 1603. Inside is splendid Baroque decoration. Notice Empoli's *Baptism of Christ,* Santi di Tito's *Francis Receiving the Stigmata,* and vault frescoes by Taddeo Gaddi (1342). In the second chapel on the right are the tombs of Count Ugolino della Gherardesca and his sons; their tombs were moved here in 1922, centuries after their tortuous death.

SAN PAOLO A RIPA D'ARNO (St. Paul's on the Bank of the Arno) was founded in 805, and its 13th-century facade imitates Pisa's cathedral. Inside, visit the Cappella Sant' Agata behind the apse. This tiny pyramid-roofed octagonal chapel is a separate structure attributed to Diotisalvi and reflects foreign tomb construction.

SAN SEPOLCRO mimics the design of the church of the Holy Sepulchre in Jerusalem. Diotisalvi designed the pyramid-roofed octagonal structure (1153) possibly for the Knights Templar. Today the church has sunk below ground level.

SANTA MARIA DELLA SPINA derives its name from a relic (now in the church of Santa Chiara) brought by a Pisan merchant from the Holy Land, a thorn *(spina)* from Christ's Crown of Thorns. Originally built (1230–1323) by the Pisanos on the edge of the Arno, it was dismantled and reassembled on higher ground in 1871 to spare it from water damage. Much of the exterior sculpture was moved to the museum and replaced by copies. Inside the church, Nino Pisano's *Madonna della Latte* has also been replaced by a copy.

SAN NICOLA was founded in A.D. 1000. Inside the church, along the south side, are Francesco Traini's *Madonna and Child,* a painting of *St. Nicholas of Tolentino Protecting Pisa from the Plague* (c. 1400), and a carved *Crucifix* by Giovanni Pisano. On the north side is Nicola Pisano's statue of the *Madonna and Child.* Be sure to find the sacristan, who will let you visit the church's 13th-century leaning tower.

The 11th-century church of SAN FREDIANO houses a notable 13th-century *Crucifix* and Aurelio Lomi's *Adoration of the Magi* (1604).

SAN MICHELE IN BORGO is a 10th-century church dedicated to the warrior archangel. It possibly stands atop the ancient site of a Roman temple to the warrior-god Mars.

The MUSEO NAZIONALE DI SAN MATTEO is housed in the former Benedictine convent of San Matteo (15th century). The order closed in 1866, and the structure was used as a prison until 1947. It was transformed into a museum with a collection of Pisan and Tuscan works from the 12th to 15th centuries.

Its vast ceramics collection highlights Islamic ceramics and local Pisan majolica works (13th–17th centuries). The tableware is juxtaposed with a renowned collection of antique metal weapons and armor. Sculpture and paintings rescued from damp Pisan churches fill the rest of the museum. Two rare signed *Crucifixes* by Giunta Pisano (one of the first medieval artists to sign his works) are among a number of 12th- and 13th-century crucifixes. A signed polyptych by Francesco Traini depicts *St. Dominic with Stories of His Life.* Simone Martini's polyptych depicts the *Madonna and Child with Mary Magdalene, St. Dominic, St. John the Evangelist, and St. Catherine.* Notice Nino Pisano's nurturing and loving nursing virgin, the *Madonna del Latte,* and the works of his pupil, Valdambrino. Among the notable paintings are Spinello Aretino's *Coronation of the Virgin* and *Three Saints,*

Agnolo Gaddi's polyptych, Taddeo di Bartolo's *Life of St. Galgan,* and Simone Martini's *Virgin and Child with Saints.* The gallery continues with a *St. Paul* by Masaccio, a *Coronation of the Virgin* by Neri di Bicci, and a *Madonna of Humility* by Gentile da Fabriano.

Two worthwhile excursions outside Pisa include the church of SAN PIETRO A GRADO (12 kilometers southwest) and the spa, SAN GIULIANO TERME (7 kilometers east). San Pietro a Grado (St. Peter on the Quay) is an 11th-century basilica built on Pisa's Roman port. The interior is decorated with scenes from the life of St. Peter and includes portraits of the popes from St. Peter through John XVII (1003).

The spa at the foot of Monte Pisano grew from the Roman spring where San Giuliano healed respiratory and digestive ailments, arthritis, and rheumatism with the spring water. Famed spa-goers include Montaigne, Byron, Shelley, and Louis Bonaparte.

PISTOIA

Situated precariously between rivals Florence and Pisa, Pistoia was influenced by the best and worst the two cities had to offer. Caught in a regional struggle for power, Pistoia developed an unstable identity. In his invective against the people of Pistoia, Michelangelo called its citizens "Friends to (their) own harm, and to (their) own neighbor." The myth of Pistoia is the myth of a quarrelsome and bellicose lot who supposedly instigated the conflict between the White and Black Guelfs. The local metalworking industry enhanced the image, producing the *pistolese* (pistol); originally a dagger, it developed into a firearm. The metal

THE CHRISTIAN TRAVELERS GUIDE TO ITALY

industry continues to thrive in Pistoia. Instead of firearms, the Breda Works produces trains and buses.

Sixty-two B.C. marks Pistoia's first conflict; here, in Roman Pistoria, a coup against the Roman Republic ended in the defeat of Cataline and his men. Pistoia developed amidst Tuscan conflict and in 1158 asserted itself as a free commune. It was occupied briefly by Florence in 1306, fell under Lucchesan Castruccio Castracani's empire from 1315 to 1328, and fell for a second and final time under Florentine control in 1329. Florence exercised strict rule over Pistoia but was powerless to stop the city's internal Guelf division between the White and Black factions from spreading to Florence. Tensions resulted in the exile of local poet and friend to Dante, Cino da Pistoia (1270–1337), for his allegiance to the Black faction. Michelangelo labeled the Pistoians the "enemies of heaven," but these so-called celestial foes managed to produce a successor to St. Peter; the son of a local noble family, Giulio Rospigliosi, reigned as Pope Clement IX from 1667 to 1669.

PLACES TO VISIT

The Duomo of SAN ZENO E JACOPO stands in the center of Pistoia, at the heart of its 14th-century diamond-shaped defense walls. It shares its central position with the adjacent Lombard defense tower, which was transformed into the Duomo's campanile (13th–16th centuries). As a result, the hybrid tower is massive and solid at its base and progressively light and delicate as it reaches heavenward, retaining both its secular and sacred aspects.

The earliest recorded cathedral on the site is a 5th-century structure that predates the tower. Destroyed by fire in 1108, the cathedral was reconstructed beginning in 1220 and continuing until the 17th century. The facade was completed in 1311. Statues of the church's patrons, Saints Zeno and James, crown either end of the pediment. Above the main entrance is Andrea della Robbia's terra-cotta, the *Virgin and Child with Two Angels* (1505).

Though exiled, Cino da Pistoia's birthplace remains his eternal home; he is entombed inside the cathedral along the south wall. His sarcophagus (1337) depicts the scholar addressing his pupils. Along the same wall is a painted *Crucifix* (1275) by Coppo di Marcovaldo.

The Chapel of St. James contains the stunning *dossale di San Jacopo* (altar of St. James), a gilded silver altarpiece modeled by master craftsmen between 1287 and 1456. Slightly less than one ton of silver was required to depict 628 figures in scenes from the Old Testament, New Testament, and life of St. James.

The Chapel of the Sacrament contains Verrocchio's only recorded work, the *Madonna di Piazza with Saints John the Baptist and Zeno* (1485); recent evidence suggests the work might be by Leonardo da Vinci or his pupil Lorenzo di Credi.

Opposite the disputed work is the *Bust of Archbishop Donato de Medici* by Antonio Rossellino. Verrocchio designed the tomb of Cardinal Niccolò Forteguerri (1476–83). Do not miss the *Coronation of the Virgin with Saints Baronto and Desiderio* by Caravaggio's pupil Mattia Preti, and Maso di Bartolomeo's bronze candelabrum (1440).

The sacristy leads into the adjacent 14th-century PALAZZO DEI VESCOVI (Bishop's Palace), which houses the MUSEO DELLA CATTEDRALE DI SAN ZENO. The cathedral's treasures have long appealed to the virtuous and sinners alike. The temptation of sacred treasure was too great for Vanni Fucci, the 13th-century political-troublemaker-come-thief, who stole some sacristy treasures. Dante relegated Fucci to the depths of hell to curse God from a pit of snakes (Inferno, Canto XXIV).

The museum offers archaeological and historical insight into the cathedral and Pistoia. The archaeological collection in the basement includes locally found Etruscan and Roman remains. Stunning reliquaries by Rombolus Salvei (1379), the *Reliquary of San Zeno* (1369) by Enrico Belandini and the *Reliquary of St. James* (1407) by Lorenzo Ghiberti and his workshop are evidence to the irresistible lure of riches that certainly plagued Fucci. The tour continues into the Cappella San Nicolò, a deconsecrated room that was formerly the bishop's private chapel (13th century). Pleas for freedom scratched into

the 14th-century frescoed walls were made by prisoners held in the room in the 15th century. The adjoining room contains carefully monitored dry tempera frescoes painted in 1868 by Giovanni Boldini.

The BATTISTERO DI SAN GIOVANNI IN CORTE (1337–59) is an octagonal structure designed by Andrea Pisano and built by Cellino di Nese. Above the entrance of the striped white and green marble structure are carved reliefs by Tommaso and Nino Pisano depicting the *Madonna and Child Between Saints John the Baptist and Peter*. Inside the sparse interior is the finely carved inlaid font (1226) by Lanfranco da Como.

The church of SANT' ANDREA remains unfinished despite 8th-century origins and an expansive 12th-century reconstruction program. The few decorations on the incomplete facade include three scenes above the doorway depicting the *Journey of the Magi, Herod Told of the Birth of Christ,* and the *Adoration of the Magi* signed in Latin by Gruamonte and his brother Adeodato in 1166.

The simple interior contains two treasures by Giovanni Pisano, a gilded wooden crucifix and a pulpit. On the pulpit, reminiscent of his father's work in Pisa and Siena, slender columns stand atop dramatically carved lion, eagle, and human bases that support the octagonal podium. Marble panels depict the *Annunciation, Nativity, Adoration of the Magi, Massacre of the Innocents, Crucifixion,* and the *Last Judgment.*

P

Dedicated to Pistoia's patron saint, the **BASILICA DELLA MADONNA DELL' UMILTÀ** (Basilica of Our Lady of Humility) is far from a humble structure. Built by local architect and student of Bramante, Ventura Vitoni (1495–1522), it is an important model of High Renaissance architecture. In 1562, Giorgio Vasari crowned the octagonal church with a massive dome. In the heart of the sanctuary is the reason for the structure's existence, the miraculous 14th-century fresco by Bartolomeo Cristiani, the *Madonna of Humility*.

The **OSPEDALE DEL CEPPO**, founded in 1277, gets its name from the Tuscan practice of collecting alms for the destitute and sick in a hollow log called a *ceppo*. Michelozzo added the Renaissance portico in 1514, imitating the design of the Ospedale degli Innocenti in Florence. Here, too, the della Robbias contributed the facade decoration. The terra-cotta frieze (1514–25) by Giovanni della Robbia depicts the *Seven Works of Mercy* framed between the *Cardinal* and *Theological Virtues;* they are *The Clothing of the Naked, Welcoming the Stranger, Prudence, Visiting the Sick, Faith, Visiting Prisoners, Charity, Burying the Dead, Hope, Feeding the Hungry, Justice,* and *Giving Drink to the Thirsty.*

The 12th- to 14th-century church of **SAN GIOVANNI FUORCIVITAS** (St. John outside the Walls) cannot be missed—literally! Hypnotic green and white stripes and abstract lozenges along the facade contrast the dark inte-

rior; however, its hidden treasures are enlightening. The stunning pulpit (1270) carved by Nicola Pisano's student, Fra Guglielmo of Pisa, depicts the *Life of Christ and the Virgin,* while Nicola's son, Giovanni, contributed a carved holy water stoup with representations of the *Cardinal and Theological Virtues.* Along the north wall is Luca della Robbia's terra-cotta *Visitation.*

The now deconsecrated church of **SANT'ANTONIO ABATE DEL TAU** (1360) was inhabited by the Franciscan Order of the Hospitallers, monks dedicated to attending the sick. The monks wore the symbol of the Greek Tau "T" on their tunics. The frescoes were whitewashed when the chapel was purchased privately in the 16th century. Fortunately, restored scenes from the *Life of St. Anthony the Abbot, The Story of the Sacred Girdle, The Creation* and *Original Sin* can still be admired.

The church of **SAN DOMENICO**, built in 1280, is known for its deceased occupants and their funerary monuments. Two notable works include the tomb of *Beato Lorenzo da Ripafratta* and the tomb of Dante's friend Filippo Lazzari by Bernardo and Antonio Rossellino depicting the scholar lecturing to a group of students. Benozzo Gozzoli is buried in the cloister (location unknown). The painter died of the plague in Pistoia in 1497 while painting a fresco in the church. The adjoining museum contains the *Journey of the Magi* begun by Gozzoli. Also in the collection is *St. Jerome Kneel-*

ing, by Verrocchio and a 14th-century Sienese *St. Mary Magdalene.*

The church of **SAN BARTOLOMEO IN PANTANO** (St. Bartholomew in the Marsh) was founded in 761 and rebuilt in 1159. The Benedictine monastery was built atop a marsh that is slowly consuming it. A self-portrait of the artist Guido da Como can be seen on a carved pulpit from 1250. The kneeling stone figure seems to struggle against the marshy ground and the weight of the marble pulpit it supports.

The Jesuit father Tommaso Ramignani designed the church of **SANTO SPIRITO** (1647). When the native Pope Clement IX was elected in 1667, he commissioned Gian Lorenzo Bernini to sculpt the high altar and Pietro da Cortona to paint the accompanying altarpiece, the *Apparition of Christ to St. Ignatius,* as a gift to his hometown.

SAN FRANCESCO (1289) contains a number of notable frescoes, including a Giottoesque cycle of St. Francis, a Sienese *Triumph of St. Augustine,* and a *Tree of Life with Crucifixion* attributed to Pietro Lorenzetti.

Inside the Palazzo del Commune (1294) is the **MUSEO CIVICO,** housing a vast collection from the 13th century to 19th century. Earlier works include a panel painting of *St. Francis* (c. 1260), an anonymous *Madonna and Child with Saints* (1310), and four Renaissance Sacred Conversations, one by Lorenzo di Credi, one by Ridolfo del Ghirlandaio, and two by Gerino Gerini. Later works include a *St. Sebastian and St. John the Baptist* by Sigismondo Coccapani, the *Vision of St. John* by Piero Paolini, and *Susanne and the Elders* by Mattia Preti.

The Museo Diocesano in the Palazzo Rospigliosi (owned by the local noble family of Pope Clement IX) houses a collection of 17th-century works, including numerous paintings by the native Pistoian artist, Giacinto Gimignani (1611–81).

PRATO

A thriving textile industry established in the Middle Ages and famed throughout Europe afforded the Pratese the opportunity to spend money on art to beautify their city. The Prato native Francesco di Marco Datini (1330–1410) contributed the art of accounting not only to his city but also to Europe and the world. Iris Origo's *The Merchant of Prato* made his financial savvy famous. He managed to balance faith and finance in his work, adding to all his documents the words "For God and Profit." For God and Love could have been the motto for the father

143

of Prato-born Filippino Lippi (1457/8–1504), son of the sinning Fra Lippo Lippi, an ex-monk who fell in love with and married the beautiful blonde-haired Lucretia Buti. The former monk was notoriously unfaithful to all his vows.

Prato first appears in records in the 9th century. Originally called Borgo al Cornio, the Lombard city took its name from a bustling market in a nearby meadow (Italian "prato"), which might have been the site of an earlier Etruscan camp. Large markets defined the city's commercial character. From 1140 to 1350, Prato was a free commune until Florence purchased it from its Neapolitan landlord. Prato's greatest sights predate its Florentine domination.

PLACES TO VISIT

At the heart of 10th-century Prato was the **PIEVE DI SANTO STEFANO DI BORGO AL CORNIO**; this small market town church rose in stature and status and by 1653 was raised to a cathedral and the see of a bishop. Begun in 1211 by Guido da Como, construction continued through 1457. A glazed terracotta *Madonna and Saints Stefano and Lorenzo* (1489) by Andrea della Robbia crowns the main entrance.

Perched on the exterior right corner is the *Pergamo del Sacro Cignolo* (Pulpit of the Holy Girdle) by Donatello and Michelozzo. This pulpit is reserved to display Prato's most revered relic, the Virgin Mary's Holy Girdle. The girdle or *cintola* symbolizes the Virgin Mary's chastity. Proverbs 31 provides biblical reference to the ancient practice of girdle making by virtuous, chaste women (presumably they also wore the girdles). According to legend, to convince him of her assumption, the Virgin Mary dropped her girdle to the doubting St. Thomas as she ascended into heaven. In 1141 the girdle arrived in Prato from the Holy Land, part of the dowry of a woman from Jerusalem named Mary who married Michele Dagonari, a local returning from the First Crusade. After his wife died he dared not tell anyone about his treasure. He hid the girdle under his mattress in hopes that no one would discover it, but angels sent from God rescued the girdle while Michele slept and entrusted it to the Pieve di Santo Stefano, Umberto. To today it remains in the possession of the church and the city. On feast days the guarded relic is released from its protective chapel. Three keys are required to unlock the reliquary; one is held by the bishop, another by the mayor, and the third by the carabinieri chief. The girdle is then displayed to devout throngs from its outdoor perch. The Virgin's undergarments can be seen from the stunning pulpit only five times a year: Easter, May 1, August 15, September 8, and Christmas.

The girdle is housed at all other times within the church in the Chapel of the Sacred Girdle. Constructed between 1385 and 1390, two bronze screens (1438) by Maso di Bartolomeo enclose the chapel. Atop the altar is a statuette of the *Madonna and Child* (1317) by Giovanni Pisano. Agnolo Gaddi's wall frescoes depict the *Life of the Virgin* and the *Legend of the Holy Girdle.*

Frescoed walls (1452–66) in the choir behind the main altar are enhanced by another local tale. Fra Lippo Lippi's cycle of the *Life of St. Stephen* and the *Life of St. John the Baptist* are the monk's first significant works, and their execution played a significant role in the brother's personal life. Portraits of Lippi and his assistant Fra Diamante are depicted in the fresco as humble mourners at the death of St. Stephen, an indication of the license granted artists by both patrons and the church. The model for the dancing figure of Salome was the local novice nun at the church of Santa Margherita, Lucretia Buti, who became both Fra Lippo's muse and lover. She bore him a son, and after much scandal the pope granted them a release from their vows and they were wed. This was a clear sign how art was indulged by the church.

Artistic representations of St. Stephen throughout the church are certain to rouse the devout as effectively as St. Stephen's famous sermon (Acts 7:2–53). Notable among them are the works of Paolo Uccello and Andrea di Giusto in the Chapel of the Assumption depicting the *Life of the Virgin and St. Stephen.*

The beautifully carved marble pulpit (1473) by Mino da Fiesole and Antonio Rossellino also depicts scenes from the *Lives of St. Stephen and St. John the Baptist.* Do not miss Giuliano da Maiano's *Madonna dell'Olivo* (1480), the Madonna of the Olive in the south transept.

The MUSEO DELL'OPERA DEL DUOMO contains more of the original venerated girdle's accouterments, including a reliquary which once enshrouded the sacred girdle by Maso di Bartolomeo (1446). The original seven panels (1428–38) which once adorned the Pulpit of the Sacred Girdle have been replaced by copies. The collection also includes Fra Lippo Lippi's *Death of St. Jerome* and his son Filippino's *St. Lucy.*

The CASTELLO DELL'IMPERATORE (Imperial Castle) is a symbol of impenetrable Ghibelline sentiment and the Holy Roman Emperor, Frederic II Von Hohenstaufen's, papal defiance. He was excommunicated twice, but his fortress attests to his enduring power and presence. The fortress (1237–48) is a defensive stronghold along the route from Germany to his inherited lands in Southern Italy and Sicily.

The church of SANTA MARIA DELLE CARCERI (1485) stand atop the site of a former prison *(carcere)* on whose walls in 1484 a miraculous image of the Virgin spoke. Based on Albertian and Brunelleschian architectural principles, Giuliano da Sangallo's plan falls short of the order, harmony, and proportion of model Renaissance churches. A terracotta frieze and medallions of the four evangelists by Andrea della Robbia decorate the austere interior.

The "Merchant of Prato," Francesco di Marco Datini, is buried near the altar steps of his patron saint's church, the 13th-century Romanesque SAN FRANCESCO. The chapter house, or the Cappella Migliorati, is decorated with frescoes (1395) by Niccolò di Pietro Gerini depicting the *Lives of St. Anthony the Abbot and St. Matthew.*

The GALLERIA COMUNALE E MUSEO CIVICO is housed in the Palazzo Pretorio. Founded in 1850, the collection focuses on 14th- and 15th-century Florentine schools. Filippino Lippi's gift to his mother, the *Madonna del Mercatale* tabernacle (1498), originally stood on the corner of his widowed mother's house. A bombing casualty of World War I, it was transferred to the museum and restored. On the second floor is another local favorite, Bernardo Daddi's *Story of the Sacred Girdle* (1337). Marian devotion is evidenced in numerous paintings of the Madonna by Lorenzo Monaco, Luca Signorelli, Filippino Lippi, Andrea di Giusto, and Francesco Botticini. Look for Filippo Lippi's *Madonna del Ceppo* with the figure of

Francesco Datini, whose fortune provided the means to found the local charity del Ceppo in 1410.

The church of SAN DOMENICO was begun in 1283 and completed in 1322 by Giovanni Pisano. Inside is a *Crucifix* by Niccolò di Pietro Gerini and various works depicting famed Dominicans St. Thomas and Philip Neri.

The MUSEUM OF MURAL PAINTING (next door) was home to two Dominicans, artist Fra Bartolomeo and the infamous Savonarola. The museum houses works salvaged from local churches, including Niccolò di Pietro Gerini's *Tabernacle of the Ceppo* and Paolo Uccello's sinopia underdrawings from the Duomo's Cappella dell'Assunta (15th century).

Visit SAN FABIANO, one of Prato's oldest churches, whose mosaic pavement decoration suggests the presence of an earlier pagan site. Nearby, in the church of SANT'AGOSTINO, is Empoli's *Sacred Conversation* and *Immaculate Conception.* Do not miss the small painting collection in the PALAZZO DEGLI ALBERTI that includes the masterful *Crucified Christ* by Giovanni Bellini.

RAVELLO

Once the see of a bishopric, the small resort town of Ravello is renowned for its breathtaking vistas and tranquil beauty, and boasts a splendid cathedral. Seemingly hovering between the sky and the sea, the tortuously winding Bacchic road up to Ravello is like journeying through a grapevined purgatory to reach heaven.

Built in the 9th century, Ravello's prosperity peaked in the 13th century.

The city gained independence from Amalfi in 1086 and maintained its self-rule until 1813. It was at the cathedral in Ravello that Adrian IV, during his flight from Rome, crowned William the Bad of Sicily (1149).

PLACES TO VISIT

The cathedral of SAN PANTALEONE, Ravello's patron saint, is dedicated to an early Christian martyr who was beheaded in Nicomedia on July 27, 290. The saint's chapel, within the cathedral, houses a miraculous relic: a vial of San Pantaleone's blood that boils on his feast days, May 19 and August 27.

Built in 1086 and renovated 700 years later, the church retains much of its original splendor. Bronze doors (1169) by Barisano da Trani contain portraits of saints, scenes from Christ's Passion, and biblical inscriptions. The church treasures include two marble pulpits with intricate mosaic decoration called *ambones*. The larger ambo, with beautifully carved spiral columns and lions, dates 1272, while the smaller ambo, depicting Jonah and the whale, dates 1130.

RAVENNA

Renowned for its rich mosaics and Byzantine churches, Ravenna's artistic heritage reveals insight into the empires of the East and West that met and clashed in the Italian city, and whose spirit shaped Christian civilization. Ravenna reached political, cultural, and economic prosperity under the rule of three different empires between the 5th and 8th centuries. As their capital, Ravenna hosted the Western Roman Empire, the Visigoth Empire, and the Byzantine Empire. What remains of its past glory are religious edifices that proclaim the divinely instituted union of political and spiritual authority.

Commanding a strategic harbor on the Adriatic, Ravenna, under Emperor Augustus, was home to the fierce Roman naval fleet. Here, ships controlled trade routes between East and West. This role of peacekeeping and tolerance proved essential to Ravenna's future prosperity.

In A.D. 402 Emperor Honorius moved the capital of the western Christian and Roman Empires from Milan to Ravenna. When Rome fell in 476, the city was briefly ruled by the barbarian King Odoacre, who, in 493, was ousted by King Theodoric. An Arian, Theodoric ruled the Christian majority in Ravenna with a spirit of tolerance. (The followers of Arius denied the dual nature of Christ, thus opposing Nicean Catholic orthodoxy.) Theodoric died in 526, but the Goths retained control of Ravenna until

R

DANTE ALIGHIERI (1265–1321). Born in Florence in 1265, Dante Alighieri is considered the finest Italian writer of the medieval period. Dante was a man of action. Actively involved in local politics, he was a member of the White Guelfs, who opposed the Church's claim to temporal power. In 1302 Dante was condemned to exile by the city's new leaders under the guidance and support of Pope Boniface VIII. Forced never to return to his native city again, Dante, humiliated and poor, wandered through Northern Italy and finally settled in Ravenna.

Dante's works bridge the gap between the spiritual world of the medieval period and the secular world of the Renaissance. His writings include the *Vita Nuova* (*The New Life*, 1293–4), the *Divina Commedia* (*The Divine Comedy*, 1304–21), the *De vulgari eloquentia* (1307), a treatise on language, the *Convivio* (1307), a discussion of wisdom, and the *Monarchia* (1317), a defense of the emperor. The *Divine Comedy* is Dante's best-known work, considered one of literature's great masterpieces.

The *Divine Comedy* is like a travel guide. The poem is divided into three parts—the Inferno (Hell), Purgatorio (Purgatory), and Paradiso (Paradise)—and Dante is a spiritual pilgrim journeying through each realm. The classical poet Virgil leads Dante through Hell and Purgatory while Beatrice, a young woman who died in Dante's youth and became a miraculous influence in his life, leads Dante through Paradise. The three form a complex allegory, with Dante as the symbol of mankind, Virgil as the symbol of human reason, and Beatrice as the symbol of God's love.

During his journey Dante undergoes moral and spiritual conversion. In witnessing and experiencing sin and its punishment, Dante and the reader prepare for an eventual spiritual union with the Lord. Ever politically minded, however, Dante includes a great deal of political invective in the *Divine Comedy*. He excoriates the papacy for its corruption, criticizes the leadership of Florence for its despotism, and condemns all those who abuse their authority.

Despite its secular emphasis on history and politics, the *Divine Comedy* is concerned with mankind's spiritual situation. Dante's journey is the symbol of man's search for salvation and revelation.

they were overrun in 540, when the city came under the control of the Byzantine Empire.

The Byzantine emperor Justinian drove the Goths out of Italy and sought to drive the Arian church out with them. His Orthodox faith and victory over heresy are expressed in Ravenna's Byzantine churches. Justinian exerted his political dominance in Ravenna by representing himself as the link between the kingdom of God and his kingdom on earth.

In 751 the city fell once again, this time to the Longobards. Its golden age ended, but the city's artistic wealth survived to touch Italy's greatest Christian poet, Dante. Exiled to Ravenna in the 14th century, he completed his *Divine Comedy* in this atmosphere of spiritual splendor. Dante's journey to the celestial sphere in the *Paradiso* was surely aided by the golden visions in Ravenna's heavenly mosaics.

PLACES TO VISIT

The MAUSOLEUM OF GALLA PLACIDIA, dating from A.D. 425–50, is both a martyrium and an imperial tomb. Galla Placidia, sister to the last Roman emperor Honorius and wife to the first barbarian emperor Ataulfo, ruled Ravenna and the Western Empire as empress and regent after her husband's death. Though she died in Rome and was probably buried there in 450, she initially intended the mausoleum to house the remains of her royal family.

Outside, the simple cross-shaped, domed structure and red brick exterior give no clue to the rich mosaic decoration preserved within. Redemption and the promise of eternal life, the focus of the decorative program, reinforces the function of the mausoleum.

Representations of St. Lawrence the martyr meeting his death on the fiery grill and Christ as the good shepherd tending his flock lead the viewer's eye up to the heavenly dome. Ninety-nine stars surround the cross of Jesus. Four beasts make up the corners: a winged man, a winged lion, a winged ox, and a winged eagle (symbols of the four evangelists, Matthew, Mark, Luke, and John, respectively) as described in Revelation 4:6–8. They accompany the sign of Christ in the Second Coming.

The NEONIAN BAPTISTERY (c. A.D. 450) and the ARIAN BAPTISTERY (end 5th century A.D.) reveal the similarities between the Orthodox and Arian faith and liturgy through structure and decoration. Both are plain brick octagonal buildings with rich mosaic interiors; both have cupolas decorated in three zones with similar subjects. At their center is the baptism of Christ, followed by the twelve apostles, and along the outer edge, an empty throne surmounted by a cross (subtle differences and additions appear at this level). The cross enthroned symbolizes earthly anticipation of Christ's coming and the Last Judgment. Notice the different focal points for the two thrones: in the

R

149

Arian representation it is seen right side up so the faithful entering can see it; conversely, the Neonian throne is only seen right side up by the priest. Which is the more promising vision?

Upon his return from Constantinople in A.D. 549, Archbishop Maximian consecrated the BASILICA OF SANT' APOLLINARE IN CLASSE, approximately three miles south of Ravenna. The church glorifies his vocation and power as intercessor in the Christian West.

Dedicated to Ravenna's first bishop (St. Apollinarius first brought the gospel to the region), the church links Maximian to Ravenna's religious history. St. Apollinarius dominates the apse mosaic as the good shepherd. Hands raised in the Orant position (in an attitude of prayer), he invokes Christ and gives praise to the mosaic cross hovering above. An abstracted Transfiguration scene, Moses and Elias flank the cross. Christ and the symbols of the four evangelists look on the scene from the arch above. Between the windows in the apse, representations of past bishops reinforce the continuity of ecclesiastical authority in Ravenna.

The BASILICA OF SANT' APOLLINARE NUOVO received its name in the 9th century when the relics of St. Apollinare housed in Classe were moved to Ravenna to protect the crypt's sacred remains from pirate raids. Built by Theodoric in the early 6th century and dedicated to Christ the Redeemer, the church was rededicated to St. Martin of Tours when the Arians fled Ravenna. The rededication was especially fitting; St. Martin was known for his fight against heresy. Each rededication meant redecoration. A procession of virgins, led by the three wise men, march toward the Virgin and Child enthroned on the right wall of the nave while on the left, St. Martin leads martyrs toward Christ. Above the solemn processions, apostles, prophets, and patriarchs hold scrolls and books. Christ's miracles (left) and Christ's Passion (right) crown the nave mosaics. As you enter church and proceed toward the vision of Christ enthroned at the altar, you participate in the regal procession of virgins and martyrs and share in their hope for salvation.

The BASILICA OF SAN VITALE, begun during the Ostrogoth domination (c. A.D. 526), was built on Imperial (Byzantine) private property likely with Justinian's permission. The patron was a wealthy banker who supported the emperor's policies. Its construction was a deliberate attempt to make the politics and religion of Byzantium physically present in the West before Imperial troops arrived.

The structure combines the Byzantine centralized plan and the Western basilican plan. Inside, Eastern and Western building styles are again combined; notice the triangular insertion (known as dosserts) between the column capitals and the arch. These dosserts are typical of Byzantine architecture and are seen in many of Ravenna's churches.

Glimmering mosaics proclaim Christ's triumph over death and his promise for eternal life. The Eucharist is symbolically celebrated in the arcade above the altar where Old Testament images of Abraham sacrificing Isaac, Abel offering a lamb, and Melchizedek sacrificing bread and wine refer to the body and blood of Christ. The Apocalyptic Christ reigns atop the earth in the apse. On his right, San Vitale receives a martyr's crown, and on his left Bishop Ecclesius presents a model of the church.

Emperor Justinian and his court and Empress Theodora and her court appear in the mosaic panels surrounding the apse. Never to come to Ravenna, their figurative presence is commemorated during every Mass, and their sacred and secular power is confirmed. In San Vitale, the power of the heavenly and earthly courts is proclaimed.

Ravenna's CATHEDRAL was formerly the Basilica Ursiana, built by Archbishop Ursus in the beginning of the 5th century. It was demolished and rebuilt in 1734 by the architect G. Francesco Buonamici from Rimini. Inside, be sure to visit the Chapel of the Sacrament where Guido Reni and his workshop painted Christ in glory in the dome.

Ravenna's museums are as rich as its church's mosaics. At the MUSEUM OF THE ARCHBISHOP is the ivory throne of Archbishop Maximian. Carved in the beginning of the 6th century, it is of eastern craftsmanship and might have been a gift from Justinian. The NATIONAL MUSEUM began in the 18th century when the monks in Classe collected and classified art as their pastime; it houses coins, weapons, icons, textiles, and ivories. The ACADEMY GALLERY contains local 15th- and 16th-century paintings, including works by Niccolò Rondinelli and Francesco Zaganelli da Cotignola.

DANTE'S TOMB now rests in a neoclassical temple erected in 1780 by Camillo Morigia. Dante Alighieri died in Ravenna in 1321, and his funeral was held in the nearby church of San Francesco.

ROMA
(ROME)

In Paul's letter to the Romans (1:8), he praised the early Christian community in Rome, "whose faith [was] reported all over the world," for its generosity, steadfast leadership, and spiritual strength. Established in the ancient capital of the world, Rome's Christian community sought recognition and fellowship in an environment where the state and religion were the same. Nonetheless, Christian roots in the city were deep; its claim to the martyred saints Peter and Paul linked Rome to the root of Christ's physical and spiritual church. Soon, the City of the Caesars was the City of the Church.

Rome's political primacy was transformed into religious primacy. Today, the city itself is the keeper of an empire of ruins, relics, art, monuments, churches, palaces, myths, legends, power, and faith that proclaim the supremacy of its secular and sacred worlds. Rome's rich cultural heritage offers an intimate link to the past, and its vast and varied appeal offers the keys to a heavenly world for artists, philosophers, scientists, businessmen, pilgrims, tourists, saints, and heretics alike.

Romulus and Remus, twin brothers suckled by a she-wolf and reared on the Palatine Hill, mark Rome's mythical founding in 753 B.C. Rome's historical genesis began two centuries earlier. A small settlement along the Tiber, the inhabitants struggled for independence from and supremacy over the all-powerful Etruscans. The settlement, ruled by an elected monarchy, grew and spread beyond the Palatine to occupy Rome's other legendary hills: the Capitoline, the Aventine, the Quirinal, the Esquiline, the Caelian, and the Viminal. In 509 B.C., a patrician revolt led by Lucius Junius Brutus overthrew the ruling monarchy and inaugurated Rome's Republic.

In 390 B.C., the Gauls of Brenno sacked Rome. The city emerged from the devastation with newfound zeal and determination. Rome attacked and conquered the Mediterranean world, organ-izing successful campaigns against Sicily, Sardinia, Macedonia, Spain, Greece, and Carthage. Its military prowess was complemented by Rome's unparalleled engineering practices. While they conquered the world, Romans constructed aqueducts, invented cement, and developed the arch, the vault, and the dome. By the end of the 1st century B.C., excessive luxury, lax morals, political conflict, and civil unrest plagued the city. In 44 B.C., Julius Caesar, who attempted to reestablish the monarchy with himself as king, was assassinated. His death resulted in the end of five centuries of Rome's Republic and the beginning of a seemingly limitless empire.

Octavian Augustus, staunch defender of the republic and Roman morals and values, rose to become Rome's first emperor, their deified leader. He ushered in a period of peace and prosperity, Rome's Golden Age. His famed and infamous imperial successors included enlightened rulers, crazed tyrants, skilled generals, spoiled madmen, Christian persecutors, corrupt murderers, and eventually, believers in Christ.

Rome's Christian citizens planted and nourished the seed of faith while pagan emperors sought to uproot the movement. Nero, Domitian, and Diocletian were the most notorious Christian persecutors. While countless Christian martyrs fell under the empire, persecutions were not practiced or enforced by all emperors. Finally, under Constantine I (306–37), the empire was converted from pagan to Christian. Constantine's victory over Maxentius at the Milvian Bridge, granted through God's grace and won under the sign of the cross, resulted in the Edict of Milan (313), which granted tolerance towards Christianity. The successful unification between Church and State is Constantine's legacy; ironically, the emperor did not receive baptism until the end of his life, long after his empire's conversion.

Soon after, the seat of the empire was moved from Rome to Constantinople. In 395 the empire was divided between East and West, with Constantinople and Ravenna successively as its capitals. By 476, the Western empire was no more; 21 years after the sack of Rome in 455, Romulus Augustus, the last western emperor, was deposed.

In the next century Rome's population plummeted. The papacy relinquished its dependence from the East, and Pope Leo III asserted papal temporal power by crowning Charlemagne in St. Peter's in 800. During the Middle Ages the Holy See sought to maintain its control. It struggled for supremacy over the Holy Roman Emperor, powerful Roman families, and its political allies.

In 1309, Pope Clement V removed the papal court from Rome to Avignon in France. The so-called Babylonian Captivity lasted until 1377 with Pope Gregory XI's return to Rome. His return divided European sentiment, resulting in the Great Schism (1378–1417) and the rise of three rival popes.

Pope Martin V's reign marks the end of the schism and the rise of Rome's

R

CHARLEMAGNE (742–814). King of the Franks, a Germanic tribe of the Rhine region, and the first Holy Roman Emperor. His conquests greatly extended his kingdom, stemming the spread of Islam and reducing Viking raids into Europe. He is remembered for the enlightened reforms, revival of learning, and extensive building program by which he began the slow restoration of Europe after centuries of chaos and barbarism.

HOLY ROMAN EMPEROR. The first Holy Roman Emperor was Charlemagne (c. 721–814), crowned in Rome by Pope Leo III on Christmas Day in the year 800. He established the Holy Roman Empire. The coronation was a symbolic act to underscore an alliance between the church and state. It set out to revive the Roman Empire with a Holy Roman Emperor. Some scholars believe the Holy Roman Empire was comprised of central Europe, chiefly of German-speaking peoples, established with the crowning of Otto I as emperor in 926 and ending with the resignation of Francis II of Austria in 1806.

Renaissance. Papal patronage and vision would soon rival the city's ancient imperial splendor. The papacy wished to attract visitors to its city. Accommodating pilgrims was of primary importance. Hotels were constructed, roads widened, bridges restored, and guidebooks printed. Focus concentrated on the pilgrimage churches and the journey to St. Peter's.

Rome's transformation continued throughout the 15th century, embellishing the sacred and secular realms. Grand palaces rose, churches were built, markets and shops opened and flourished, and once-dry fountains sprang to life. As Rome's political and ecclesiastical worlds grew, humanists, architects, artists, and philosophers flocked to the city.

The sack of Rome mounted by the Holy Roman Emperor Charles V in 1527 devastated the city. Ten thousand died and 30,000 buildings were destroyed. The publication of Luther's 95 Theses ten years earlier encouraged the already widespread discontent over papal extravagance and worldliness; the sack was merely the climax of mounting disapproval. Soon after, the Church recovered from the assault and responded to the northern Protestant challenge. The result was the Counter-Reformation, which arose from the Council of Trent (1545–63) intent to reaffirm papal authority, denounce Protestant claims, defend Catholic practice, and revitalize faith.

Despite the artistic restrictions imposed by the Council of Trent, the 17th and 18th centuries in Rome reached an artistic zenith and at times, decorative excess. However, a failing papal economy in the end of the 18th century could no longer sustain its splendid vision. Church power continued to diminish. Between 1809 and 1814, Napoleon annexed the papal states. When papal power was finally restored under Pope Pius VII (1815), the papacy had all but lost its artistic and cultural momentum.

In 1849 Rome was proclaimed a Republic. The pope fled the city only to return the following year in defeat, forced to surrender his papal power and lucrative papal states and retreat to the Vatican. Rome became capital of the unified Italy in 1870 and remains its glorious and eternal capital.

PLACES TO VISIT

THE VATICAN. On February 11, 1929, an agreement between the Italian government and the pope was reached; it recognized the Vatican as the world's smallest independent and sovereign state with the pope heading its legislative, executive, and judiciary branches. The Vatican City issues its own currency and stamps, prints a daily newspaper, operates its own broadcasting station, runs a railway station, and commands a small army which includes the Swiss Guards (their uniforms are allegedly designed by Michelangelo).

This small state includes the largest square (St. Peter's Square), the most sumptuous palace (the Vatican Palace), and the largest Catholic Church (St. Peter's). In the Middle Ages, Pope Gregory XI (1330–78) moved the papal residence from the Lateran palace to a simple building near St. Peter's basilica. Over the decades the building was rebuilt and embellished by Bramante, Raphael, Ligorio, Fontana, and Bernini. The papal and court apartments occupy a small part of the palace's 1,400 rooms, halls, and chapels. Vast libraries, archives, and museums occupy much of the palace.

THE CHURCH OF OLD ST. PETER'S.

Christian emancipation during Constantine's reign resulted in a move away from domestic to official church building. No official Christian churches existed prior to A.D. 300; instead, the faithful, fearing persecution, gathered at Christian homes.

Old St. Peter's (so called because it was torn down completely in the early 1500s and replaced by New St. Peter's) was one of the largest churches in all Christendom. The monumental structure accommodated pilgrims journeying in multitudes to venerate the relics of the apostle Peter. Begun in 320, it was consecrated by Pope Sylvester I and completed after Constantine's death. The edifice rose atop the site of a pre-existing church built around St. Peter's tomb. This ancient church had, in turn, been constructed atop a cemetery. The plan of Old St. Peter's was derived from ancient Roman basilicas. A basilica was a large assembly hall, an administrative center. At each end was a hemicycle with a statue of the emperor. Old St. Peter's modified this plan. The church consisted of an apse at the east end (the altar area), a nave (where the congregation gathered), and a transept (the crossing at the apse and nave). The design resembled Christ's Cross, reminding the congregation of his death and promise of salvation. The five-aisle church had a large entrance hall and many mosaic and fresco decorations.

NEW ST. PETER'S.

After nearly a thousand years of use, Old St. Peter's was in a state of disrepair and in danger of collapse. In 1452 Pope Nicholas V decided to rebuild the basilica, but it wasn't until 1506 that work began under Pope Julius II. Julius's architect, Bramante, began work on the new design, choosing a Greek cross plan (with four equal-length arms) over the original Latin-cross design (a cross with three short arms and one long arm). Successive architects (Raphael, Baldassare Peruzzi, Antonio da Sangallo the Younger, Michelangelo, Vignola, Pirro Ligorio, Giacomo della Porta, and Domenico Fontana) wavered between the Greek and Latin designs. Finally, in 1603 Carlo Maderno was appointed architect and ordered by Pope Paul V to alter the structure into a Latin cross plan for liturgical reasons. On November 18, 1692, Pope Urban VIII reconsecrated the grandiose new center of faith, 1,300 years after its first consecration.

PIAZZA SAN PIETRO,

St. Peter's Square, harmonizes the diverse elements

R

155

POPE JULIUS II (1443–1515). Humble beginnings did not deter Giuliano (Julius) della Rovere from achieving epic grandeur. Born on December 5, 1443, to poor parents, Julius was rescued from his indigence by faith, vigor, luck, and nepotism. When, in 1471, Julius's uncle became Pope Sixtus IV, he named Julius the bishop of Carpentras. Julius soon acquired other bishoprics. Though his papal favor continued and he helped secure the election of Pope Innocent VIII (1484–92), Julius encountered a grave enemy in the Borgia pope, Pope Alexander VI (1492–1503). Forced to flee for his life, Julius absconded to France, where he remained until Pope Alexander's death. The papal successor, Pope Pius III, survived only 21 days after his election. Julius acted quickly, securing popularity through lavish bribes; as a result he was unanimously elected pope at the next conclave.

It was Julius's bellicose nature that best served the Church. His attempts to restore and extend papal power through diplomatic and military means necessitated an active role. He personally led his armies to victory, capturing Perugia and Bologna in 1506. Julius excommunicated and defeated Venice in 1509 and subsequently joined the League of Cambrai formed by France, Germany, and Spain. Through 1512 he continued to engage in one campaign after another, warring against Ferrara, Modena, and Ravenna, to name a few.

Nicknamed "the terrible"; Julius was irascible, difficult, and ruthless. Ironically, this military pope was also a great lover of the arts. He was a triumphant patron of the greatest artists and architects of the period, using their talents to glorify himself and the Church. However, Julius could never abandon his pugnacious nature, and he expected his artists and architects to be obedient soldiers of the Church. He employed Michelangelo to build his tomb (1505) and forced him to return to Rome from Florence to paint the Sistine Chapel ceiling (1508–12); he commissioned Raphael to paint the Stanza della Segnatura (1508–11); and he hired Bramante to design the new Church of St. Peter's (1505). Only Julius, a man who rose from poverty to papal privilege, would have the audacity to tear down the most sacred church in Christendom and replace it with an edifice grander than the original.

of church facade, church dome, enormous obelisk, and two fountains into a coherent whole. Gian Lorenzo Bernini began the square in 1656 and completed it in 1667. Built to accommodate massive crowds gathering on special occasions, particularly for the Easter Sunday papal blessing *Urbi et Orbi* (given to Rome and the world), the oval square represents the open arms of the Church of Rome embracing the faithful. Two-hundred-eighty-four columns define the embrace, while atop the colonnade 140 life-size statues of saints and martyrs look down on the faithful.

Commanding the center of the square, the Obelisco Vaticano (Vatican Obelisk) towers 83 feet above the throngs. Caligula transported the 331-ton obelisk from Alexandria to Rome in A.D. 37. Until the 15th century it stood in the Circus of Nero, where, in A.D. 64, tradition holds the apostle Peter was martyred.

OBELISKS

The Roman Empire chose to commemorate its triumph and power over the Mediterranean world by moving massive ancient obelisks to Rome and reerecting them as monuments to Roman glory and immortality. During the Middle Ages, the Roman obelisks were broken and buried; only the one in the Vatican remained standing. In the 16th century the popes took on the process of reerection. Pope Sixtus V (1585–90) was instrumental in the effort to restore these ancient symbols of omnipotence and continuity. His successor followed his example, and their efforts survive today. Thirteen obelisks stand in modern Rome. They are the Lateran obelisk, the Vatican obelisk, the Piazza del Popolo obelisk, the Fountain of Four Rivers obelisk, the Piazza del Pantheon obelisk, the Monte Cavallo obelisk, the Axum obelisk, the Esquiline obelisk, the Piazza della Minerva obelisk, the Piazza di Montecitorio obelisk, the Pincio obelisk, the Sallustiano (Trinità dei Monti) obelisk, and the Dogale obelisk.

Rome's most impressive of these monoliths is the Lateran obelisk; at 105 feet it is the tallest in the world. It originally stood in one of the courtyards at the Temple of Karnak in Ancient Egypt (1501 B.C.), where it remained until A.D. 330 when Constantine decided to move it to the city of Byzantium. However, the obelisk was never transferred farther than Alexandria, and in 357 Constantius, the successor to Constantine, transported the nearly 460-ton monument to Rome and erected it in the Circus Maximus. In 1587 the same obelisk was discovered buried beneath the ground of the circus. It took 500 men to dig it out. A year later it was erected in the Lateran Square, where it stands today.

R

In the late 16th century Pope Sixtus V commissioned Domenico Fontana to move the obelisk to its present location. The transfer and reerection proved difficult and dangerous. Quick thinking by a local workman named Breca, who threw water on the strained ropes to prevent breakage, saved the obelisk from falling and smashing to pieces. In reward, he and his descendants were given the right to provide the palms used in St. Peter's on Palm Sunday.

No hieroglyphic inscription decorates the obelisk. Its plinth is inscribed by Sixtus V, who believed it was his duty to eradicate paganism while propagating Christianity. Each side of the plinth is given a dedication; the north side is dedicated to the Cross; the south side is dedicated to the area of the apostles; the east side warns those hostile to Christ to leave; and the west side proclaims the triumph and rule of Christ. Atop the obelisk is a cross containing a relic of the True Cross.

The **BASILICA DI SAN PIETRO** (St. Peter's Basilica), 610 feet long and 446 feet high at the cupola, is certainly an earthly paradise grander than St. Peter could conceive for his humble community. Statues of Rome's two patron saints, St. Peter (left) and St. Paul (right), flank Bernini's three-tiered staircase leading up to the church. Nine balconies divide Carlo Maderno's facade. From the central balcony, the *Loggia delle Benedizioni,* come papal blessings and the announcement of a newly elected pope. Atop the balustrade are statues of Christ, St. John the Baptist, and the apostles.

The portico leads to the church's five entrance doors. The *Porta Santa* (Holy Door), to the right, is only open during Holy Years. Above the door is an inscription and bull by Pope Boniface VIII commemorating the inaugural Jubilee year, 1300.

As you enter the church, on your right is Michelangelo's masterpiece, the *Pietà* (1497–1500). The vision of the dead Christ in his mother's lap is Michelangelo's only signed work (notice his name carved upon the Virgin's sash). Serene and beautiful, the youthful Virgin seems no older than her Son does. Michelangelo, in his biography by Condivi, claims "a pure woman retains her youth longer" and "the body is the reflection of the soul." Hence, Michelangelo's Virgin is physically and morally beautiful. The same applies to Christ. Observe that the Virgin does not appear to grieve over her dead Son; instead, she simply bows her head in understanding—her Son's death was inevitable for humankind's redemption and salvation.

On the pavement near the nave entrance is the porphyry disc upon which Charlemagne knelt and was crowned in 800 by Pope Leo III. Successive pavement markings lead toward the altar, indicating the length of other great Christian churches.

As you approach the altar, on the last right pillar in the main aisle sits the venerated bronze *Statue of St. Peter* by Arnolfo di Cambio (13th century), awaiting reverence from the faithful. Over the centuries devout kisses have worn away St. Peter's right foot.

The highest dome in Rome, Michelangelo's cupola hovers above the main altar. Its majestic mosaics (1605) depict God the Father at the center surrounded by Christ, the Virgin, St. Paul, St. John the Baptist, the apostles, popes, and Church Doctors. At the base of the four massive pillars supporting the dome are four colossal statues of saints and their relics. They are *St. Helena with the True Cross* (1639) by Bolgi; *St. Veronica with the Sudarium* (the veil Veronica used to wipe Christ's perspiration as he carried the cross) by Mochi (1632); *St. Andrew Crucified on an X-shaped Cross* (1640) by François Duquesnoy; and Bernini's *St. Longinus* (1629–38). Above each saint is a loggia containing the corresponding relics: a piece of the True Cross, the Sudarium, St. Andrew's head, and the Holy Lance.

Bernini's triumphal canopy, the *Baldacchino* (1624–33), erected above St. Peter's crypt, provides a glittering focal point. The monument, while a crowning tribute to St. Peter, equally glorifies Urban VIII. Commissioned by Pope Urban VIII Barberini, the gilt bronze structure required so much metal that the pope allowed Bernini to melt down church candelabras, bronze sculptures, and the Pantheon's bronze-lined dome. Critics disgusted by the extravagance decried *"Quod non fecerunt I bar-*

bari, I fecerunt I Barberini" (What the barbarians did not do, the Barberini did). Barberini's emblems—the bees and laurel—appear all over the monument. Atop the columns angels hold the papal tiara and keys, symbolizing papal authority. Crowning the structure is a cross atop a globe, symbolizing the Church Triumphant.

Bernini encased the *Cattedra Petri,* St. Peter's wooden bishop's throne, in a gilt bronze reliquary (1657–66). His work provided a sumptuous enclosure in the relic and a culminating point in the pilgrim's journey across the Bridge of Angels through St. Peter's Square into the church and past the triumphant canopy. As if by divine will, the throne appears to hover in midair. Carved in relief on the back of the throne is Christ's command to Peter, *"Pasce oves meas"* (Feed my sheep). On either side are four bronze figures—St. Ambrose, St. Athanasius, John Crysostom, and St. Augustine—representing the East and the West.

The old and new sacred Vatican grottoes, the **GROTTE VECCHIE** and the **GROTTE NUOVE**, lie beneath the basilica floor. Created during St. Peter's reconstruction, the grottoes occupy the space between the present church floor and the old church floor. The grottoes contain numerous papal tombs and 13th–15th-century frescoes.

Deep below the basilica, beneath the grottoes, is the **NECROPOLI PRECONSTANTINIANA**, the Pre-Constantinian Necropolis (seen only by appointment made through the Ufficio Scavi della Fabbrica di San Pietro). The 2nd-century pagan and Christian cemetery is the foundation for Constantine's St. Peter's. St. Peter is allegedly buried on the site, though by the time of the 16th-century church construction the tomb's existence was forgotten. The exact location of St. Peter's burial place among the graves is yet unknown.

The MUSEO STORICO ARTISTICO—TESORO DI SAN PIETRO (the Sacristy and Treasury of St. Peter) displays precious religious objects. Do not miss Pollaiuolo's bronze masterpiece, the *Monument to Sixtus IV* (signed 1493), and the 4th-century sarcophagus of the Roman prefect Junius Bassus, depicting Old and New Testament scenes.

The Vatican palaces house the splendid and varied VATICAN MUSEUMS. In the 18th century the papal collections were established and arranged according to period. They include the Museo Gregoriano Egizio (Egyptian artifacts; founded in 1839 by Gregory XVI); the Museo Chiaramonti (ancient statuary and inscriptions; founded by Pius VII); the Museo Pio-Clementino (Greek and Roman sculpture; founded in 1771 and named after Clement XIV and Pius VI); the Museo Gregoriano Etrusco (Etruscan works; founded in 1837 by Gregory XVI); the Stanze di Raffaello (Nicholas V's apartments); the Appartamento Borgia (the Borgia apartments); the Cappella Sistina (the Sistine Chapel); the Pinacoteca Vaticana (paintings; founded in 1816 by Pius VI); the Museo Grego-

rian Profano (pagan art; founded in 1844 by Gregory XVI); and the Museo Pio Cristiano (catacomb excavations; founded by Pius IX).

Commissioned by Pope Julius II (1503–15), Raphael and his assistants redecorated the former apartments of Pope Nicholas V (1447–55) between 1508 and 1525. Now known as the STANZE DI RAFFAELLO in honor of the master artist, the apartments were originally decorated by Piero della Francesca, Signorelli, and Perugino.

The STANZA DELL'INCENDIO (Room of the Borgo Fire) was frescoed during the pontificates of Leo III and Leo IV. The Leos are glorified in the scenes depicting *The Fire in the Borgo* in 847 which Leo IV put out by making the sign of the cross; *The Coronation of Charlemagne by Leo III,* in 800 at St. Peter's; *The Battle of Ostia,* where Leo IV was victorious over the Saracens; and *The Oath of Leo III.* Painted in the vault is Perugino's *Glorification of the Trinity.*

Julius II's office and library, the STANZA DELLA SEGNATURA (Signature Room), was painted by Raphael between 1509 and 1511. In the lunettes Raphael depicts the *School of Athens* (philosophy), the *Disputà* (theology), the *Virtues* (law) and *Mount Parnassus* (poetry), thus linking together Christian revelation and secular learning.

The *School of Athens* depicts ancient philosophers in a fictive setting that recalls the Basilica of Maxentius and Constantine and the Pantheon. Under the arch are Plato and Aristotle. Plato (an allegorical portrait of Leonardo da Vinci) holds his book the *Timaeus*. The text, which explored the creation of the world, the nature of the soul, and the return to God, influenced Christian humanists. Aristotle holds his *Ethics*, also widely read among sacred and secular scholars. Plato points heavenward suggesting that all inspiration is divine, while Aristotle's hand is palm downward suggesting an exploration of the world and moderation. The various philosophers that surround Plato and Aristotle are identified as Euclid, holding a compass (possibly a portrait of Bramante); Pythagoras, writing in a book; Diogenes, seated on the steps; and Heraclitus, seated, looking melancholy, hand against his head in thought (allegorical portrait of Michelangelo).

The *Disputà*, literally the Dispute, depicts the Affirmation of the Holy Sacrament. This represents a well reasoned, well argued justification of the doctrine of Transubstantiation, that is, the belief that the body and blood of Christ are contained in the Eucharist, crucial to Roman Catholic belief and espoused by Julius II. At the center of the picture is the Host, symbolizing Christ. Surrounding the Host are apostles and prophets (upper tiers), Christ flanked by John the Baptist and the Virgin (central tier), and saints and Church Doctors (lower tier). Thus, Christ is the center of light, life, and knowledge.

Atop *Mount Parnassus*, ancient and Renaissance poets (Homer, Virgil, and Dante) gather around Apollo and the nine muses. It was believed that poets and philosophers were able to ascend to heaven aided by the muses they honored in life.

The *Virtues* depicts three of the four cardinal virtues accompanied by the three theological virtues. Fortitude is dressed in armor, Prudence holds up her mirror, and Temperance reins in her passions. Justice, the fourth cardinal virtue, appears in a separate lunette above. Putti personify the three theological virtues: Faith points upward, Charity holds her burning torch, and Hope collects acorns from the oak. The figure of Pope Gregory IX represents canon law, while Justinian symbolizes civil law.

Church history is glorified in the **STANZA DI ELIODORO** (the Heliodorus Room) decorated between 1512 and 1514. Representations include the *Meeting of Leo the Great and Attila*, the *Mass at Bolsena*, the *Expulsion of Heliodorus*, and the *Mass at Bolsena*.

The **SALA DI COSTANTINO** (Room of Constantine) is a large public audience chamber. Frescoed between 1519 and 1524, the narratives depict the life of the first Christian emperor, Constantine the Great (306–70). The four scenes are the *Vision of Constantine*, the *Battle at the Milvian Bridge*, the *Baptism of Constantine*, and the *Donation of Constantine*.

One of the oldest papal rooms, the **CAPPELLA DI NICCOLÒ V**, decorated by

R

Fra Angelico (1448–50), illustrates the lives of the *Martyrs Stephen and Lawrence.*

The **BORGIA APARTMENTS** were decorated by Pinturicchio and Pietro da Cortona for Alexander VI Borgia between 1492 and 1495. The *Hall of the Sibyls* contains paintings of prophets and sibyls; the *Hall of the Creed* depicts the Twelve Apostles each holding scrolls with sentences from the Creed; the *Hall of Liberal Arts* contains allegories of grammar, dialectics, rhetoric, geometry, arithmetic, music, and astronomy; the *Hall of the Lives of the Saints* was decorated by Pinturicchio; the *Hall of the Mysteries* illustrates the mysteries of faith; and the *Hall of Popes,* the largest of the apartments, in which there are various works of art depicting popes. The lower floor includes the *Collezione d'Arte Religiosa Moderna* inaugurated by Pope Paul VI in 1973 to house modern religious art. Contributing artists include Matisse, Rodin, Casorati, Carrà, Kandinsky, De Chirico, Klee, and Picasso.

The **CAPPELLA SISTINA** (Sistine Chapel) is the papal palace chapel, used to celebrate special masses and to accommodate the College of Cardinals when the conclave assembles to elect a new pope. Built by Pope Sixtus IV (1437–83) between 1475 and 1481, the massive barrel-vaulted chapel (130 feet long by 42¼ feet wide by 65 feet high) was decorated by the period's leading artists. Between 1481 and 1483 Sixtus IV commissioned Botticelli, Signorelli, Perugino, Ghirlandaio, Pinturicchio, and Piero di Cosimo to fresco the side walls with parallel narrative stories depicting the life of Moses (signifying the world under law) and the life of Christ (signifying the world under grace). The episodes are *Moses' Journey to Egypt, Moses and the Young Women, Moses' Youth, Crossing the Red Sea, The Ten Commandments, The Punishment of Kore, Dathan and Abrion,* and *The Death of Moses* (on the left), and *Baptism of Christ, Healing of the Lepers and the Temptation of Christ, Vocation of the Apostles Peter and Andrew, The Sermon on the Mount, Christ Giving the Keys to St. Peter,* and *The Last Supper.*

SIBYL was a seeress from antiquity whose utterances were subsequently interpreted by Christian theologians as foretelling the coming of the Messiah.

A sibyl is the pagan counterpart of the Old Testament prophet. As prophets link the Jewish world with Christianity, the sibyls tie together the Roman world with the Christian age. There are 12 sibyls whose names indicate their place of origin: Persian, Libyan, Erythraean, Cumaean, Samian, Cimmerian, European, Tiburtine, Agrippine, Delphic, Hellespontic, and Phrygian.

In 1508, Julius II commissioned Michelangelo to fresco the Sistine Chapel ceiling with stories from the book of Genesis. Michelangelo's trials and tribulations during the project are well known. In addition to his family constantly badgering him for money and alleged plots against his life by rival Bramante, Michelangelo had to endure the unending goading by Julius, who on at least one occasion stood atop the scaffold behind Michelangelo and hit the artist with a cane in order to make him work faster.

The painting began in January 1509, and on New Year's Day 1513, the frescoes were unveiled. The ceiling decoration combines religion and philosophy. Nine central panels contain ten scenes. The first three panels (directly above the altar) dealing with the origin of the world depict *God Separating Light from Dark, Creation of the Sun and Planets,* and *Parting of the Seas.* The following three scenes depict four stories from the life of Adam and Eve: *Creation of Adam, Creation of Eve, Temptation,* and *Expulsion from the Garden.* In the last three scenes are stories from the life of Noah: *Sacrifice of Noah, Deluge,* and *Drunkenness of Noah.* Thus, even the man whom God has saved to carry forth the human race is prone to sin. Man is now in need of deliverance, a theme taken up in the ceiling corners, which illustrate *David Slaying Goliath* (deliverance of the Israelites from the Philistines), *Judith and Holofernes* (deliverance of the Israelites from the Assyri-

ans), *Moses and the Brazen Serpent* (deliverance of the Israelites from snakebites during their Exodus) and the *Crucifixion of Haman* (deliverance of the Israelites from persecution).

The ceiling is also read in reverse chronology beginning with the *Drunkenness of Noah.* Michelangelo, a devotee of Plato, wished a reverse reading to suggest the progression of the soul imprisoned in the body through to the soul's final release and union with God the Father.

In 1536, Pope Paul III commissioned Michelangelo to paint the *Last Judgment* on the end wall behind the altar. Completed in 1541, the extraordinary and original work depicts Christ, the supreme judge, flanked by the Virgin, St. John the Baptist, martyrs, and saints. Above Christ, angels hold the instruments of his Passion. Below the heavens, the good and evil take their count. Angels combat devils for possession over souls, while Minos, the prince of hell, surveys the scene. Minos is also a contemporary portrait; Michelangelo's revenge on Pope Paul III's chamberlain, who annoyed the artist daily, was to depict him as the horrible demon. The well-known story tells that when the chamberlain saw himself as Minos, he begged Paul III to intervene. Upon seeing the portrait his Holiness replied, "Son, if Michelangelo had put you into purgatory, I could do something about it. But since you are in hell, it is outside my authority."

R

163

The PINACOTECA VATICANA houses a stunning painting collection. Among the masterpieces in the chronologically arranged gallery are works by Giotto, Pietro Lorenzetti, Simone Martini, Gentile da Fabriano, Filippo Lippi, Benozzo Gozzoli, Fra Angelico, Carracci, Guido Reni, and Carlo Maratta. Do not miss Giotto's *Stefaneschi* polyptych, Benozzo Gozzoli's *Virgin and St. Thomas,* and Lucas Cranach the Elder's *Pietà.* Raphael figures prominently with ten tapestries (1515–16), his *Transfiguration* (completed by Giulio Romano), his first large-scale work *Coronation of the Virgin* (1503), and *Madonna di Foligno* (1512–13). Leonardo da Vinci's *St. Jerome* (c. 1480) is followed by Titian's *Madonna dei Frari* (1528), Caravaggio's *Deposition* (1602–1604), Guido Reni's *Crucifixion of St. Peter,* and Pietro da Cortona's *David and Goliath.* The collection ends with statuary models by Bernini and a small gallery containing Byzantine and Russian religious objects.

In the 17th century pilgrims to Rome crossed the PONTE SANT'ANGELO (Bridge of Angels) en route to St. Peter's. Centuries earlier, Romans crossed the ancient bridge, *Pons Aelius* (133–34), built by Hadrian, to reach the emperor's mausoleum. The reconstructed bridge incorporates three of its ancient arches, which suffered structural damage from overcrowding during the 1450 Jubilee. Between 1667 and 1671, Bernini and various sculptors carved ten angels, each holding an instrument associated with Christ's Passion to remind viewers of his suffering for man's redemption. Two angels designed by Bernini—one holding the superscription "I.N.R.I.," the other holding the crown of thorns—were so beautiful they were moved from the bridge to the church of Sant'Andrea delle Frate.

CASTEL SANT'ANGELO (Castle of the Holy Angel), once the Emperor Hadrian's mausoleum (2nd century A.D.), was transformed into a prison and fortress (A.D. 241) and, after the recognition of papal temporal authority in Rome, it became a defensive outpost. It subsequently passed between public and papal ownership and provided papal refuge in 1527 during the sack of Rome.

The present name derived from an event in Pope Gregory the Great's (590–604) life. While leading a procession to intercede for delivery from the plague of 590, the pope envisioned an angel sheathing his sword atop the mausoleum, a sign the plague had ended. Atop the castle is a bronze sword-wielding *Archangel Michael* (1752) by Van Verschaffelt commemorating Gregory's vision.

The MUSEO NAZIONALE DI CASTEL SANT' ANGELO brings together ceramics, weaponry, and Renaissance paintings. Its highlights include the *statue of the Archangel Michael* (1554) by Raffaello da Montelupo; a *St. Sebastian* (patron saint of those suffering from plague and disease) and *St. John the Baptist* by Niccolò di Liberatore; the *Virgin Mary with*

Christ Child and Saints by Luca Signorelli; and a *St. Jerome* by Lorenzo Lotto.

The 17th-century church of SANT' AGNESE IN AGONE was built atop the site of the virgin martyr's beheading. The non-Christian son of a Roman prefect zealously pursued St. Agnes, a devout Christian. She dismissed his advances. Overcome with unrequited love, he resolved to rape her. Instead, he was killed by a demon, and Agnes was condemned to burn as a witch. When the flames did not scathe her she was beheaded.

Pope Innocent X chose to reconstruct the earlier 8th- and 12th-century sanctuaries to glorify his own reign. Work begun in 1652 by Giacomo and Carlo Rainaldi was modified by Borromini, then Bernini, and subsequently finished by the one who began it, Carlo Rainaldi.

The interior has several enormous marble altarpieces, the most significant being the high altar by Domenico Guidi representing the *Holy Family.* The frescoed cupola depicts the *Glory of Paradise* (1689) by Ciro Ferri, while Baciccia frescoed the *Cardinal Virtues* (1665) along the spandrels. Ruins from Domitian's Circus can be seen beneath the church.

In front of the church, also commissioned by Pope Innocent X, is the FONTANA DEI FIUMI (Fountain of the Four Rivers). Begun in 1648, Bernini's travertine fountain includes rocks, animals, and four enormous marble figures personifying the four continents. The Danube (Europe) is associated with a horse, the Rio della Plata (Americas) is seen with an armadillo, the Nile (Africa) sits with a lion, and the Ganges (Asia) is shown with a snake. The Danube adjusts Innocent X's coat of arms, the Rio della Plata holds up his hand to shield himself from the supposedly unstable church of Sant'Agnese (based on a false claim that Bernini didn't trust the workmanship of the rival architect, Borromini), the Nile covers his head because its source was unknown, and the Ganges steers the ship of the Church. An Egyptian obelisk, transferred from the circus of Maxentius, stands atop the fountain and is crowned a dove (representing the pope's coat of arms). The meaning of the Four River fountain, not unlike the ancient Rivers of Paradise, suggests the new Rome, ruled by Pope Innocent X, will again dominate the world, not through force but through faith.

Consecrated the French National Church in Rome in 1589, SAN LUIGI DEI FRANCESI (St. Louis of the French) houses among the greatest religious paintings in Catholic Reformation Rome the Matthew cycle in the Contarelli Chapel, by one of the most violent and seemingly impious artists of the period, Caravaggio (1573–1610).

Constantly cited in city police records, Caravaggio arrived in Rome in about 1590 and proceeded to beat a

R

THE FOUNTAINS OF ROME

At the time of Constantine the Great (306–337), the city of Rome was home to 1212 fountains. However, the individual most responsible for the plethora of spouting water was Marcus Agrippa, who erected 500 fountains and even more hundreds of basins and pools. Eleven aqueducts leading to Rome built from 272 B.C. to A.D. 226 literally quenched the thirst of the ancient city. Unfortunately, in 537 the Goths destroyed Rome's aqueducts and stifled the city's water supply. Those fountains that did not crumble largely remained dry for almost another 1000 years. Finally, in 1453, Pope Nicholas V. (1447–55) reestablished Rome as the city of fountains. Of Rome's six modern aqueducts, the popes financed four.

Every visitor to Rome should see the Trevi Fountain (1732–62), named for the three streets (*tre vie*) that merge at the fountain. The custom of throwing a coin over one's shoulder into the fountain is a relatively modern practice dating no later than the late 19th century. Also visit the Fountain of Moses (1587), which was carved by Prospero Antichi, who allegedly committed suicide after hearing the howls of laughter which greeted his work; the Triton Fountain (1642–43) by Gian Lorenzo Bernini; and, in the Vatican Gardens, the Fountain of the Galleon (1620) by Jan van Santen, an extraordinary 15-foot-long model of a 17th-century three-masted galleon. The galley is lead, the sails are brass, and the rigging is copper.

Take a stroll along any of Rome's ancient streets and you'll likely happen upon a delightful fountain. Some treats include the Fountain of the Turtles, the Fountain of the Bees, the Fountain of the Naiads, and the Fountain of the Moors.

rival painter with a cane, engage in street brawls, conceal weapons, attack his landlady, fight over a prostitute, and kill a man over a Bocce game. He also created numerous masterpieces for churches, popes, and private patrons.

Inside the church, at the 5th chapel on the left, the Contarelli chapel, are Caravaggio's *St. Matthew and the Angel*, *The Martyrdom of St. Matthew*, and *The*

Calling of St. Matthew (1597–1602). *St. Matthew and the Angel* is Caravaggio's second version of the scene; the first was rejected. The second version relies on a traditional medieval representation depicting Matthew writing the Gospel guided and inspired by an angel. *The Calling of St. Matthew* illustrates the account from Matthew 9:9: "Jesus saw a man named Matthew sitting at the tax collector's booth. 'Follow me,' he told him, and Matthew got up and followed him." *The Martyrdom of St. Matthew* depicts Hirtacus's henchmen slaying Matthew. Matthew had forbidden Hirtacus, king of Ethiopia, a non-Christian, to marry Iphigenia, the former king's daughter who converted to Christianity.

Visit the beautifully frescoed chapel depicting the *Life of St. Cecilia* (second chapel on the right) by Domenichino (1616–17). Behind the altar is a copy of Raphael's *St. Cecilia and Four Saints* by Guido Reni.

The **PANTHEON** (All the Gods) was built by Marcus Vipsanius Agrippa in 27 B.C., rebuilt by Hadrian between A.D. 118 and 125 (his inscription can be read in the pediment), and restored by Septimius Severus and Caracalla in 202. In 608 the Emperor Phocas gave the temple to the Church; Pope Boniface IV gave it a new name, Santa Maria Rotunda, and dedicated it to the Virgin and all the martyrs. In 1870 it became the mausoleum for the kings of Italy.

Entombed among Italy's monarchs in an ancient sarcophagus is the artist Raphael. The Latin inscription on his tomb reads: *"Ille hic est Raphael, timuit quo sospite vinci, rerum magna parens et moriente mori."* (Here lies Raphael by whom, when he was alive, nature, the great mother of all things, feared being outdone; when he died, nature feared death). Above the tomb stands a sculpture of the *Madonna del Sasso* (1520), commissioned by Raphael before his death.

Rome's only Gothic church, **SANTA MARIA SOPRA MINERVA** (St. Mary above Minerva) was rebuilt above the ancient temple to Minerva Calcidica (the goddess of wisdom, Greek = Athena). The structure housed an 8th-century Greek convent before the Dominicans occupied it in the 13th century. The structure underwent significant changes and restorations in the 16th, 17th, and 19th centuries.

Numerous treasures and tombs lie inside the church. Notice the funerary monuments of *Pope Clement XII* and *Pope Leo X* by Antonio da Sangallo (1536–41) the Younger and the tomb of *Francesco Tournabuoni* (1408) by Mino da Fiesole. Michelangelo's *Risen Christ* (1518–21) near the main altar presents a marble Christ holding the cross, the instrument of his Passion. An object of great devotion, the faithful have literally kissed away one of the Savior's toes. Beneath the high altar rests the body of St. Catherine of Siena (copatron of Italy with St. Francis).

The Cappella Carafa (Carafa Chapel) is one of the most beautiful in Rome. Painted by Filippo Lippi between 1498 and 1493, and dedicated to the Virgin Annunciate and St. Thomas, its altarpiece depicts the *Annunciation*. Above the altarpiece, the heavens open for the *Assumption of the Virgin*. On the sides are scenes from the *Life of St. Thomas,* a Dominican, author of the *Summa Theologica* and one of the greatest medieval minds.

R

In front of the church is Bernini's *Elephant Carrying an Obelisk* (1666–67) raised in homage to Pope Alexander VII. A contemporary 17th-century poem recounts that an elephant carried the obelisk to Alexander VII as a gift and represents the pope's wisdom.

The 17th-century church of SANT' IGNAZIO DI LOYOLA (St. Ignatius of Loyola) is dedicated to the founder of the Society of Jesus (the Jesuit Order) who was canonized in 1622. Ignatius was a Spanish soldier who was disabled in 1521; he subsequently underwent a mystical conversion and became a spiritual soldier for Christ and the Virgin. Pope Paul III officially recognized the Jesuit Order in 1540, and the Church recognized Ignatius's *The Spiritual Exercises* in 1548. The text suggests individuals should attempt to feel what martyred saints felt, to experience their passion and devotion. Ignatius urged the reader to use all his senses to realize and reenact the Passion, the torments of hell and martyrdom, and heavenly bliss.

Inside the church above the nave is Rome's largest ceiling fresco. Painted by the Jesuit mathematician and theoretician Andrea del Pozzo in 1694, it represents St. Ignatius's entrance into heaven. Visitors must stand at a designated point to see the dome in proper perspective. During the church construction the Jesuits ran out of funds to complete the dome, so a *trompe l'oeil* took its place.

Rome's principal Jesuit church, IL GESÙ or SANTISSIMO NOME DI GESÙ (Most Holy Name of Jesus), was constructed between 1568 and 1584 funded by a gracious donation by Cardinal Alessandro Farnese. The church is not only dedicated to Jesus, but also to God and the Virgin. At the time of dedication, the church's name, Jesus, was considered shocking, even blasphemous. Pope Sixtus was convinced it was sacrilegious; there had been churches dedicated to Christ the Redeemer, but this was the first to use his name. Despite the controversy, the name remained. It is the first Catholic Reformation church in Rome and as such emphasized all that the Protestant church rejected: it promoted the cult of the saints and the cult of the Virgin, facilitated numerous daily Masses to encourage public reform, and emphasized decorative richness and ceremony as a means to uplift the devout masses.

Baciccia's frescoed vault (1679) depicting the *Adoration of the Name of Jesus* dominates the massive interior. The subject is important to the order's belief; according to Jesuit writers, the name of Jesus is more beautiful than the dawn and the light, its power irresistible—every knee bends before it.

The order's founder, St. Ignatius, lies buried in a chapel to the right of the altar. Above the chapel altar is a statue of the saint, to the left is a sculpture representing the *Triumph of Faith Over Paganism,* and to the right sculptures depict *Religion Overthrowing Heresy.*

Behind the altar is a depiction of *Christ's Circumcision.* According to the gospel of Luke (2:21), eight days after his birth, Christ was circumcised and named Jesus, a named chosen for him by an angel before he was conceived. The Feast of the Circumcision is on New Year's Day.

Novice Jesuits were posted at the church of SANT' ANDREA AL QUIRI-NALE (1658–70) across from the Quirinal Palace, which was the papal summer residence from 1592 to 1870, the residence for the kings of Italy from 1870 to 1946, and since then, the presidential residence. Bernini's small oval Jesuit church, known as the Oval Pantheon, is a Baroque masterpiece.

Inside the elliptical church, above the high altar, is Guglielmo Cortese's *Crucifixion of St. Andrew*. Between the altar and the dome, Antonio Raggi's statue of *St. Andrew* depicts the saint crashing through the architectural pavement as he ascends to heaven.

The church of SAN CARLO ALLE QUATTRO FONTANE (St. Charles at the Four Fountains) stands at the intersection of four fountains; they depict two male figures, the Tiber and the Arno, and two female figures, Strength (symbolized by a lion) and Fidelity (symbolized by a dog). The church was commissioned by the Spanish Discalced Trinitarians, founded in 1597 and dedicated to promoting the Trinity. The church is dedicated to San Carlo Borromeo, a Trinitarian and champion of the Council of Trent reforms.

Borromini built the church between 1641 and 1667. The painting above the main altarpiece by Orazio Borgianii depicts *The Holy Trinity with San Carlo and Trinitarian St.*, emphasizing the Trinity, the cult of saints, and saintly visions.

SANTA MARIA DELLA VITTORIA (St. Mary of the Victory) was built in honor of an image of the Virgin invoked for protection and victory over Protestant Prague in 1620. Built between 1610 and 1612 on Carlo Maderno's plans, its attraction is the *Cornaro Chapel* executed by Bernini between 1647 and 1652. The chapel depicts the *Ecstasy of St. Teresa;* witnesses to the miraculous event, members of the Cornaro family, discuss the scene, read, and pray. St. Teresa of Avila, an important Spanish reformer, is seen undergoing a mystical experience. In her autobiography, Teresa relates how an angel pierced her heart with a fiery arrow of the divine love of God. Bernini depicts Teresa in the throes of spiritual ecstasy. Her head falls back in a deep swoon, her fingers seem to tremble, and her toes curl as God's love sweetly flows through her body.

The 15th-century church of SANTA MARIA DEL POPOLO (St. Mary of the People) is named after the citizens of Rome who funded an earlier 13th-century church atop the site. Rebuilt by Pope Sixtus IV (1471–84) between 1472 and 1480, additions and alterations continued through the 17th century.

The people's church is full of divine works. The Della Rovere chapel contains the tombs of Sixtus IV's nephews, Cristoforo and Domenico, with a medallion of the *Virgin* by Mino da Fiesole. Frescoes depicting the *Life of St. Jerome* and the *Adoration of Christ* (1485–89) by Pinturicchio decorate the chapel walls. In the choir are Andrea Sansovino's funerary monuments for *Cardinal Ascanio Sforza* (1505) and *Cardinal Girolamo Basso Della Rovere* (1507). The frescoed vault by Pinturicchio depicts the *Coronation of the Virgin with Evangelists, Sibyls, and Church Doctors* (1508–10). To the left of the altar is Annibale Carracci's *Assumption* (1601) flanked by Caravaggio's masterpieces, the *Conversion of St. Paul* (1601–02) and the *Crucifixion of St. Peter* (1601–02). The Chigi Chapel is a family mausoleum designed by Raphael and built between 1510 and 1515; notice Bernini's sculptures depicting *Habakkuk and the Angel* and *Daniel in the Lion's Den* (both 1655–61) and Sebastiano del Piombo's *Birth of Mary* (1533–34).

One of the earliest churches dedicated to the Virgin in Rome, SANTA MARIA IN TRASTEVERE, was begun under Pope Calixtus (221–27) and completed during the papacy of Julius I (341–52). According to legend, when Christ was born a fountain of oil sprung up at the site; thus, the church was known as the Church of the Fountain of Oil. The *fons olei,* in the church presbytery, marks the miraculous oil spring. In 1140 the church was renovated using stone from the Baths of Caracalla.

A 13th-century mosaic representing the *Madonna and Child Enthroned with Two Donors and a Procession of Female Figures* adorns the facade. Inside, 22 ancient columns terminate in a spectacular apse. Its mosaic decoration depicts the *Coronation of the Virgin.* Here, Christ and the Virgin sit together on a heavenly throne, in his hand is a book with the words, "Come my chosen one, I shall place thee on my throne," and written on the Virgin's scroll is a response from the Song of Songs, "His left hand raises my head, his right arm embraces me." Other mosaics depict *Pope Innocent III with a Model of the Church, The Candelabra of the Apocalypse, The Mystical Lamb,* and scenes from the *Life of the Virgin Mary.* Domenichino completed *The Assumption of the Virgin* (1617) set in the carved gilt ceiling.

Built atop the 5th-century home of St. Cecilia and her husband, St. Valerius, the church of SANTA CECILIA IN TRASTEVERE was built by Pope Paschal I in the 9th century and renovated in the 12th, 13th, 15th, and 18th centuries. The patrician couple were martyred in the 2nd century under Marcus Aurelius's reign. Cecilia, a virgin, took a vow of chastity and convinced Valerius, her soon-to-be husband, to also practice abstinence. He agreed to the condition provided Cecilia reveal to him her guardian angel. The angel appeared and presented the couple with a crown of roses and lilies. Condemned to death by suffocation, Cecilia survived, was administered three axe blows to the neck, and lived another three days, attending the sick and poor. A corridor within the church leads to the room where Roman guards attempted to suffocate Cecilia for three days. Within the same room is Guido Reni's *Decapitation of St. Cecilia,* the act that led to her successful, yet slow, martyrdom.

Beneath the altar is Stefano Maderno's statue of *St. Cecilia* (1600); it depicts Cecilia's miraculously preserved body as it looked when exhumed in 1599. Atop the altar is Arnolfo di Cambio's *ciborium* (1293) and above it, the apse mosaic depicting *Christ Giving a Benediction with St. Paul, St. Cecilia, St. Paschal I, St. Peter, St. Valerius, and St. Agatha.*

Perched at the edge of the Roman forum, the basilica of SANTI COSMA E DAMIANO (Saints Cosmas and Damian) was constructed in 527 by amalgamating two existing structures from the ancient center. Honoring the two brothers, physicians and martyrs, Pope Felix IV joined the Biblioteca del Foro della Pace (Library of the Forum of Peace) and the temple of Divus Romulus (the God Romulus) into the forum's first Christian church. According to legend, the twin brothers offered free medical service to all in need. On one occasion, the brothers amputated a man's diseased leg and replaced it with the leg of an African who had recently died. If true, the account documents the first successful transplant. Invoked against sickness and plague, the persecuted saints survived drowning, crucifixion, stoning, and burning. They were finally beheaded in northern Syria. The beautiful church mosaics depict the *Apocalypse with the Mystical Lamb* and *Saints Peter and Paul Presenting Saints Cosmas and Damian to Christ.* Atop the altar sits a 13th-century panel painting of the *Virgin and Child.*

Originally a 2nd-century Christian home where the faithful gathered to worship (called a *titulus*), the BASILICA DI SAN CLEMENTE (Basilica of St. Clement) was constructed atop the early Christian residence in the 4th century. St. Clement (88–97?) was a celebrated early Christian author and Rome's third bishop. He refused to renounce his faith and was banished to Crimea to labor in the marble quarries; he was martyred there, hurled into the sea with an anchor tied about his neck. During a 9th-century reconstruction, his relics were returned to his church in Rome. After Norman destruction in 1084, Pope Paschal II rebuilt the church atop the original structure, maintaining the early Christian three-aisle plan.

A golden mosaic in the apse and vault dominates the upper church. The *Triumph of the Cross* (12th century) depicts a crucifix (symbolizing life through Christ) with 12 doves (representing the apostles) flanked by the Virgin and St. John the Baptist. Deer drink from a stream flowing from the cross (representing the soul's thirst for God), while a snake taunts a small stag (representing temptation) in the foreground. In the triumphal arch is Christ with the symbols of the Evangelists flanked by

R

St. Lawrence, St. Paul, the prophet Isaiah, and the City of Bethlehem representing the New Testament (left) and St. Peter, St. Clement, the prophet Jeremiah, and the City of Jerusalem representing the Old Testament (right). In the lower register, the *Agnus Dei with Twelve Lambs* symbolizes the apostles adoring Christ.

The lower basilica includes the fourth original basilica, a 3rd-century Mithraeum, and 1st-century Roman buildings. Notice the Romanesque fresco depicting the *Miracle of St. Clement,* a legend claiming that a chapel appeared floating atop the Black Sea to protect the martyred pope's remains. Ninth-century frescos illustrate the *Virgin and Child, The Wedding at Cana, The Crucifixion,* and *The Descent into Limbo.*

Rome's cathedral, the pope's titular seat, and the city's earliest church is the **BASILICA DI SAN GIOVANNI IN LATERANO** (St. John Lateran), known as the *caput et mater omnium ecclesiarum,* the mother and head of all churches in the city and the world. The basilica is dedicated to *SS. Salvatore e SS. Giovanni Battista e Giovanni Evangelist* (the Most Holy Savior and Saints John the Baptist and John the Evangelist) but takes its common name from the family to which the land originally belonged, the Plauzi Laterani. Constantine obtained the land and donated it to the basilica's founder, Pope Melchiade (311–14); little remains of his original church, which suffered successive barbarian destructions and devout reconstructions. In 1650, Pope Innocent X commissioned Borromini to remodel the church for the Jubilee year; in 1735, Clement XII ordered the facade redesigned; and in the late 19th century, Pope Leo XIII reorganized the apse.

On the balustrade atop the church facade are 15 twice-life-size statues representing Christ, St. John the Baptist, St. John the Evangelist, and the Doctors of the Church. The bronze doors in the central doorway were taken from the Roman forum. The far right door is the *Porta Santa,* open only during Jubilee years.

Borromini rebuilt the 130-meter nave between 1646–50 and 1656–57. Twelve colossal statues of the *Apostles* (1703–18) loom from their massive niches between the central pilasters. Encased in silver high atop the Gothic tabernacle are the heads of Rome's beloved apostles, St. Peter and St. Paul. Below, at the altar where only the pope can say Mass, is the early Christian wooden altar believed to be used by St. Peter and St. Sylvester, the Church's first popes. The 13th-century apse mosaic (restored 1884) by Jacopo Torriti and Jacopo da Camerino depicts Christ standing atop Jerusalem, the source of four rivers (the Gospels) which nourish sheep and deer (Christ's followers).

The **PALAZZO DEL LATERANO** (Lateran Palace) or *Patriarchium* (papal residence) dates primarily from the 6th century except for two rooms, the Aula

172

Magna and the Sala Consilii, built during Leo III's rule (795–816). The medieval structure was demolished by Pope Sixtus V (1585–90), who thought the palace was overwhelmingly ugly. He commissioned Domenico Fontana to erect a new one. Only the original Chapel of San Lorenzo (the Sancta Sanctorium) was left untouched. The once papal residence was transformed into a hospital, then an archive, and finally in 1967 it became the vicariate of Rome. The palace includes the **APPARTAMENTO PAPALE** (Papal Apartments) and the **MUSEO STORICO VATICANO** (Historical Museum). The apartments include sumptuous reception halls, while the museum documents papal history through paintings, armaments, costumes, and pontifical collectibles.

Near the palace is the Lateran Baptistery dedicated to **SAN GIOVANNI IN FONTE**. Built by Constantine, it was completely restored and altered by Urban VIII in 1637. Within the octagonal interior is a basin used for baptism by full immersion. Notable works include 5th–7th-century mosaics, an altar by Carlo Rainaldi, a plaque by Borromini, and 12th-century bronze doors.

The **SCALA SANTA** (Holy Staircase) contains the Sancta Santorum (the ancient papal chapel of San Lorenzo), which was moved from the second floor of the Lateran palace, and the Scala d'Honore (Stair of Honor), named after a tradition that claims Jesus ascended the stairs to meet Pilate during his trial. Pope Nicholas III's words are inscribed

on the structure claiming, "There is not a holier place in the entire world." In 1589 Sixtus V enclosed the chapel and staircase in a building designed by Domenico Fontana.

Constantine's mother, St. Helen, brought the Holy Staircase to Rome from Jerusalem. The 28-step relic is covered with wood to avoid wear. Out of respect and obligation, visitors climb the stairs on their knees. The stairs terminate at the Chapel of San Lorenzo. Atop the altar is a portrait presumed to be a contemporary picture of *Christ as Redeemer* believed to be painted by an angel (an acheropita image—not painted by hand).

SAN PIETRO IN VINCOLI (St. Peter in Chains), also called the Basilica of Eudosia, was built by Emperor Valentinian's wife, Eudosia, to house the chains that bound St. Peter. Medieval legend claims two chains, one used to shackle the apostle in Jerusalem and the other used for the same purpose in Rome, miraculously merged together when placed side by side. The fused chains are exhibited at the high altar. Consecrated in 439 by Sixtus III (432–40), the church was subsequently renovated in the 16th, 18th, and 19th centuries.

The basilica houses Michelangelo's unfinished *Mausoleum of Julius II*. In 1513 Pope Julius II (1503–15) commissioned Michelangelo to construct an enormous tomb glorifying his life and pontifical reign. Intended to stand beneath the dome of St. Peter's in the Vatican, Julius's death and pressure from

Pope Leo delayed the project's completion. Though the tomb is incomplete, its 44 colossal figures unrealized, the statue of Moses alone is worth a trip to Rome; Vasari, in his *Lives of the Artists,* claimed, no "work will ever equal it in beauty." The statue of *Moses* depicted with two horns (to symbolize rays of light) is flanked by the figures of Rachel and Leah, representing the active and contemplative life respectively.

In the sacristy is Domenichino's *Liberation of St. Peter* (1604), and in a nearby chapel is Guercino's *St. Margaret.* Beneath the high altar, a gilt bronze reliquary containing St. Peter's chains is opened annually on August 1 for visitors and pilgrims.

Built atop an early Christian home (489 A.D.) used for worship, called a titulus, SANTA PRASSEDE was erected in 822 under Pope Paschal I (817–24) to commemorate the daughter of the Roman senator Pudens, St. Peter's protector. Honored for their piety, Santa Prassede and her sister Santa Prudentiana offered refuge and protection to fellow Christians. A porphyry disk in the pavement supposedly marks the well into which Santa Prassede poured the blood of the martyrs.

Inside the *Chapel of San Zenone,* sometimes called the "Garden of Paradise," are the most beautiful and important Byzantine mosaics in Rome. Built by Paschal I to honor his mother Theodora, the mosaics depict *Christ Borne by Angels, Christ Flanked by Paschal I and Valentinian,* and *The Virgin and Child Enthroned with Saints Prassede and Prudentiana.* To the right, the *Column of the Flagellation,* brought by Santa Prassede from Jerusalem in 1223, is said to be a fragment from the column against which Christ was scourged.

Mosaics decorating the triumphal arch depict the *Adoration of the Multitude of Saints in Heaven* from Revelation 19. Within heavenly Jerusalem, Jesus stands among the Virgin, St. John the Baptist, and the apostles. On the inner arch is the *Adoration of the Lamb* and in the apse is *Christ Flanked by Saints Peter and Paul* (representing Prassede and Prudentiana respectively).

SANTA MARIA MAGGIORE (the Church of Mary Major), also known as the Basilica of Santa Maria ad Nives (St. Mary of the Snows) or the Basilica Liberiana (after Pope Liberius), is Rome's fourth patriarchal basilica. According to legend, during Pope Liberius's reign (352–66), a Roman nobleman and his wife who were unable to have children offered all their worldly possessions to the Virgin. On the eve of August 5, the Virgin appeared to the couple requesting they build a basilica in her honor atop a snow-covered hill. Despite being the middle of the summer, the next day when the couple awoke they discovered snow atop the Esquiline hill. The miraculous event is celebrated annually on August 5 in Santa Maria Maggiore, during which thousands of white flower petals are dropped from the ceiling into the nave, reenacting the wondrous snowfall.

During the Middle Ages heretical books were burned atop the long flight of steps leading into the church. The church, constructed principally under Sixtus III (432–40) commemorates the decision made at the Council of Ephesus (431) to bestow the title "Mother of God" upon the Virgin. The structure has undergone numerous renovations but the upper walls of its nave and roof date back to its early Christian origins.

Inside, the mosaics on the triumphal arch (sometimes called the Ephesian arch because it celebrates the dogma of the Virgin and Christ's virgin birth) are among the most exquisite Roman mosaic narratives. They majestically depict the *Annunciation, Presentation, Nativity,* and *Adoration of the Magi.* The earliest representation of the Trinity is seen in the nave. Here Abraham welcomes three angels (without wings following Jewish tradition), an event the early Church fathers regarded as prefiguring the Trinity. Atop the sanctuary arch is the first representation of an empty throne, symbolizing Christ's Second Coming. The symbol derives from a passage in Revelations, which foretells of his kingdom on earth and vividly describes a heavenly throne. Jacopo Torriti's apse mosaics (1295) represent an extravagant *Coronation of the Virgin;* here, Mary is the Queen of Heaven. The Latin inscription below refers to the feast of the Assumption of the Virgin, celebrated on August 15.

In 1585, shortly after his election to the papacy, Sixtus V commissioned Domenico Fontana to erect a funerary chapel, the *Cappella Sistina* (Sistine Chapel) or Cappella del Santissima Sacramento (the Chapel of the Most Holy Sacrament), to entomb Sixtus V (1588–90) and his predecessor, Pope Pius V (1556–72). The Communion container is the chapel's focal point, underscoring the Council of Trent's (1545–63) demands that the faithful focus their worship on the Host.

The *Pauline Chapel,* commissioned by Pope Paul V (1605–21), commemorates the church where he was a chaplain. Built by Flaminio Ponzio (1610–13) and assistants including Bernini's father, Pietro, the chapel houses the pope's tomb and an icon of the Virgin Mary known as the *Salus populi romani,* the salvation of the Roman people. Purportedly painted by St. Luke, the icon allowed the Catholic Church to justify erecting religious images in churches. The chapel frescoes celebrate the triumph of the Counter-Reformation and glorify the Virgin and saints.

Gian Lorenzo Bernini's modest tomb, marked only with a simple family burial stone, is also housed in the basilica to the right of the altar.

SANTA CROCE IN GERUSALEMME (the True Cross in Jerusalem) was built atop the 4th-century Sessoriano Palace, home to St. Helen, the mother of Constantine, who brought to Rome the relics of the True Cross from Jerusalem and

R

kept them in her palace. The church, built A.D. 320, provided a worthy sanctuary for the relics. In 1144 Pope Lucius II completely rebuilt the structure, and in 1743, Pope Benedict XIV (1740–58), much interested in restoring Rome's early Christian churches, again remodeled the church.

Vault frescoes depict the story of the relics, including the *Discovery of the True Cross by St. Helen, The Recovery of the True Cross by Heraclius,* and *Christ Giving a Blessing.* On the right behind the nave a stairwell descends to the Chapel of St. Helen; beneath its pavement is soil from Mt. Calvary carried to Rome by Helen. Its stunning mosaic vault (c. 1480) by Melozzo da Forli is a copy of the original early Christian vault decoration. On the left behind the nave a second stairwell leads to the Chapel of the Relics, which houses the most sacred relics associated with Christ's Passion: three pieces of wood from the True Cross, a nail that was driven through Christ's flesh and into the cross, part of the inscription nailed to the cross, and two thorns taken from the crown of thorns.

One-hundred-twenty-four steps, built by the Romans in 1346 in thanksgiving for deliverance from the plague, lead up to SANTA MARIA IN ARACOELI. The church dates much earlier than the endless staircase. According to legend, Augustus constructed a temple atop this same spot after a sibyl stood here and predicted Christ's birth. A 6th-century Benedictine monastery was later constructed atop the site, which was reconstructed and transferred to Franciscan rule between 1285 and 1287.

Inside the church are numerous fresco cycles. The most celebrated cycle is in the Bufalini Chapel decorated by Pinturicchio (1485) and illustrating the *Life of St. Bernard of Siena.* Other decorated chapels include the works of Pietro Cavallini, Pomarancio, and Benozzo Gozzoli. Notable 15th-century funerary monuments are the *Tomb of Cardinal Lodovico d'Albret* by Andrea Bregno and the *Tombstone of Giovanni Crivelli* by Donatello. Atop the main altar is the venerated 10th-century image of the *Virgin Mary with Christ Child.*

The 6th-century church of SANTA MARIA IN COSMEDIN served a Greek community that fled to Rome to escape persecution by Byzantine emperors. The church derives its name from the Greek word *kosmidion,* meaning ornamented.

The church's main attraction is a classical drain cover known as the *Bocca della Verità* (Mouth of Truth). Fable claims that liars who stick their hands into the Mouth of Truth will have them bitten off by the river god depicted on its face.

Inside note the Gothic baldachino, 8th-century pavement, and 11th-century wall frescoes. In the sacristy look for an 8th-century mosaic originally from Old St. Peter's.

SAN PAOLO FUORI LE MURA (St. Paul Outside the Walls) rose above the private family burial ground of a young

Christian girl who was entrusted with St. Paul's body after he was beheaded in A.D. 64. His tomb, a popular pilgrimage site, marks the spot where Constantine built a church dedicated to Paul and second only in size, plan, and beauty to St. Peter's. Rome's patrons, Peter and Paul, were honored with similar basilicas after, according to legend, the beloved pair were led outside the city gates to prison and martyred on the same day. Consecrated by Pope Sylvester I in A.D. 324, it was successively rebuilt and reconsecrated in 390 by Pope Siricius and completed by Honorius, the first emperor of the West, in 395. Destroyed by fire in 1823, it was reconsecrated a third time by Pope Pius IX in 1854.

Inside the church, above the central aisle, are frescoes depicting the *Life of St. Paul* with 262 mosaic portraits of popes below. Arnolfo di Cambio's *ciborium* (1285) marks the high altar. Among the stories represented on the Gothic canopy are *Adam and Eve After the Fall, Cain and Abel,* and *The Abbot Bartolomeo Offering the Tabernacle to St. Paul.* The nearby *Paschal Candelabrum* depicts scenes from the *Life of Christ.* Before the high altar, a triumphal arch, decorated for Pope Leo the Great (440–61), represents *Christ Pantocrator with Beasts of the Apocalypse and the 24 Church Elders.* The apse mosaic depicts *Christ Blessing Between St. Peter, St. Andrew, St. Paul, and St. Luke.*

The adjacent art gallery contains 16th-century Umbrian works, and the museum (in the adjacent monastery) contains papal portraits and Christian inscriptions.

Constantine built the patriarchal basilica of San Lorenzo Fuori le Mura (St. Lawrence Outside the Walls) in A.D. 330 to accommodate throngs of pilgrims journeying to St. Lawrence's tomb in the Verano catacombs. Lawrence, a Christian martyr of Spanish origin, was put to death in Rome in A.D. 248. Tradition claims that Lawrence, on Pope Sixtus II's instructions, gave away the church's treasures. While doing so, a Roman prefect ordered him to surrender the valuables, to which Lawrence replied, pointing at the poor and sick around him, "Here are the treasures of the Church." As a result, Lawrence was roasted alive on a grill.

Often destroyed and rebuilt, the church suffered a final assault during Allied bombing on July 19, 1943. The church structure incorporates two basilicas, the 6th-century incorporation of the adjacent church dedicated to the Virgin and a 13th-century reconstruction. Inside notice the Cosmatesque floor, the *Paschal candelabrum* (Easter candelabrum) and the mosaic-decorated *Bishop's Throne* (1254). The *ciborium* (triumphal canopy) above the crypt is the first signed work by Roman *marmorari* (marble carvers) dated 1148. St. Lawrence's interred remains can be visited in the Catacomb of Ciriaca through the adjoining cloister.

Originally dedicated to the Apostles Peter and Paul, the 4th-century

177

basilica of SAN SEBASTIANO FUORI LE MURA (St. Sebastian Outside the Walls) offered a temporary refuge for the apostles' sacred remains from Emperor Valerian's persecutions (A.D. 258). After his persecution under Diocletian, St. Sebastian's martyred remains were also hidden here. By the 9th century the church was officially named after St. Sebastian, whose remains are still interred in the crypt. St. Sebastian was a Roman officer who, when condemned for his faith, was riddled with arrows, survived, was rescued, and recovered, only to be condemned to death again. He was clubbed to death in A.D. 290. He is one of Rome's most venerated martyrs and the patron saint for protection against the plague.

Sebastian's church has always provided refuge for sacred relics. In the Chapel of the Relics is one of the arrows that pierced St. Sebastian and the post he was tied to. The most revered relic is Christ's footprint. The impression is believed to have been made during the *Domine quo vadis?* (Lord, where do you go?) as first related in the early *Acts of Peter*. In his account, Peter, urged by fellow Christians, left Rome to avoid Nero's persecutions. Along the Appian Way he envisioned he met Christ. He said to him, "Lord, where do you go?" and received the reply, "I go to Rome to be crucified again." Peter immediately understood its meaning; he would return to Rome for his own crucifixion. The nearby church of the Domine Quo Vadis was built atop the supposed spot where Peter met Christ in his vision.

Rome's churches are too numerous to take in on one trip, but if you are staying for an extended time do not miss the following sanctuaries. SANT' AGOSTINO (1479–83) houses Caravaggio's *Madonna of the Pilgrims* (1605) and Jacopo Sansovino's *Madonna del Parto* (Madonna of Childbirth, completed 1521). SANT' ANDREA DELLA VALLE (1591–c. 1660) contains a stunning Baroque fresco depicting *The Glory of Paradise* (1625–28) by Giovanni Lanfranco in the dome. Adjacent to the former headquarters of Rome's University, the 17th-century church of SANT' IVO DELLA SAPIENZA (St. Ives of Wisdom), dedicated to St. Ives of Kermartin, a 13th-century lawyer, notable for his charity, emphasizes the belief that religion is the beginning of wisdom, and that all wisdom comes from God. Borromini's rhythmic ground plan and spiraling dome are Baroque masterpieces. SANTA MARIA DELLA PACE (1482) houses Raphael's Chigi Chapel; above the chapel arch are Raphael's *Sibyls* (1514); influenced by Michelangelo's Sistine Chapel, the figures represent the Cumaean Sibyl, the Persian Sibyl, the Phrygian Sibyl, and the Tiburtine Sibyl. SANTO STEFANO ROTONDO (5th century) is Rome's oldest circular-planned church. Its shape, a combination of a circle and cross, symbolizes eternity and Christ's suffering respectively. Stephen was one of the first seven deacons ordained by the apostle Peter. SAN FRANCESCO A RIPA (10th century), where St. Francis purportedly once stayed, contains Bernini's beautiful funerary monument, the *Blessed Ludovica Albertoni.* SAN PIETRO IN MONTORIO (15th century) houses Sebastiano del Piombo's *Flagellation of Jesus,* and in its cloister, Bramante's model of Renaissance building principles, the *Tempietto.* Diocletian's bath was transformed into SANTA MARIA DEGLI ANGELI (16th– 18th centuries) and dedicated to the Virgin Mary, the angels, and the Christian martyrs who built the emperor's bath. Little remains of Michelangelo's original design for the church, but numerous noteworthy works include Domenichino's *Martyrdom of St. Sebastian.* Founded by Pope Mark in A.D. 336, SAN MARCO is one of Rome's oldest basilicas. Its apse mosaic (827–44) depicts Pope Gregory IV (who commissioned the mosaic decoration) presenting the basilica to Christ with St. Mark. The CIMITERO DEI PADRI CAPPUCCINI, the cemetery of the Capuchin monks, is decorated with the bones and skulls of over 4,000 monks. This macabre mausoleum emphasizes the importance of the cult of the dead. Earth from the Holy Land is scattered on the floor throughout the skeleton-rich chambers.

Between the 2nd and 5th centuries Roman Christians dug hundreds of kilometers of labyrinthlike subterraneous galleries to entomb their dead. During the Christian persecutions these CATACOMBS,

primarily created to celebrate funerary rites for those buried within them, also served as a refuge to celebrate Mass and partake in the Eucharist. Christians chose inhumation, paralleling Christ's burial. Christian burial practice included wrapping the deceased in shrouds and enclosing them in rectangular niches *(loculi)* covered with simple stone or marble slabs, again mimicking Christ's entombment. Tombstone inscriptions often consisted of the name of the deceased and a Christian symbol. Common symbols were the Good Shepherd (Christ with a lamb), the Orant (a figure with open arms representing divine peace), Christ's monogram (the first two letters of the Greek *Christos,* X = chi and P = ro), the fish (Christ's symbol), the dove (symbolizing a peaceful soul), the Alpha and Omega (Christ is the beginning and the end), the phoenix (symbolizing resurrection), and the anchor (symbolizing salvation). Biblical themes included Jonah and the whale (symbolizing resurrection) and Noah's ark (symbolizing salvation).

The CATACOMBE DI SAN CALLISTO (Catacombs of St. Calixtus) were built in the 2nd century under Deacon Calixtus's administration. Elected pope in 217, Calixtus officially sanctioned the complex. Subsequently, 16 popes and numerous early Christian martyrs are buried within the 20 kilometers of underground galleries. The *Cripta dei Papi* (Crypt of the Popes) entombs nine popes; Greek inscriptions indicated the places to visit of St. Anterote, St. Lucius,

R

St. Eutychian, St. Pontian martyr (MPT = consonants in Greek word for martyr), and St. Fabian martyr (MPT). The adjacent *Tomb of St. Cecelia* (the patron of sacred music) contains 9th-century frescoes; while 3rd-century frescoes depicting the Eucharist, baptism, and penance decorate the nearby *Cubicoli dei Sacramenti* (Cubicles of the Sacrament).

The four-story CATACOMBE DI SAN SEBASTIANO (Catacombs of St. Sebastian) once housed St. Sebastian martyr's tomb, whose relics now sit in his nearby church, San Sebastiano. In use from the 1st century to the 4th century, the catacombs incorporate pagan and Christian imagery.

Atop the Campidoglio, the Capitoline Hill, one of Rome's most sacred original hills, are the MUSEO CAPITOLINO (Capitoline Museum) and the PALAZZO DE CONSERVATORI (Palace of the Conservatori). The former contains masterful classical sculpture and the latter houses both classical sculpture and painting. The PINACOTECA CAPITOLINA within the Palazzo dei Conservatori, founded by Pope Benedict XIV, houses a vast collection of Italian and European painting. Its highlights include the *Baptism of Jesus* (1512) by Titian, *Romulus and Remus Suckled by the She-Wolf* (1617–18) by Peter Paul Rubens, the *Burial and Glory of S. Petronilla* (1623) by Guercino, the *Fortune Teller* (1595) by Caravaggio, and the *Holy Family* by Dosso Dossi. Veronese, Guercino, Tintoretto, Pollaiuolo, and Pietro da Cortona are among other featured artists.

Pope Innocent X Pamphili established the GALLERIA DORIA PAMPHILI in 1651. Housed in the 18th-century family palace, the painting collection is dispersed throughout the sumptuous palace apartments. The collection's treasures are Lorenzo Lotto's *St. Jerome,* Caravaggio's *Rest During the Flight into Egypt* and *Mary Magdalene,* Bellini's *Virgin Mary and Christ Child,* and Velazquez's portrait of *Pope Innocent X.*

The world-renowned collections in the MUSEO BORGHESE and GALLERIA BORGHESE are housed in the Casino Borghese (1613–17), built by Cardinal Scipione Borghese to house his personal art collection. Ancient, Renaissance, and Baroque sculpture and painting fill the vast collection.

The Museum's masterpieces are a *Venus Victorious* (1805) by Antonio Canova; several works by Gian Lorenzo Bernini, including his *Apollo and Daphne* (1624); the *Dead Christ with Angels* by Taddeo Zuccari; and *Amor Sleeping* by Luca Cambiaso.

The Gallery displays Raphael's *Deposition,* Fra Bartolomeo's *Sacred Family,* Perugino's *Virgin and Christ Child,* Bronzino's *John the Baptist,* Lorenzo Lotto's *Sacred Conversation,* Caravaggio's *Young Man with a Bowl of Fruit* and the *Madonna dei Palafrenieri,* Jacopo Bassano's *Adoration of the Magi* and the *Last Supper,* Correggio's *Danae,* Titian's *Sacred and Profane Love* and Antonello da Messina's *Portrait of a Man.*

R

SAN GALGANO

The ruined Cistercian abbey of San Galgano is a stone jewel in a densely wooded forest. Often skipped by tourists, it is a peaceful and picturesque site for any weary traveler.

Born to a noble family from nearby Chiusdino, San Galgano Guidotti (1148–81) abandoned a military career for hermetic solitude after he received a vision of St. Michael on the slopes where he later built his hermitage. In a symbolic gesture to renounce his past life, Galgano attempted to break his sword against a stone. Miraculously, he drove the sword through the rock, where it remains today. Galgano continued to work miracles and was canonized only four years after his death by Pope Urban III. In the 14th century the hermitage fell under a corrupt administration. Only the abbot remained in the monastery in 1397 when Sir John Hawkwood and his mercenaries stormed the abbey. A few monks later resurfaced, but the abbey was again abandoned in the 17th century. Since 1973, Olivetan nuns have administered the site.

PLACES TO VISIT

The **ABBEY CHURCH** (1218–88) is the largest French-Cistercian Gothic structure in Tuscany. The monks, who were known to be savvy administrators, agriculturists, and accountants, were also skilled architects; they built the church themselves. The roofless ruin is perhaps the most apt place for prayer—it is a church open to the heavens.

Atop the Monte Sepi is the **CHAPEL OF SAN GALGANO** (1182). It was here that San Galgano lived, was buried, was canonized, and left the steadfast symbol of his renunciation of the profane world for a sacred one—his sword in the stone. A 14th-century side chapel decorated by Ambrogio Lorenzetti depicts Galgano's life and his vision of St. Michael.

SAN GIMIGNANO

San Gimignano's 13th-century appellation, the "citta delle belle torri" (the city of beautiful towers), continues today to define the city's characteristic beauty and appeal. It retains its medieval character more than any other Tuscan town, preserving 15 of its original 76 towers. Constructed for defense, the towers attest to civic power and prosperity during its cultural and historical climax. San Gimignano is also known for its local white wine, La Vernaccia. This legendary bouquet is noted in Dante's *Purgatory* as Pope Martin IV's marinade for roasted eels.

St. Geminianus (a 4th-century bishop of Modena) became the patron and namesake of San Gimignano in the 6th century when the townspeople prayed to him to deliver the city from the Goth invasion. San Gimignano interceded, appearing to the attackers as a golden knight from the heavens. Originally an Etruscan settlement, the town grew and prospered through the Middle Ages owing to its position along the Via Francigena (the "Franks Road"). This road was an important trade and pilgrimage route between Rome and Northern Europe. It emerged in the 12th century as an independent commune and suffered 200 years of internal rivalry between its two most powerful families, the Ardinghelli (ardent Guelf supporters) and the Salvucci (loyal Ghibellines). In 1299 Dante visited San Gimignano as an ambassador for Guelf-allied Florence, and by 1353 it fell under Florentine control. In the 15th century the pilgrim's road was rerouted to the Elsa Valley, contributing to its commercial decline. As a result, the present city seems a vision of eternal, though aging, medieval splendor.

PLACES TO VISIT

The COLLEGIATA DI SANTA MARIA ASSUNTA is San Gimignano's principal church. The city is no longer the see of a bishop, and as a result the church lost its title of Duomo. The Romanesque (11th century) structure was transformed into its current plan in 1475 by Giuliano da Maiano. The decorative interior compensates for the unimpressive facade.

A *Last Judgment* (1410) on the entrance wall by Taddeo di Bartolo is meant to provoke those exiting the church to examine their own life and future judgment. Below is Benozzo Gozzoli's fresco, the *Martyrdom of St. Sebastian* (1465), flanked by two statues of the Virgin Mary and angel Gabriel (1420) by Jacopo della Quercia.

Two fresco cycles representing Old Testament and New Testament stories adorn the side walls. Barna da Siena depicted the *Life of Christ* (1335–40) on the south aisle. According to Vasari, Barna was killed when he fell from the scaffolding while painting the *Crucifixion*. Bartolo di Fredi executed the cycle on the north wall unharmed. It includes scenes of the *Creation* and the stories of *Noah, Moses,* and *Job*.

The CAPPELLA DI SANTA FINA celebrates the city's unofficial patron saint (Santa Fina was never canonized). The chapel was built by Giuliano da Maiano in 1468 and decorated with stories from her short life by Domenico Ghirlandaio in 1475. Legend tells that a ten-year-old Fina encountered a boy on the way to a well and accepted an orange from him. Scolded by her mother for her sin and overwhelmed with guilt, devout Fina fell ill on the kitchen table and remained there in prayer for the next five years. St. Gregory appeared to her to announce her death in 1254. At the moment of death, the table that she lay on and the city's towers bloomed with yellow pansies. Three miracles occurred during her funeral service and are depicted in the chapel: a blind boy regained sight, her nurse's paralytic hand regained strength, and angels rang the church bells.

The MUSEO D'ARTE SACRA, to the left of the Collegiata, houses a collection of paintings, sculptures, and ecclesiastical objects. The building also houses the MUSEO ETRUSCO, a small collection including urns, vases, and coins.

The MUSEO CIVICO is located in the upper floors of the Palazzo del Popolo. Built between 1288 and 1323, it was the site of the local government through the 13th century and continues to serve as the town hall.

The Sala del Consiglio is allegedly where Dante, in 1300, appealed to the citizens on behalf of the Guelf league. Today in the same room, a *Maestà* (1317) by Lippo Memmi appeals to the viewer's emotions. In 1466, Benozzo Gozzoli added two saints to Memmi's arrangement of the Madonna in majesty.

Works by 13th-century to 15th-century Florentine and Sienese painters comprise the collection in the Pinacoteca upstairs. The most notable works are: a 13th-century *Crucifix* by Coppo di Marcovaldo, Guido da Siena's *Madonna and Child Enthroned* (1280), Benozzo Gozzoli's *Madonna of Humility* (1466) and *Madonna and Child with Saints* (1466), Filippo Lippi's two tondos of the

Annunciation (1482), and Pinturicchio's *Madonna in Glory with Saints George and Benedict* (1512).

Climb the 200 steps up the adjacent TORRE GROSSA (Big Tower) for a splendid view. This is the tallest tower in San Gimignano.

The brick church of SANT'AGOSTINO was built between 1280 and 1298. Inside, the Cappella di San Bartolo is dedicated to yet another of the city's patron saints. In 1494, Benedetto da Maiano constructed a marble altar around the saint's tomb; statues of the three Theological Virtues stand above frescoed scenes of the *Life of San Bartolo* (1228–1300).

The choir decoration by Benozzo Gozzoli (1464–65) depicts the life of the church's namesake, St. Augustine (354–430). Also by Gozzoli, a cycle on the left wall illustrates the *Life of San Gimignano.* It was commissioned in gratitude to San Gimignano for interceding with an army of angels against illness during a plague in 1464.

Other notable works include Lippo Memmi's *Madonna Enthroned* (1330), Sebastiano Mainardi's *St. Bernard Giving a Blessing* (1487) and Pollaiuolo's altarpiece, *The Coronation of the Virgin* (1483).

Smaller churches to be explored are SAN PIETRO, decorated with Sienese paintings, SAN JACOPO, a Romanesque church built by the Templars with a beautiful *Crucifixion* by Memmo di Filippuccio, and the Romanesque SAN BARTOLO.

The TORTURE MUSEUM in the Torre del Diavolo (Devil's Tower) also houses

S

the Museum of Medieval Criminology and the Inquisition. Racks, chastity belts, and breast rippers are among the collection of torture devices.

The small 12th-century church,

PIEVE DI CELLOLE, lies just outside San Gimignano. Set upon a cypress grove, its beauty inspired Puccini's *Suor Angelica* and provides a serene respite for the tired traveler.

SANSEPOLCRO

Sansepolcro is an industrial town famed for producing fine lace and Buitoni pasta. Thousands of visitors come to the town yearly simply to pass a few hours in the civic museum and see the famed works of its equally famous native son, Piero della Francesca (1410–92). Though he worked in Florence, Ferrara, Rome, and Urbino, Piero spent most of his life in his hometown. During the last 20 years of his life, blind and unable to paint, Piero wrote two treatises—*On Perspective in Painting* and *On the Five Regular Bodies.* Sansepolcro is for the art lover.

According to legend, Sansepolcro was settled and named by two pilgrims, Arcano and Egidio, on their return from Jerusalem. They arrived in Sansepolcro with relics from the church of the Holy Sepulchre. In 1012 an abbey was established; it rose to the seat of a bishopric in 1520.

PLACES TO VISIT

Piero della Francesca's works are the star attractions in the MUSEO CIVICO. The museum is housed in the 14th-century Palazzo Pretorio. Piero della Francesca painted a *Resurrection* on the palace walls in 1463 which was later moved to its present location in 1480. The Gospels do not recount the moment of Christ's resurrection, but ample artistic representations illustrate the mystery. Piero's follows the traditional representation, with Christ holding the white and red banner of the Resurrection above his open tomb while three guards are fast asleep before him. Piero's serene divinity seems to have saved Sansepolcro from ruin in World War II. In 1944 a British army officer, having read Alduous Huxley's praise for the work, withheld orders to bomb Sansepolcro. The war soon ended, and the painting and city remained unharmed.

SANT' ANTIMO

The only rival to the captivatingly beautiful Romanesque abbey of Sant'Antimo is the alluring Gregorian chant that resounds from the church during the daily celebration of Mass. Among the most breathtaking abbeys in Tuscany, its setting, sights, and sounds are not to be missed. Be sure to visit in July or August for the annual organ concerts.

Founded in 781 by Charlemagne, the original Benedictine monastery came into being after the emperor's prayers for his troops' well-being were answered. In a vision, an angel revealed the remedy for Charlemagne's ailing troops, an herb called *Carolina*. The cure worked, and the abbey was constructed and dedicated to Sant'Antimo, whose sacred relics were possessed by Charlemagne (a gift from Pope Hadrian I). In the 13th century the abbey fell into financial crisis followed by spiritual degeneration. In 1439, Pope Eugenius IV incarcerated the abbot, and in 1462, Pope Pius II subdued the abbey. It remained uninhabited until the 19th century. Today, Cistercian monks administer the abbey.

PLACES TO VISIT

Built in 1118, the **ABBEY CHURCH** combines French, Spanish, and Lombard influence. The earlier 9th-century Carolingian church and crypt form the sacristy. The baptismal font can be seen through an oculus at the base of the older church. Inside the lofty structure are beautifully carved column capitals with geometric and vegetal reliefs. A representation of *Daniel in the Lion's Den* is among the most delicate column reliefs. The upper gallery or *matroneum* (literally women's gallery) dates from a time when gender separated the congregation. The luminous ambulatory and radiating chapels incorporate delicate onyx and alabaster stone. Atop the high altar is a 13th-century painted wooden crucifix and a 13th-century wooden statue of the *Madonna del Carmine.*

Little else remains of the complex, its wealth and privilege lost in spiritual and physical ruin. At its peak it would have included a large community with monk's quarters, a refectory, a chapter house, barns, and visitor accommodations.

S

SIENA

Siena's mythic origins are linked to Rome's vanquished cofounder, Remus. According to legend, his sons Senius (from which Siena gets its name) and Ascius founded the city. Each rode a horse—Senius's was black and Ascius's was white—and these colors decorate the city shield. Also seen throughout the city is the she-wolf suckling the twins Romulus and Remus (more commonly associated with Rome), the sign of their birthright.

Three hills define the city and divide the layout into thirds, called *terzi*. Areas within each *terzo* are divided into wards, called *contrade*. Each *contrada* is an administrative center with its own head-quarters, church, and museum. Each of the 17 *contrada* is named after an animal and has its own flag and motif. Citizens baptized in a Sienese church are baptized a second time in an open-air fountain in their *contrada*.

The PALIO DELLE CONTRADE, Siena's famous festival and tournament, encourages rivalry, pitting each ward against the others in a furious three-lap horse race around the city's central square, the Piazza del Campo. It was first recorded on August 16, 1310. A second race was added in 1649 on July 2. The palios are now held annually on July 2 (the Feast of the Visitation) and August 16 (the day after the Feast of the Assumption); however, the only seemingly sacred elements are the horse blessings and a banner of the Virgin Mother.

Siena's illustrious natives include Pope Alexander III (d. 1181) and St. Catherine of Siena (1347–80). Architects Lorenzo Maitani (1275–1330), Francesco di Giorgio Martini (1439–1502), and Baldassare Peruzzi (1481–1556) are all natives. Its most celebrated painters are Guido da Siena (13th century), Bartolo di Fredi (1353–1410), Domenico Beccafumi (1486–1551), Domenico di Bartolo (1400–1446), Duccio di Buoninsegna (1260–1319), Ambrogio Lorenzetti (d. 1348), Pietro Lorenzetti (d. 1348), Lorenzo Monaco (1370–1425), Simone Martini (d. 1344), Matteo di Giovanni (1435–95), and Lippo Memmi (1317–49).

A tribe of Gauls settled ancient Siena, naming it *Sena Etruria*. The Roman emperor Augustus founded a military colony on the site and named it *Sena Julia*. It endured Frankish and Carolingian rule, during which time it was a major stop along the Christian pilgrimage route from Northern Europe to Rome, the Via Francigena. In 1125 it became a free commune, developing both a sophisticated banking system and communal government. In 1186, citizens-turned-soldiers fought against Barbarossa under Sienese Pope Alexander III. Siena began to expand its territory and engage in fierce competition with Florence in the wool trade. The struggle for supremacy over art, commerce, and textiles is at the heart of their historic rivalry. Ironically, it was exiled Guelf Florentines who helped Ghibelline Siena defeat Florence at the battle of Montaperti in 1260. While the victory inaugurated Siena's Golden Age, their supremacy was short-lived. In 1270, Charles of Anjou defeated the Ghibellines. A papal excommunication forced many Ghibellines to shift to Guelf allegiance. A new government was established under Guelf rule. Art, commerce, and peace prospered until the Black Death arrived in May, 1348. By October, one-third of the population was decimated. The plague was followed in 1355 by 14 years of war with Charles IV and ended under the rule of Gian Lorenzo Visconti in 1399. Florentine rivalry flourished and unstable rule reigned. Various rulers seized control, including Pandolfo Petrucci and Cosimo I. Pietro Leopoldo's 18th-century rule established stability.

PLACES TO VISIT

The city's DUOMO is a tribute to Sienese ambition and a physical reminder of the ravages of both the plague and regional politics, which resulted in the end of Siena's golden era. A 9th-century church originally stood on the spot. In 1179 a second church was built and consecrated. In 1215, the third and present structure was begun. It was completed in 1263 only to be enlarged again in 1316. However, Sienese builders and citizens

aspired to greater worldly and sacred glory, embarking in 1339 on new plans to make their cathedral the greatest in Christendom. Citizens who contributed to the building by hauling marble in their own carts were granted indulgences by the local bishop. Under the new plan, the existing church would simply become the nave wall. However, the plan was not realized; ambition succumbed to two merciless enemies, the bubonic plague and Tuscan politics.

Giovanni Pisano contributed the lower facade decoration (1284–85 and 1296–97), carving images of prophets, philosophers, and patriarchs (replaced by copies). The upper facade was completed between 1382 and 1390, 70 years after the six-story campanile was constructed. In the 19th century the Venetian mosaics were finally added to the facade.

Inside, resist the temptation to look up at the cathedral's coffered dome; instead, look to the floor at the stunning inlaid marble pavement. Completed between 1373 and 1547, the entire church floor is divided into 56 designs. The earliest are simple black outlines on white marble, others are inlaid black-and-white marble, and later designs are colored. Over 40 artists executed the biblical and secular scenes. The most stunning are the *Ten Sibyls,* the *Hill of Virtue* by Pinturicchio, and the *Massacre of the Innocents* by Matteo di Giovanni. The entire floor can only be seen from August 7 to 22; the rest of the year many panels are covered.

S

187

The venerated painting of the *Madonna del Voto* (13th century) is housed in the circular Cappella Chigi (1659–62), designed by Bernini for Alexander III. The painting is revered for its miraculous power to save the city and was invoked for protection on the eve of the battle of Montaperti. Citizens continue to place the city keys before the image and pray for deliverance from destruction.

A bronze ciborium (1467–72) by Vecchietta crowns Baldassare Peruzzi's high altar (1532). A stained-glass window (1288) in the apse is possibly based on Duccio's drawings.

Nicola Pisano's octagonal pulpit (1265–68), constructed with the help of his son Giovanni and Arnolfo di Cambio, offers representations of *Philosophy, The Liberal Arts,* and *Christian Virtues.* Its seven panels illustrate the *Redemption,* scenes from *The Life of Christ,* and scenes from *The Last Judgment.*

A model for 14th-century tomb design is Tino da Camaino's *Tomb of Cardinal Riccardo Petroni* (d. 1313). Before it is a bronze pavement tomb by Donatello for Bishop Giovanni Pecci (1426).

The Cappella di San Giovanni Battista (1492), by Giovanni di Stefano, includes frescoes by Pinturicchio depicting the *Life of St. John the Baptist* and Donatello's bronze *St. John the Baptist* (1457).

Michelangelo contributed four statues (1501–04)—*St. Peter, St. Pius, St. Gregory,* and *St. Paul*—to Andrea Bregno's Piccolomini altar (1480). Jacopo della Quercia's earliest work, a *Madonna and Child* (1397–1400), crowns the altar.

The BIBLIOTECA PICCOLOMINI (access through the left nave) is a Renaissance library founded by Cardinal Francesco Piccolomini (later Pius III) to house Pius II's (his uncle's) library. Pinturicchio's frescoes depict the life of the beloved uncle, humanist scholar, diplomat, geographer, poet, politician, and pope, Aeneas Silvius Piccolomini (1404–64). His life's endeavors, prayer and womanizing among them, were both spiritual and worldly. The ten frescoes include *Aeneas Being Crowned a Poet, Named a Bishop, Made a Cardinal and Elected a Pope.* Notice the nephew's prize acquisition, a Roman copy (3rd century) of the *Three Graces* by Praxiteles. Also displayed are liturgical accessories as well as the cathedral's 15th-century illuminated choir books.

The MUSEO DELL'OPERA METRO-POLITANA is housed in the structure originally intended to be the right aisle of the ambitious and unrealized new church. A gallery for the cathedral works, its treasures include: Duccio's *Maestà* (1308–11), a two-sided work showing the *Madonna and Child Enthroned* and the *Story of the Passion* (taken from the cathedral high altar in 1505), Pietro Lorenzetti's *Birth of the Virgin* (1342), a wooden crucifix (1250) by Giovanni Pisano, and the *Madonna dagli Occhi Grossi* (Madonna of the Big Eyes) by the Sienese "Maestro di Tressa" (1220–30).

A 15th-century stair extends beneath the cathedral apse, leading to the **BAPTISTERY OF SAN GIOVANNI BATTISTA** (1345). Built to support the planned cathedral extension, the structure is almost entirely covered by mid-15th-century frescoes depicting scenes from the *Life of Christ* and figures of the *prophets and sibyls*. The hexagonal baptismal font (1417–30), designed by Jacopo della Quercia, depicts the life of St. John the Baptist in gilded relief panels. Lorenzo Ghiberti sculpted two panels, *The Birth of Christ* and *St. John in Prison,* and Donatello added *Herod's Feast*. Donatello also contributed the representations of the virtues *Faith and Charity* to the sides of the font.

The church of **SANT'AGOSTINO** (1258) was closed in 1982, but a custodian will let you in on request. Often used as an exhibition site, the church's own works are worth viewing. Adorning the remodeled neoclassical interior (1749) are a *Crucifixion* (1506) by Perugino, an *Epiphany* (1518) by Sodoma, a *Massacre of the Innocents* (1482) by Matteo di Giovanni, and a lunette of the *Madonna and Saints* by Ambrogio Lorenzetti. In the Cappella Bichi, frescoes by Francesco di Giorgio Martini, discovered in 1978, depict the *Birth of the Virgin and the Nativity.*

Built atop the piazza where he preached his sermons, the **ORATORIO DI SAN BERNARDINO** (15th century) is dedicated to the Franciscan preacher, St. Bernardino (1380–1444). Known as the founder of the "cult of devotion to the name of Jesus," while preaching he displayed the monogram of Jesus (I.H.S.) as a symbol of a unified Italy under the church. Bernardino's use of the symbol led Pope Martin V to accuse him of heresy, but the accusation was dropped and Bernardino continued to preach his lengthy sermons as before—in the name of Christ. His apt motto—"Make it clear, short, and to the point"—led to his being named as the patron saint of advertising in the 1980s.

The oratory's upper chapel is decorated with 14 frescoes depicting the *Life of the Virgin* (1496–1518) by Sodoma, Beccafumi, and Girolamo del Pacchia. Francesco Vanni, Domenico Manetti, Ventura Salimbeni, and Rutilio Maneti decorated the lower chapel with 17th-century scenes from Bernardino's life.

SAN DOMENICO (1226, 1262–65), a massive and austere church, is a typical Dominican structure; however, the saint venerated within its walls is extraordinary. St. Catherine of Siena (1347–80) was a devout and holy woman who experienced visions in her youth and received the stigmata. Though she never became a nun, in 1378 she was asked to intercede on behalf of the excommunicated citizens of Florence. She journeyed to France and convinced Pope Gregory XI to return the papacy to Rome. Catherine received various honors: she was canonized in 1460, named patron saint of Italy (shared with St. Francis) in 1939, and in 1970 Catherine was declared a Doctor of the Church.

S

According to tradition, Catherine experienced ecstasies in the Cappella della Volte. Within the chapel, a niche with shallow steps marks the spot she received the stigmata. Above it, her friend Andrea Vanni painted Catherine's portrait. Parts of her holy corpse were spread throughout Italy when she died; Siena received her head, which is kept locked in a golden reliquary in her shrine, the Cappella di Santa Caterina (1488). Sodoma frescoed the chapel with scenes from her life, including her episodes of religious fervor and her miracles.

Significant works throughout the church include a *Nativity* by Francesco di Giorgio Martini, a tabernacle with two angels (1475) by Benedetto da Maiano, and a *St. Barbara Enthroned with Angels and St. Mary Magdalene and Catherine* by Matteo di Giovanni. Take in the beautiful terrace-top view of the Duomo and city center.

Nearby is St. Catherine's home, CASA E SANTUARIO DI SANTA CATERINA. She was born here on March 25, 1347 (the Feast of the Annunciation), the 24th of 25 children in a family of cloth merchants. The house was converted into a sanctuary and purchased by the city in 1466. Inside, frescoes depict her life and works.

A flight of stairs will take you to the oratory of SANTA CATERINA IN FONTEBRANDA (1465), built atop the family's dye workshop and housing a beautiful polychrome wood statue of St. Catherine (1475) by Neroccio di Bar-

tolomeo. The "miraculous cellar" where Catherine produced wine is below the oratory.

Siena was known for its hospitality towards pilgrims traveling en route from Northern Europe to Rome along the Via Francigena. The OSPEDALE DI SANTA MARIA DELLA SCALA offered respite, shelter, and food for the weary traveler. Founded in the 9th century and first documented in 1090, legend credits Beato Sorore (9th century), a devout cobbler who devoted his life to charitable works. Plans to convert the hospital into the new Pinacoteca Nazionale are progressing slowly. The hospital's 1,000-year history of generosity and charity have ended, but a beautiful record remains in the Sala Pellegrinaio (reception hall) where frescoes (1440–44) by Domenico di Bartolo, Jacopo della Quercia, and Vecchietta depict the hospital's history and daily life.

The hospital's church, SANTISSIMA ANNUNCIATA (rebuilt 1466), was constructed with money from donations. Inside is Vecchietta's bronze *Risen Christ* (1476) and the shadowed Cappella di Santa Caterina della Notte, where the saint went to pray at night.

Works by Sienese artists abound in the PINACOTECA NAZIONALE. Five centuries of art arranged chronologically offer an excellent understanding of the development of the Sienese school. The collection begins with an altar frontal depicting scenes from the *Legend of the True Cross* (1215); attributed to the "Master of Tressa," it is the first datable piece from the Sienese school. Among numerous works by Guido da Siena is a beautiful *Madonna and Child* (1262–67). Numerous Madonnas by Duccio da Buoninsegna (1260–1319) and his followers include the *Madonna dei Francescani* (1285). Do not miss Simone Martini's famed *Madonna and Child* and his *Pala di Beato Agostino Novello.* Significant works by brothers Pietro and Ambrogio Lorenzetti include a plethora of enthroned Madonnas. Giovanni di Paolo's *St. Nicholas of Bari* (1453), Matteo di Giovanni's three *Madonna and Child with Saints,* and Vecchietta's *Madonna and Child with Saints* are notable 15th-century works. Numerous pieces by Sodoma and Beccafumi include *St. Michael and the Rebel Angels* (former), the *Scourging of Christ* (former), and cartoons for the duomo pavement (latter). The top floor highlights 15th- and 16th-century works by Northern Italian and European artists.

The Palazzo Publico houses municipal offices on its ground floor and a superb collection of Sienese works in the **Museo Civico** on the upper floor. The palace frescoes by Bartolo di Fredi, Vecchietta, Simone Martini, Ambrogio Lorenzetti, and Sodoma rival the excellent museum collection. Among the stellar works are Spinello Aretino's scenes from the *Life of Pope Alexander III* (1407–8); Beccafumi's frescoed vault depicting heroism in ancient Greece and Rome; Simone Martini's earliest work, the *Maestà* (1315); Sodoma's *Saints Victor and Ansanus;* and Ambrogio Lorenzetti's *Allegory of Wise and Evil Government* (1338–40).

SPOLETO

S

Situated along the banks of the Torrente Tessino (River Tessino), Spoleto is surrounded by thick woods and is graced with cool summer breezes. Cicero likened the Umbrian town to a star in the heavens, calling it "fixed and illustrious among the highest." Inhabited since prehistoric times, Spoleto retains much of the cultural and artistic splendor of its three stellar periods, Roman, medieval, and Renaissance.

The Romans colonized *Spoletum* in 241 B.C. and rewarded the town for its allegiance after the Punic Wars with the title of *optimun jure* (magistrate) in 90 B.C. After successive barbarian invasions Foroaldo I chose the city as a Longobard dukedom in A.D. 569. The Longobards enlarged the territory of the dukedom to the outskirts of Rome. It passed into Frankish power and later into the hands of a local duke, Guido III, who gained the imperial throne. Spoleto was destroyed by Barbarossa and endured a period of bloody conflict between local Guelfs and Ghibellines. In 1354 Cardinal dell'Albornoz reestablished Spoleto's church ties. He made it an important center of the papal state, governed for a term by Lucretia Borgia (1499), and inaugurated a final period of cultural favor and artistic splendor.

PLACES TO VISIT

Spoleto's DUOMO is a testament to the enduring spirit and faith of the townspeople. Dedicated to Santa Maria Assunta, it was built in the 12th century on the site of a previous cathedral destroyed by Barbarossa. Pope Innocent III consecrated the new church in 1198. The typical Umbrian facade is divided into three horizontal zones. At the lowest zone, the beautiful Romanesque portal is preceded by a Renaissance porch (1491) and framed by pulpits at either end. A large rose window in the central zone is surrounded by symbols of the four evangelists and flanked by four smaller rose windows. The facade is crowned by three Gothic arches with a Byzantine mosaic in the central arch of *Christ Blessing with the Virgin and St. John* (1207). Its 12th-century bell tower incorporates materials from its three greatest periods.

The interior was restored in the 17th century by Luigi Arrigucci, architect to Pope Urban VIII, whose pontifical image is captured in a bronze bust by Bernini that sits above main door.

In the CAPPELLA EROLI OR SACRO CUORE (Sacred Heart), first chapel on the right, is a *Pietà,* an altar fresco by Pintoricchio from 1497. Through a door in the Eroli chapel are the family tombs

of bishops Constantino and Franco. Its frescoed walls are attributed to Jacopo Siciliano.

Fra Lippo Lippi's frescoes (completed with the help of two assistants) depicting the *Life of the Virgin* decorate the PRESBYTERY (1467–69). Notice the small group of figures on the right of the *Dormition of the Virgin;* they are portraits of Fra Lippo, his son Filippo (also a painter), and his two assistants, Fra Diamante and Pier Matteo d'Amelia.

The TOMB OF FRA LIPPO LIPPI is in the right arm of the transept on the left wall. It was erected and paid for by Lorenzo Il Magnifico and designed by Filippo Lippi.

In the CAPPELLA DELLA SANTISSIMA ICONE is a Byzantine icon of the *Madonna* (12th century), said to be painted by St. Luke and saved from the destructive rampage of the iconoclasts. In 1185, Federico Barbarossa gave it to the city as a token of peace.

The CORO D'INVERNO (1548–54) in the Cappella della Relique, the sixth chapel along the left nave, is a beautifully inlaid wooden choir with tiny frescoed panels. The work is by two local artists. To the right of the choir is a *Crucifix* by Alberto Sozio (1187). This Byzantine work, made with parchment paper attached to wood, is the church's oldest treasure.

The ARCHIVO CAPITOLARE (Capital Archives) houses important documents and codices and a prized letter to Fra 'Leone signed by St. Francis of Assisi.

Enclosed within the courtyard and structure of the bishop's palace is the 12th-century church of SANT' EUFEMIA. Galleries above the side naves, unusual for a small church, make it unique among Umbrian churches. The galleries (called *matroneum*) possibly belonged to the bishops or were used to segregate the female congregation. The original church was a Benedictine monastery founded by an Italian named Gunderada. He chose this spot as the burial place of San Giovanni, a local bishop and martyr, after rescuing it from the Goths (980). In 1017, Emperor Henry II gave the monastery over to a count, and in the 12th century it became the site of the bishop's palace.

The history of the church of SAN GREGORIO MAGGIORE is well-documented. Begun in 1079 and consecrated in 1146, it has suffered the ravages of fire, floods, and war. An inscription on the facade refers to human devastation, recalling 10,000 martyrs allegedly buried at this spot. The 12th-century facade is modeled on the Duomo and includes a 16th-century porch that covers the Cappella degli Innocenti (Chapel of the Innocents). Now a baptistery, the chapel is decorated with frescoes of the *Life of Sant' Abundatius*, whose body is buried within the crypt inside the church.

Various 12th–15th-century Umbrian artists decorated the walls inside the main church. The Cappella del Sacramento (Chapel of the Sacrament) provides a decorative contrast to the simple, sparsely orna-mented church. The beautifully carved TABERNACLE decorated with stone angels and floral motifs is by the 16th-century Pistoian artist, Benedetto da Rovezzano.

SAN NICOLÒ stands above the former 13th-century church, Chiesa della Misericordia (Church of Mercy). Of interest in the lower church are a 14th-century *Crucifixion* and a so-called "clothed crucifix," a work draped in cloth. The upper church was built in 1304 and burned in 1849; it is no longer used today.

SAN DOMENICO, originally San Salvatore, is a single-naved 13th-century church decorated with 14th–15th-century votive frescoes. Like many Dominican churches, a chapel is dedicated to the pride of the order, St. Thomas Aquinas. Inside a niche on the first altar to the right is a 15th-century representation of the *Triumph of St. Thomas Aquinas* with the saint displaying an open text to his disciples, bishops, and cardinals.

However, the real source of pride in the church is a relic in the left transept. A silver reliquary in the CAPPELLA DEI MONTEVECCHIO encases a nail from the True Cross; the blessed Gregory brought it to Spoleto.

The PONTE SANGUINARIO (Bloody Bridge) is a Roman ruin that was buried after the Tessino River was rerouted. The ponte was unearthed in 1817. The name "sanguinario" comes from the tradition that the blood of many Christian martyrs flows under this bridge. Presumably they were sacrificed in the nearby amphitheatre (2nd century).

S

The **ARCO DI DRUSO** (Arch of Drusus), erected in honor of Tibrius's son, Drusus, marks the entrance to the ancient Roman forum. The arch flanks the church of **SANT' ANSANO**, constructed atop a Roman temple. Below the temple's cella is a crypt dedicated to St. Isaac and St. Martial; both monks sought refuge from persecution in the hills surrounding Spoleto. The walls of this 7th-century Christian church are decorated with frescoes, including the *Decapitation of John the Baptist, Christ in Glory,* and *The Last Supper.*

Crowning Monte Elia is the **ROCCA**, a bleak fortress built to keep a protective watch over the city and act as a stronghold for the papacy. Commissioned by Cardinal Albornoz (1355–67), it was a defensive castle for the papal kingdom after the Avignon residency. Among its most notable temporary residents were Lucretia Borgia and Popes Nicholas V, Pius II, Sixtus IV, Julius II, and Valentino. The castle is now a prison.

The **PINACOTECA COMUNALE** in the Palazzo Comunale houses a collection of paintings from the 13th–18th centuries. The most notable works include a 16th-century polyptych of *Saints John the Baptist and Gabriel,* the *Madonna delle Grazie* by Niccolò Alunno, a *Magdalene* (1636) by Il Guercino, and a *Crucifixion with the Madonna and St. John* by Lo Spagna.

The **MUSEO CIVICO** is an eclectic collection of Roman and medieval sculpture, portrait busts, architectural fragments, inscriptions, and reliefs. The **LEX SPOLETINA** are the most valuable pieces in the collection. They are two tablets (c. 240 B.C.) that mark the "sacred grove" and warn woodcutters of the consequences of cutting hallowed shrubbery.

MONTELUCO (804 meters), 8 kilometers outside the city, is Spoleto's mountain and the site of the sacred grove. The name comes from *lucus,* meaning sacred forest. The forest has ancient Roman religious significance. It was here in the 5th century that Saints Isaac and Martial sought refuge and where St. Francis, in 1218, caused a spring of water to appear. The Benedictines gave him their church to commemorate the miracle, and Francis used it to house one of his first convents.

Various churches on the outskirts of Spoleto are worth visiting. **SAN PIETRO** (5th century) is built on the site of a cemetery of Iron Age origins. Bishop Achillus had the church built to house a relic: St. Peter's chain. The relic has since disappeared.

The elaborately carved 13th-century facade instructs the viewer on the power of redemption to cleanse the soul of sin. The central door is framed by 14 panels, six panels in two sets of three. There are symbolic sculptures of *Men Driving Oxen* (representing human labor as the result of sin), *A Hind Milking Her Young and Devouring a Servant* (representing redemption through Christ), and *A Peacock Eating Grapes* (representing immortality through Christ). The surrounding larger panels represent *Christ Washing St. Peter's Feet, Christ Calming the Waters of Lake Tiberias, The Fox Feigning Dead and the Ravens* (the fox symbolizes the Devil and the ravens represent the soul succumbing to the flesh), *Brother Wolf and a Ram Fleeing* (a comment on monastic life), *A Lion Chasing a Dragon* (the lion represents Christ and the dragon, evil), *The Death of the Just Man, The Death of the Sinner, The Lion and the Woodsman, The Man Kneeling Before the Lion,* and *The Lion Attacking the Soldier.* This is a facade dedicated to the religious edification of the faithful.

SAN SALVATORE is a Paleo-Christian (4th century) structure. The facade fuses classical and oriental architectural elements. Within, the presbytery mimics the architecture of an ancient Roman temple. Between the 11th and 16th centuries the church was called San Concordio after a saint entombed in the church. After the 16th century it was referred to as "del crocifisso," in recognition of the 9th-century jeweled cross behind the altar.

SAN PONZIANO is dedicated to a local martyr and patron of the city who was killed under the rule of Emperor Antoninus. The 12th-century Romanesque church is built above the catacombs of Santa Sincleta, where San Ponziano was laid to rest in 175.

SUBIACO

Not far from Rome, two twins left their mark on another city in the Lazio region. St. Benedict (480–c. 543) and his twin sister St. Scholastica (480–c. 530) were not suckled by a she-wolf (like Rome's Romulus and Remus) but nurtured by the isolated mountains and woods of the Roman countryside. The twins were a devout, pious, and holy pair. Benedict founded the Benedictine order, and Scholastica founded the first community of Benedictine nuns. According to legend, the bond between the twins was so great that when Scholastica died, Benedict, praying in his cell, envisioned her soul in the form of a dove ascend to heaven.

The birthplace of Latin monasticism, ancient Subiaco (*Sublaqueum,* "under the lakes"), began as a worker's village for crews constructing a nearby villa for Nero. An early Christian monastery dedicated to St. Clement was established in the 4th century. A century later, Benedict arrived to live a hermetic life in three years of silence and prayer. During this time, he lived in a cave known as the *Sacro Speco* (Holy Grotto), where he fed ravens with his own food. News of Benedict's piety spread quickly, and followers flocked to Subiaco. With Scholastica's help he constructed the monastery, only to leave after a confrontation with a monk named Fiorenzo. Three ravens then

S

led Benedict to Monte Cassino where, in A.D. 529, he founded another monastery.

The monks that remained in Subiaco constructed a second convent dedicated to Saints Cosmas and Damian, which was rededicated to St. Scholastica after her death. The monasteries prospered in the 11th and 12th centuries, diminished in the 14th century, and were subsequently ruled by abbots from the Colonna, Borghese, and Barberini families.

PLACES TO VISIT

Climb the "Via dei Monasteri" (Way of the Monasteries) up 2.5 kilometers to the MONASTERO DI SANTA SCHOLASTICA. Here in the Middle Ages, power and privilege necessitated the construction of three cloisters, the large cloister (1569–80), the second cloister (1450), and the third cloister (1210–43). Each reveals a portion of the convent's history.

The church of SAN SCHOLASTICA was built in the 7th and 10th centuries

and rebuilt in 1770 by the architect Giacomo Quarenghi. Inside are remnants from the earlier church and Nero's villa. The church library boasts the first two books printed in Italy and a splendid archive that houses 30,000 books, papal bulls, and state documents.

Continue up the road to the MONASTERO DI SAN BENEDETTO or SACRO SPECO (Holy Grotto). Carved into the hillside, the church is part of the mountain. The upper church (c. 1350) is decorated with 14th-century Sienese frescoes of the life of Christ, while the lower church decoration depicts the life of St. Benedict.

A flight of steps leads to the Holy Grotto, a natural cave in which stands a statue of *St. Benedict* (1657) by Antonio Raggi. The Chapel of St. Gregory houses a portrait of St. Francis from Francis's visit in 1210. The Scala Santa follows the path St. Benedict took to his grotto, and the Grotto dei Pastori (Grotto of the Shepherds) commemorates the cave where St. Benedict preached to shepherds.

TODI

Atop a hill and obscure from view, Todi looks down upon the Tiber and surrounding sea. Its landscape dictated the city's military destiny; it played a strategic defensive role for the Umbrians, the Etruscans, and the Romans. It also resisted an attack by Totila. In the 12th century it was a free town at war with its neigh-

bors, Orvieto, Narni, and Spoleto. In 1237 it became part of a Guelf alliance, resisting attack by Emperor Frederick II. In the 14th century it passed through the grasp of various families and finally into the hands of the church.

Todi is the birthplace of Pope Martin I (649–53), but its most famous citizen is Jacopone (Ser Jacopo Benedetti), a

Franciscan, a poet, and author of the laudi (praises). Born in 1230, Jacopone was a wild young man. At age 32 he lost his wife in a tragic accident. The loss led him to live a monastic life among the Franciscans. His conversion was likely influenced by the discovery that his wife was secretly wearing a rough penitential skirt under her dress when she died (following St. Francis's practice, self-mortification). Against official Franciscanism and the Vatican, Jacopone became a *fraticello* and openly opposed dogma and theology. His laude are evidence to his praise for life. Jacopone's most famous laude, the *Pianto della Madonna,* recounts Mary's search for her son and discovery of Christ on the cross.

PLACES TO VISIT

The walk up the 29 steps to the **DUOMO OF SANTISSIMA ANNUNCIATA** is a symbolic reenactment of the struggle of the faithful, which parallels Christ's own arduous struggle. The 12th-century structure might be constructed atop an ancient temple to Apollo.

Inside the church, notice the column capitals carved with representations of various saints. Approach the wooden inlaid choir in the apse, decorated in 1530. The decorative seats include representations of doorways, courtyards, windows, books, crucifixes, hourglasses, musical instruments, birdcages, and buildings. The *Annunciation* decorates the central throne.

As you exit the church, notice the *Last Judgment* fresco by da Faenza (1562–1645) on the back wall imitating Michelangelo's treatment of the same subject in the Sistine Chapel. Last Judgment scenes are often the last works one sees when exiting a church and are intended to encourage the viewers to contemplate how their own actions will be judged.

Two Romanesque lions guard the unfinished facade of **SAN FORTUNATO.** Begun in 1292, work terminated in 1458 when Giovanni di Santuccio abandoned work on the facade. The portal (1420–36) juxtaposes columns with floral motifs and bishops with naked figures. Statues in the flanking niches represent Gabriel and the Virgin Annunciate.

Inside, in the fourth chapel on the right, is one of Masolino's last works, a *Madonna and Child with Two Angels.* In the last chapel along the same aisle, pilgrims have left penciled prayers for peace and happiness on the walls. Todi's infamous monk, Fra Jacopone, is buried in the church's crypt.

The Palazzo del Capitano houses the city's **GALLERY AND ARCHITECTURAL MUSEUM.** The most notable works in the collection include a *Coronation of the Virgin* (1507) by Lo Spagna, a Byzantine crucifix, and a variety of other sculptures and paintings. In the archaeological museum is a collection of Etruscan and Roman finds including columns, sarcophagi, bronzes, and objects used in daily life.

Smaller churches in Todi are worth a visit. The Gothic church of **SAN NICOLÒ** has a unique wooden ceiling painted by a local priest who inscribed

T

the beams with excerpts from Scripture arranged in a rhythmical verse. SANTA PRASSEDE has a simple 14th-century exterior and subdued Baroque interior. Luther sojourned here en route to Rome. Just outside the city is SANTA MARIA DELLA CONSOLAZIONE, a Renaissance church now open only one day of the year. Its simple, serene structure, perhaps based on a design by Bramante, encourages reflection and contemplation as a means to serenity and peace.

TORCELLO

Mother and daughter, you behold them both in their widowhood—Torcello and Venice." (John Ruskin, *The Stones of Venice*). Parent city to Venice, Torcello rose in the 5th century as a refuge colony for the people of Altinum fleeing mainland invasions. It rose to become the busiest island in the lagoon, only to be overshadowed by Venice. It is now a peaceful and pleasant escape from its overcrowded "daughter." All that remains of its past glory echoes in the deserted remains of its cathedral and ruined edifices.

Following the mass exodus, Bishop Paolo Altinum transferred the bishopric of Altinum and its treasures, including the relics of St. Heliodorus, to Torcello in 639. The town prospered and gave rise to Venice—ensuring its own demise. Once a thriving center for wool manufacturing with a populous of 20,000, a malaria epidemic and growing Venetian supremacy in the 15th century left Torcello all but abandoned by the 17th century.

PLACES TO VISIT

One of the lagoon's oldest churches and tallest campaniles stand side by side; the cathedral of SANTA MARIA DELLA ASSUNTA (Our Lady of the Assumption) was begun in 639, and its detached square bell tower dates from the 11th to 12th centuries. Remains of the original 7th-century baptistery still stand before the facade.

Its foundation stone laid in 639, the cathedral aspired heavenward in decoration and design in the following centuries, undergoing enlargements in 824 and 1008. The interior decoration dates between the 11th and 13th centuries. Striking mosaics decorate the floor and wall surfaces, from the *"opus Alexandrinum"* pavement (11th century) to the Byzantine *Last Judgment* (11th–12th centuries) covering the west wall. Atop the elaborately paneled marble iconostasis (11th century) are local 15th-century paintings depicting the *Virgin and Apostles*. Above them hovers a wooden Gothic *Crucifix*.

In the central apse a Byzantine mosaic of the *Madonna with Christ Child* crowns the dome. The representation seems to have replaced an earlier mosaic, possibly executed at the same time as the mosaic of the *Apostles* directly beneath it. Beneath the golden dome and high altar is a Roman sarcophagus (3rd century) containing the relics of St. Heliodorus.

The relics of the early Christian martyr, Santa Fosca, were brought to Torcello before 1011 and enshrined in a church to which she gives her name. SANTA FOSCA was constructed in 1100 to incorporate an earlier structure and ground plan. The sparse and austere interior evokes serenity and contemplation.

The MUSEO DI TORCELLO (est. 1870) houses local archaeological and ecclesiastical remains. Its highlight is a 13th-century *Pala d'Oro* from the cathedral.

TORINO
(TURIN)

Industry, artistry, and culture intersect along the sprawling urban grid plan that has defined Turin since its origins. Known for its automobile industry, particularly the Fiat and Lancia factories, other industries include rubber, leather, chemical, and electrical plants. The city is also renowned for its chocolate and Vermouth. A multitude of museums with vast collections of paintings, sculpture, artillery, automotives, cinema, zoology, and Egyptology reveal the city's varied cultural interests. Stunning Baroque churches attest to the worldly city's spiritual pursuit. It was named a bishopric in 415 and rose to an archbishopric in 1510. Turin is home to the most controversial relic in Christendom, the Holy Shroud, also known as the Shroud of Turin.

Named after its founding settlers, the *Taurini,* Turin grew along the organized lines of a city grid plan established during its Roman colonization. Barbarian occupation included Lombard and Frankish rule. In 1046, the House of Savoy, through marriage between the daughter of the marchese of Turin and a son of the Savoia line, began a brief rule of the city. A short period of conflict and unrest ended in 1280, when the Savoy established supremacy. Its university was founded in 1404, during the Great Schism, by antipope Benedict XIII; in 1506, Erasmus became a Turin university graduate. Turin was named the capital of the duchy of Savoy in 1563. The city passed from Savoy to French hands until the 18th century. In 1861 it became the first capital of the united

T

Italy, only to lose the title four years later to Florence.

PLACES TO VISIT

The **CATHEDRAL OF SAN GIOVANNI BATTISTA,** dedicated to Turin's patron saint, houses the famed *Sacra Sindone* (Holy Shroud). The church, commissioned by Cardinal Domenico della Rovere and built between 1491–98, is the city's only Renaissance structure.

Two flights of black marble steps flanking the presbytery lead up to the *Chapel of the Holy Shroud* (1668–98), a Baroque jewel begun by Guarino Guarini. Also faced with black marble, the circular chapel is crowned with a six-tiered dome. At the center, the Holy Shroud sits encased in a silver casket. White marble funerary monuments (1842) dedicated to the members of the house of Savoy surround it. The powerful family received the shroud as a gift in 1453 and brought it to Turin in 1878. Their sepulchres now stand over the shroud in silent watch. The eternal Savoy vigil was interrupted on April 12, 1997, when fire swept Guarini's chapel and the nearby Royal Palace. Miraculously, the relic survived the flames.

The faithful believe the 14-foot-3-inch x 3-foot-7-inch linen cloth is the shroud Joseph of Arimathea used to wrap Christ upon his descent from the cross. It bears the image of a man with a bearded face and purportedly displays the markings from the crown of thorns, Christ's wounds, and his stigmata.

First documented in 1354, skeptics emerged almost immediately. The shroud was declared false by the bishop of Troyes in 1389. Clement VII (antipope, 1378–94) called it a "likeness" of the original shroud. However, the future church could not ignore the devout masses' faith in its originality and its obvious enigmatic appeal. In 1453 it was given to the House of Savoy and taken to Turin in 1878 after sustaining fire and water damage.

Its authenticity continues to spark debate. Scientific analysis has not revealed conclusive results, but carbon dating attributes the cloth to the 13th century. Is this the imprint of Christ? For believers, where science is uncertain, faith remains.

Guarino Guarini, an ingenious Baroque architect, enriched Turin with two ecclesiastical jewels. Built atop the site of a previous church called Santa Maria del Presepe, the church of **SAN LORENZO** was begun in 1634 by Emmanuel Philibert in gratitude for a prayer realized. Guarini completed the structure between 1668 and 1680. Its simple palacelike facade was built in the 19th century, making the structure indistinguishable from the neighboring palaces. Guarini's sumptuous interior is rich and complex. Decorating the many altars are Andrea Pozzo's *Crucifixion* (1678–79), a marble *Annunciation* (1670–80) by Giuseppe Maria and Giovanni Carlone, a *St. Lawrence* by Marcantonio Franceschini, and, atop the main altar, a carved relief by Carlo Antonio Tantardini depicting the *Vow of*

Emmanuel Philibert before the Battle of San Quintino.

The 12th-century church of Sant' Andrea was rededicated in the 17th century to the SANTUARIO DELLA CONSO-LATA, when Guarini transformed and enlarged the structure. The elaborate design includes an oval vestibule and hexagonal sanctuary that extends into four oval chapels. Do not miss the statues of *Queen Maria Teresa and Queen Maria Adelaide in Prayer* (1861) by Vincenzo Vela.

SAN DOMENICO (14th century) is Turin's only Gothic building. It was largely rebuilt in the late 18th century followed by an extensive facade renovation. Inside, visit Guercino's *Madonna of the Rosary* (1637) and the 16th-century venerated *Virgin.* The church's Gothic treasures are frescoes (1350–60) by the Maestro di San Domenico depicting the *Annunciation,* the *Virgin Enthroned with Child and St. Thomas,* the *Maestas Domini,* and the *Apostles.*

The Jesuit church, SANTI MARTIRI (1577), is dedicated to Torino's patron saints, the martyrs Solutor, Aventor, and Octavius. Its paintings include a *St. Paul* by Federico Zuccari and the *Virgin Mary and Titular Saints* (1765–66) by Gregorio Guglielmi. The small *Cappella della Pia Congregazione dei Bancheri e Mercanti* (Chapel of the Pious Congregation of Bankers and Merchants) is decorated with frescoes of *Paradise, Prophets, Sibyls, Biblical Scenes,* and wood carvings of the Doctors of the Church.

The impressive collection in the MUSEO CIVICO D'ARTE ANTICA features Piedmontese painting, sculpture, carvings, furniture, and other precious antiquities. Among its treasures are the *Virgin and Child* (1313–15) by Tino da Camaino, the *Life of St. Peter* (1410–1515) by Giacomo Jaquerio, the famed *Portrait of a Man* (1476) by Antonello da Messina, and a *St. Michael and the Demon* by Jacopo Pontormo.

The museum book collection includes the precious *Book of Hours* (1470) by Simon Marmion, a missal (1490–92) by Cardinal della Rovere, and the *Heures de Milan* (1380–1450) completed by Jan van Eyck.

The GALLERIA SABAUDA houses works acquired by the House of Savoy during their nine-century rule in Turin. The collection was first exhibited in 1832 and donated to the state in 1860.

The collection offers Piedmontese, Tuscan, Lombard, Flemish, and Dutch artists. A few of its numerous masterpieces are Fra Angelico's *Virgin and Child,* Fillipino Lippi's *Three Archangels and Tobias,* Danielle da Volterra's *Beheading of St. John the Baptist,* Bergognone's *St. Ambrose Preaching,* Gerolamo Savoldo's *Adoration of the Shepherds,* Jan van Eyck's *Stigmatization of St. Francis,* Hans Memling's *Passion of Christ,* a triptych by Jacques Iverny, Gaudenzio Ferrari's *Crucifixion,* Rogier Van der Weyden's *Visitation and Faithful in Adoration,* Veronese's *Supper in the House of Simon,* Guercino's *The Prodigal Son,* Orazio Gentilleschi's

T

Annunciation, and Peter Paul Rubens's *Deianira Tempted by the Fury.*

King Victor Amadeus II's crowning masterpiece is the BASILICA DI SUPERGA erected in thanksgiving to the Virgin to whom he prayed for deliverance from the French in 1706. His plea to the Virgin on September 6, 1706, was made as he surveyed his city from a nearby hilltop while the French and Spanish troops spoiled his city.

Commanding a view atop the mountain of Turin (10 kilometers outside Turin), the massive basilica was built by Filippo Juvarra (1717–31). The royal church, dedicated to the nativity of the Virgin Mary, houses the tombs of the kings. Its stunning sepulchres entomb Victor Amadeus II (d. 1732), Charles Albert (d. 1849), and others from the Savoy line. Also notice the marble frieze depicting the 1706 *Battle of Turin* by Cametti.

Behind the basilica a plaque commemorates the 1949 plane that crashed near the site and killed 31 people, including Turin's entire soccer team.

URBINO

Princely patronage in Urbino during the second half of the 15th century transformed the quiet town into an illustrious court and a center of military, humanist, and artistic activity. Set on a windy hill in the Marches region, Urbino existed solely on the area's poor resources and local industry until the Renaissance, when it thrived on its prince's military contracts and patronage. Urbino's "golden age" was a time of enlightened rule and cultivated art patronage that gained prestige throughout Europe. The court not only attracted the greatest painters, poets, and scholars of the time, but it also gave the world two of its native sons, Bramante and Raphael.

A visit to Urbino is an encounter with the legacy of an ideal Renaissance man. Federico da Montefeltro (1422–82), celebrated condottiere and benevolent prince, ruled Urbino from 1444 until his death and cultivated a court that harmonized secular and sacred endeavors. A military commander and learned man, he was celebrated as the model man, balancing the active and contemplative life. In 1474 Pope Sixtus IV named Federico duke of Urbino and made him *gonfaloniere* (captain of the papal army). His prowess, benevolence, and virtue also earned him international honors: from Edward IV of England, the Order of the Garter, and from Ferrante in Naples, the Order of the Ermine.

Federico devoted the great wealth he amassed in the art of war to the art of patronage, investing more money in art and architecture than any of his contemporaries. He was actively involved in his building designs and commissions, demanding they reflect the order, clarity, and dignity of his rule. Behind this great man was also a great woman; Battista Sforza was praised for her own political ability (practiced in her husband's absence), piety, and learning. She bore Federico eight daughters and one son, dying soon after the sole heir's birth in 1472. The heir, Guidobaldo, maintained the fame and atmosphere of his father's court and was celebrated in Baldassare Castiglione's *The Courtier* (1528).

PLACES TO VISIT

The heart of Urbino and of Federico's rule is the **PALAZZO DUCALE DA URBINO** (1465–79). Both a residence and a fortress, the twin-towered palace was Federico's political and social center that included court buildings, kitchens, stables, libraries, chapels, and gardens. The Dalmatian architect Luciano Laurana built the palace into the hillside for a defensive view of the surroundings and an aesthetic view of the main square before it. The inner courtyard provides a light and airy contrast to the somber facade. The combination of Corinthian pilasters and composite columns in the arcade are a model of proportion and harmony imitated in courts throughout Italy. A grand entrance leads from the entrance to the *piano nobile* (main floor above ground level) that included audience chambers and Federico's private rooms.

The **STUDIOLO** (1472–76) served as both a private study and a public wel-

coming room. Its decorative program proclaims Federico's humanist erudition, Christian devotion, and military accomplishments. Justus of Ghent decorated the upper walls with 28 portraits of learned men in two tiers, figures from antiquity and lay humanists on top and religious figures below. Interestingly, Dante and Petrarch are included among the religious men. Fourteen of these panels are originals; the rest are in the Louvre and have been replaced with sepia-colored copies. The lower wall below the portraits is decorated with illusionistic intarsia (panels of inlaid wood), possibly inspired by designs by Botticelli and Francesco di Giorgio. The intarsia depicts furniture, open and closed cupboards containing books, scientific and musical instruments, vegetal motifs, the theological virtues, and a portrait of Federico.

Directly below the studiolo are two barrel-vaulted chapels (c. 1474) respectively dedicated to God, the **CAPPELLA DEL PERDONO,** and to the Muses, the **TEMPIETTO DELLE MUSE.** They are decorated in the Albertian tradition with colored marble panels with classical columns framing the altar niche. The chapels and studiolo above them reflect the coexistence of the sacred and the secular and the harmonious marriage of humanism and Catholicism in Urbino's court and in its prince.

Two museums are housed within the palace. The **GALLERIA NAZIONALE DELLE MARCHE** displays a renowned collection of paintings including Piero

U

HUMANISM began in Italy in the second half of the 13th century. The term came from *studia humanitatis,* which denoted a liberal, literary education. In the late 1300s humanism denoted a specific course of studies which included rhetoric, grammar, poetry, and history.

The two earliest centers of humanism in Italy were Padua and Verona. In the 14th century the leader of the humanist movement was Francesco Petrarca (1304–74). The intellectual and cultural movement that developed from the study of classical Greek and Latin literature and culture helped give rise to the Renaissance. Although not incompatible with Christian belief, it emphasized human pursuits rather than religious interests.

della Francesca's *Flagellation of Christ* and *Madonna di Senigallia* and Raphael's *La Muta* (the Silent One). The *View of an Ideal City* (attributed to Luciano Laurana or Piero della Francesca) with its Albertian buildings and circular temple likely influenced Bramante, who created a similar structure in Rome. Roman stone inscriptions and archaeological artifacts can be found on the ground floor of the palace in the MUSEO ARCHEOLOGICO.

Visit RAPHAEL'S HOUSE to see the humble beginnings of the "divine one." Born in Urbino in 1483, Raffaelo Sanzio (known as Raphael) left the city after his father's death in 1494 to make his way to Rome and earthly glory. Raphael's father, Giovanni Santi, was a court painter whose works can be seen in the ducal palace and throughout the region. For a glimpse of a possible early work by Raphael, look to a fresco of the Madonna on a wall of his Urbino home. Up the hill beyond the artist's house stands a statue of Raphael, whose stone eyes gaze eternally at his native soil.

The ORATORIO DI SAN GIOVANNI BATTISTA is a small church decorated by two local brothers in 1416. Jacopo and Lorenzo Salimbeni's vision of the *Life of St. John the Baptist* and the *Crucifixion* is rarely viewed but worth the trip. Notice the number of dogs in the paintings; one can relate to the playful portrayal of our faithful friends.

End your visit to Urbino by paying your respects to the prince who is responsible for much of the splendor you've just seen. The TOMBS of Federico and his son Guidobaldo are in the church of SAN BENARDINO (1491) by Francesco di Giorgio. Allegedly, 30 years after Federico's death, his adopted grandson (Francesco Maria della Rovere) opened the duke's sealed tomb. Desiring a memento of his great ancestor, he tried to pull some hairs from the duke's chest; miraculously, they could not be extracted.

U

VENEZIA

(VENICE)

The ancient maxim of the Venetian government, *"Prima di tutto Veneziani, poi Cristiani"* (First above all Venetians, then Christians), reveals the common faith of the Venetian citizens in their own "serene" republic. La Serenissima was the embodiment of beauty, liberty, and wise government. In this mighty and cosmopolitan seaport, religion served the secular realm. The subordination of the Church to the State and the subjugation of religion to support the beliefs of the republic were the defining factors of Venetian consciousness. Venetians believe God chose their city and infused it with grace though their city's patron, St. Mark.

Venetian myth and history are inextricably linked. The lagoons surrounding Venice were first settled in A.D. 537/38. In the subsequent years the settlement was ruled by Byzantine emperors and protected by the exarch (a provincial governor) of Ravenna. The first doge (a doge is Italian dialect for the elected head of state in Venice and Genoa) was elected in 726 yet was still subordinate to Byzantine power. In the 9th century Venice rose to became a major commercial port. During this prosperous century the Venetians decided to steal the body of St. Mark

buried in Alexandria. With the success of the pious theft and St. Mark's remains secure in Venice, the Venetians replaced their city's patron St. Theodore (the symbolic link to Byzantium) with St. Mark and proclaimed their independence from the East. With the Evangelist as the new patron of the city, Venice was linked to the origins and spread of Christianity.

Venetian legend claims St. Mark stopped in the Venetian lagoons while preaching throughout Italy and formed an immediate bond to the area and its people. St. Peter supposedly sent St. Mark and a companion to preach in Northern Italy. They encountered a storm on their return to Rome and sought shelter in a Venetian lagoon. During their repose an angel came to St. Mark in a dream and said, *"Pax tibi, Marcae. Hic requiescet corpus tuum."* (Peace, Mark. Here your body will rest.) The angel told the evangelist that someday the Venetian settlers would build Mark's burial spot, and that God would grant them many gifts through the saint's intercession. The legend's many adaptations emphasize Venetian superiority, virtuosity, and piety. Through this legend, called the *praedestinato* (predestinate), Christianity came to Venice in the person of St. Mark.

V

The cult of St. Mark grew around the *praedestinato* and two other legends. The *translatio* (translation) is the legend of the theft of St. Mark's body in 828. Venetian ships blown off course sought shelter in Alexandria. Two merchants, Bruno da Malamocco and Rustico da Torcello, disembarked and befriended a monk and a priest who were members of the Christian church that housed St. Mark's body. Moslems threatened to destroy the church, so Bruno and Rustico identified St. Mark's remains by the odor of sanctity emanating from the tomb and absconded with the body. Upon arriving in Venice the two merchants presented the relics to the doge; this gift formed a permanent union between Venice's spiritual and political realms.

The cult of St. Mark combined religious and civic values, granting Venetians political authority given by God through St. Mark to the doge. The third legend, the *inventio* (invention), is the apparition of St. Mark. In 976, the church housing St. Mark's body burned. The saint's secret burial location was no long forgotten. Venetians erected a new church atop the site, and despite numerous searches, the body remained lost until 1094. The doge ordered a fast. The citizens' piety and obedience inspired a miracle; during High Mass on the third day of the fast, the ghost of St. Mark appeared and filled the church with a sweet aroma. The *inventio* symbolized the end of Venetian dependence on Byzantium and asserted St. Mark as the true patron of the city.

The autonomous city rose to international prestige and power and was granted a unique position as an impartial mediator in world affairs. In 1177 Venice arranged peace between the Holy Roman Emperor Frederick I and Pope Alexander III. Subsequently, the two universal authorities, the emperor and the pope, bestowed the gift of equality to the doge. Freedom from the emperor in temporal affairs and freedom from the pope in spiritual affairs granted Venetian citizens individual liberty.

In the 15th century the Turkish infidel invaded Italy. Venice escaped relatively unharmed and capitalized on its neighbor's losses. As a result, Pope Julius II formed a holy alliance and defeated Venice. However, the Venetians soon recuperated, presenting an indestructible and greatly admired stable and free republic.

Tension between Venice and Rome grew. On October 7, 1571, the Venetian fleets defeated the Turks at the Battle of Lepant. The Venetians defeated the enemies of Christendom. Instead of viewing the indomitable Venetians as defenders of the faith, the popes saw Venetian autonomy and glory as a horrible threat to Christendom. Venice continued to resist papal demands and assert their unique identity. Finally, in 1606, the doge accepted the rules set forth in the Counter-Reformation and agreed, in part, to be subordinate to the Church.

The end of the doge's power did not come through Rome and the pope but by way of France and Napoleon. On May 17, 1797, Doge Lodovico Manin was deposed, and decades of Venetian frivolity and opulence dethroned.

In 1866 Venice became part of the newly united Italy. No longer threatened by Turks or invading armies, today Venice thwarts even greater perils—thousands of tourists yearly, depopulation, pollution, and rising flood tides. Venice's undulating foundations, the murky lagoon waters, threaten to swallow the city whole.

PLACES TO VISIT

The heart of Venice and the core of Venetian faith and politics lie in PIAZZA SAN MARCO. The often rain-drenched or, when sunny, pigeon-filled square accommodates Venice's principal church and the doge's palace. The Basilica San Marco, the Palazzo Ducale, the Procuratie Vecchie, the Torre del' Orologio, the Procurate Nuove, the campanile, and the library face the square and follow a colonnade that opens out onto the waterfront and the ancient Venetian harbor.

Originally the doge's private chapel the BASILICA DI SAN MARCO became Venice's cathedral in 1807. Divinely instituted and intimately linked to the affairs of state, the basilica is the eternal symbol of Venetian wealth, power, history, and faith. The church is an apostolic reliquary and a storehouse for art glorifying Venetian history and the interconnectedness of state and religion. In 832 a church modeled on the Church of the Holy Apostles in Constantinople was built to house the newly acquired relics of St. Mark. Fire ravaged the church in 976, and the subsequent structure was consecrated in 1094.

The light and shadow that fall on the intricate facade are as much a part of the rich ornamentation as the delicate columns, tabernacles, and sculptures. A bas-relief on the lower level depicts heroes and warrior saints, Hercules laboring among Saints Demetrius, and George. Separating the mythical god and the soldier saints are the Virgin and the Angel Gabriel. The facade's sole original mosaic sits atop the door of Sant' Alipio and depicts the *Transfer of the Body of St. Mark to Venice* (1260–70). Above the central doorway is a mosaic of the *Last Judgment* (1836) and delicately carved arches depicting Venetian Vocations, the Months, the Zodiac, and the Virtues.

Seeking atonement, or rather, forced to submit, Holy Roman Emperor Frederick I Barbarossa knelt before Pope Alexander III in the basilica's atrium. A red marble slab marks the spot of supplication. The surrounding 13th-century mosaics illustrate stories from the Old Testament, the world before Christ's grace. The basilica's earliest mosaics above the central doorway depict the Madonna with the apostles and four evangelists.

Inside the church, glittering mosaics illustrate the New Testament, a world graced by Christ and the triumph of his

Church. Witness to religious and political ceremony, the mosaics conferred glory on the Venetian church and state. Golden scenes depict the *Ascension of the Virgin, Christ's Passion, Christ Enthroned between the Madonna and St. Mark, Agony in the Garden, Old Testament Prophets, The Life of Christ* and *The Life of St. Mark.*

The Life of St. John the Baptist decorates the 14th-century Baptistery walls. Housed within are two baptismal fonts, one designed by Jacopo Sansovino (1545) and another that marks Sansovino's tomb (d. 1570). The central 16th-century font is used today, while the inscribed granite tomb slab, transported from Tyre in 1126 and used for baptism by total immersion, was employed by priests from the earlier St. Mark's. Legend claims Christ spoke atop this stone. The baptistery leads into the Cappella Zen (1504–22), built for Cardinal Giovanni Battista Zen, whose money and state contributions bought him a funerary chamber within the church.

Flanking the bronze and silver cross, the Virgin, St. John, and the twelve apostles stand vigil atop the iconostasis (screen). Built in 1394, the figures provide an eternal watch over St. Mark's remains buried in the crypt. When the first church burned in 976, many thought St. Mark's holy relics were lost. A thorough search revealed nothing. Miraculously on June 25, 1094, while parishioners prayed for intervention to find the remains, St. Mark's arm broke through the stone to reveal his hiding place.

The sun seems to rise behind the main altar and emanate from the Pala D'Oro (10th–13th centuries), a golden altarpiece encrusted with 1300 pearls, 300 sapphires, 90 amethysts, 75 balas-rubies, 15 rubies, four topazes, two cameos, and numerous emeralds. Its bejeweled scenes depict *Christ's Passion, The Dormition of the Virgin, Christ Pantocrator,* and scenes from the *Life of the Evangelists.*

The champion of victory and the protectress of Venice is safeguarded in the Cappella della Madonna Nicopoeia (Nicopoeia means maker of victory). The icon of the *Virgin Nicopoeia* (1204) is a venerated image of the victory-working Madonna that led processions of Venetians into battle and onto victory and into church and onto heavenly glory.

The first Venetian Renaissance works, mosaics depicting the *Life of the Virgin* (1430–50), decorate the Cappella della Madonna dei Mascoli. The chapel, dedicated to the Madonna of males, was named in the 17th century for the male confraternity that worshiped within.

The TESORO DI SAN MARCO (treasury) contains Byzantine icons and precious chalices that accompany 12th- and 13th-century reliquaries and patens (a paten is a shallow plate for the bread of the Eucharist). These precious works are the few items that escaped Napoleon's rapacious grasp.

The PALAZZO DUCALE (Ducal Palace) is the home of the doge and magistrates of the Republic. Juxtaposed

V

with the Basilica of San Marco, the palace is the physical symbol of secular power, the reason for Venetian serenity. Built in the 9th century and renovated in the 14th and 15th centuries, the sumptuously decorated palace proclaims the doge's omnipotence through secular and sacred subjects.

The role of a good and just government, one that punishes immorality, defends righteousness, and upholds virtue, is suggested in the facade decoration. Carved capitals depicting the *Drunkenness of Noah, Adam and Eve,* and the *Judgment of Solomon* exemplify the need for a just sovereign who rules with the virtues of *Fortitude, Justice, Temperance,* and *Charity* personified in statues adorning the palace entrance, the Porta della Carta (1438–43).

Atop the landing of the Scala dei Giganti (Staircase of Giants) are two colossal statues of *Neptune and Mars* by Sansovino (1554). Protectors of Venice, the serene and majestic ruler of the sea and god of war stand above the spot where Venice's earthly protector, the doge, is crowned.

Sumptuous rooms in the Appartamento Ducale (the doge's private apartments) decorated by Venetian masters depict *Christ Mourned* by Giovanni Bellini, *Twelve Philosophers* by Tintoretto and Veronese, and *St. Christopher* by Titian.

Magistrates and government administrators convened on the top floor. The famed decoration includes ceiling and wall paintings by Tintoretto, particularly his *Bacchus and Ariadine Crowned by Venus,* Veronese's *Rape of Europa,* and Bassano's *Return of Jacob to His Family.* Also note Titian's *Doge Grimiani Kneeling before Faith as St. Mark looks On* (1576, completed after Titian's death) and Jacopo Tintoretto's *Venice Seated Among the Gods and Receives the Gifts of the Sea* (1581–84). Descend to the second floor and visit the remaining rooms. Masterful works include the *Coronation of the Virgin* by Guarineto (1365–67), *Paradise* by Domenico Tintoretto (1588–92), and *Venice Surrounded by Gods and Crowned by Victory* by Veronese (1588).

Two bronze Moors sound each hour from the TORRE DELL'OROLOGIO (clock tower) built by Mauro Codussi from 1496 to 1499. The figures are actually shepherds who after years of exposure to the elements have darkened. The astronomical clock tracks the sun and moon through the signs of the zodiac. During the celebration of the Ascension and the Epiphany, when the hour tolls, figures of the two Magi pop out of doors that flank the statue of the Madonna and bow before her.

St. Mark's CAMPANILE (bell tower) collapsed without warning on July 14, 1902. The structure, begun in the 9th century and completed in the 12th century, was rebuilt and reopened on April 25, 1912. An angel crowns the structure. Two lions and two figures representing Venice stand beneath the figure of Justice. While the top of the tower offers visitors a fabulous view, Galileo

V

used the peak in 1609 to gaze at the stars through his telescope. The *Loggetta* (1537–46) at the tower's base by Sansovino includes bronze statues of Athena, Apollo, Mercury, and Peace.

Repeated bloodshed in the Gothic church of SANTO STEFANO (14th–15th centuries) necessitated six reconsecrations. Today the fear of death strikes only tax-plagued citizens entering the adjacent monastery, which was transformed into the Ministry of Finance in 1810.

The exceptional wood ceiling within, constructed by Fra Giovanni degli Eremitani (a member of the church's founding order, the Eremitani Agostiniani) imitates the form of a ship's hull. Among the numerous funerary monuments within the vast interior are a monument to *Giacomo Surian* (1694) depicting the physician kneeling before the Virgin, the tomb slab of *Giovanni Gabrieli,* a Venetian composer and church organist, the tomb slab of *Doge Francesco Morosini*, the Renaissance tomb of *Giacomo Surian* (1493), and Antonio Canova's funeral stele of *Giovanni Falier* (c. 1808).

Three dynamic canvases by Jacopo Tintoretto in the sacristy depict the *Agony in the Garden, Christ Washing the Disciples' Feet,* and the *Last Supper* (c. 1580). They hang alongside Paolo Veneziano's painted *Crucifix* (1348).

Outside is Venice's tallest bell tower, the leaning *Campanile* of Santo Stefano. Begun in the 15th century and completed in the next century, the tilt-ing tower looks as though it could topple at any moment.

Jacopo Sansovino redesigned the church of SAN ZULIANO (Venetian for San Giuliano) in 1553. Founded in 829 and rebuilt in the 12th century, the new structure glorified its patron Tommaso Rangone, a wealthy physician from Ravenna, who paid for the entire church reconstruction. Exalted in a bronze statue above the church entrance, he is shown in his study among his books and spheres.

While the scholar Giuliano is honored on the church facade as a worldly intercessor, within the church his patron saint, St. Giuliano, is extended the glory of heaven. A vision of the *Apotheosis of St. Julian* (1585) by Palma the Younger seems to hover, weightless, above the simple rectangular interior. The richly decorated church houses numerous paintings including Paolo Veronese's *Pietà with Three Saints,* Palma's *Virgin of the Assumption,* and, at the high altar, *Coronation of the Virgin* by Girolamo da Santacroce flanked by Antonio Zanchi's *Miracle of St. Julian* and *Martyrdom of St. Julian.*

Before the church of SAN SALVATORE is a tabernacle marking the spot where Pope Alexander III slept *al fresco* when he secretly visited Venice in 1177. Had he visited five centuries later perhaps the pope would have sneaked into the church begun by Giorgio Spavento in 1507 and completed by 1534 by Sansovino. The pope would have experi-

V

enced a most harmonious slumber under the elegant domes and barrel vaults within San Salvatore. The church's most notable monument to eternal slumber is the *Monument to Doge Francesco Venier* (1556–61) with statues of *Hope* and *Charity,* two of the three theological virtues (1 Corinthians 13:13), sculpted by Jacopo Sansovino in his late seventies. Alessandro Vittoria contributed two statues, patrons of the sick and plague stricken *St. Roch* and *St. Sebastian,* to the church circa 1600. Three luminous paintings add richness to the serene interior; Titian's *Annunciation* (1566), Titian's *Transfiguration* (1560) above the high altar, and the *Supper at Emmaus* attributed to a follower of Giovanni Bellini.

SANTA MARIA GLORIOSA DEI FRARI, the glorious church built by the Franciscan Minorite friars, is no minor edifice. Founded in 1250, the original church was torn down in 1330, and a new and grander structure was completed in 1492. Its grandeur is one of spaciousness, simplicity, and sacred stillness—an ideal setting for Franciscan friars to minister to a large congregation. However, the august interior is not without stunning paintings and serene sepulchres.

The *Coro dei Frati* (1468), the monk's choir, divides the nave and the transept. The 124 choir stalls were carved and decorated by Marco Cozzi and Lorenzo and Cristoforo Canozzi. Pietro Lombardo's stone screen depicts a *Crucifixion with the Virgin and St. John the*

Evangelist with Reliefs of the Apostles, Saints, and Prophets. Along the left side of the nave is the monument to Jacopo Pesaro (d. 1547), bishop of Paphos, who commanded the Venetian navy in a victory against the Turks in 1502. Above the bishop's effigy is Titian's *Madonna di Ca' Pesaro* (1519–26). The vibrant composition depicts the Madonna and Child with saints surrounded by members of the Pesaro family. The kneeling armored crusader is Bishop Pesaro, who presents Turkish converts to St. Peter. The Canova monument to Titian, a pyramidal tomb, was designed in 1794 and completed after Antonio Canova's death in 1822. The Carrara marble actually encases Canova's heart. Titian is buried directly across the way in a tomb designed by Canova's followers.

Many masterpieces adorn the numerous chapels in the transept. Among them is a polyptych by Bartolomeo Vivarini depicting the *Virgin and Child with Saints* (1482), a wooden statue of *St. John the Baptist* by Donatello, a *Madonna and Saints* by Bernardino Licinio, and a triptych of *St. Mark* (1474) by Bartolomeo Vivarini. In the sacristy is Giovanni Bellini's celebrated *Virgin and Child with Saints Nicholas, Peter, Benedict, and Paul* (1488) and Nicolò Frangipane's *Pietà.* In the main altar is Titian's *Assumption* (1516–18), a revolutionary and dramatic work, vibrantly illustrating the apocryphal story from the *Golden Legend.* "The soul came to the body of Mary, and issued

V

gloriously out of the tomb, and thus was received in the heavenly chamber, and a great company of angels with her."

The clinking of wine glasses at a dinner table in Italy is often accompanied with the toast "Salute!" meaning both health and salvation; the church of SANTA MARIA DELLA SALUTE (1631–81) is the Venetian toast to their protectress the Virgin Mary, a thanksgiving for deliverance from the plague. Baldassare Longhena won the commission to build the structure one year after the plague claimed a third of the Venetian populace, almost 50,000 citizens. He planned the church in the form of a crown suitable for the Queen of Heaven, thus fulfilling a vow made by the Senate should the Virgin deliver Venice from the epidemic. Atop the church, a statue of the Virgin Mary, baton in hand, commands the lagoon.

On November 21 the Festa della Salute, the feast day of the presentation of the Virgin, Venetians flock to the church in procession and celebration. Inside the church, on the pavement, is the inscription *"unde origo inde salus"* (whence the origin, thence the salvation and health), referring to the Virgin's protection of the lagoon's original inhabitants. Throughout the church, decorations celebrate the Virgin. Of particular interest are the Byzantine icon (12th–13th centuries) depicting the *Madonna and Child* and the masterful statue by Juste le Corte depicting the *Virgin Mary with Christ, Casting the Plague from Venice.* The decrepit old woman represents the fleeing plague.

Numerous important paintings are housed within the sacristy. Titian's *St. Mark Enthroned Between Saints Cosmas, Damian, Roch, and Sebastian* was painted to commemorate an earlier plague from 1510. This votive acknowledges St. Mark's protection aided by the efforts of the two plague saints, Roch and Sebastian, and two miracle-working doctors, Cosmas and Damian. Three other Titians include *Cain and Abel, The Sacrifice of Abraham,* and *David and Goliath.* Also note Jacopo Tintoretto's *Marriage at Cana* (1561).

Founded in 1350 and originally dedicated to St. Christopher, the church of the MADONNA DELL' ORTO was rechristened in 1377 after a miraculous statue of the Madonna and Child was discovered in a nearby garden ("orto" in Italian). The rich 15th-century terracotta facade and delicate tracery windows define the Venetian Gothic. Notice the exterior statues of the *Apostles, The Madonna and Gabriel,* and *St. Christopher.* This is Jacopo Tintoretto's parish church. The simple interior houses numerous works by this famed parishioner, including his humble tomb. Its numerous chapels are richly decorated, like a garden in full bloom. Tintoretto's many canvasses include the massive *Worship of the Golden Calf* and *Last Judgment* (both c. 1546), his theatrical *Presentation of the Virgin at the Temple* (1551) in the sacristy, and the

V

painting of *Agnes Raising Licinius* (c. 1579) in the Contarini Chapel. Cima de Conegliano's *St. John the Baptist Between Saints Peter, Mark, Jerome, and Paul* (1493) and Giovanni Bellini's *Madonna and Child* (1478) are celebrated Renaissance masterpieces.

Rivalry between the Mendicant orders in Venice is expressed in their respective churches; SAN ZANIPOLO or church of SANTI GIOVANNI E PAOLO is the Dominican response to the Franciscan church of I Frari. Both edifices are among the first large-scale Gothic churches built in Venice. Begun in 1246 and consecrated in 1430, the church faces a prominent square unrivalled by the square surrounding the Franciscan church. Adjacent to San Zanipolo is the splendid Scuola di San Marco; its ornamental facade closes off the piazza and faces the grand Colleoni Monument, which forms a third "wall" to frame the square. The monument to the condottiere (mercenary) Bartolomeo Colleoni (1400–1475) fulfills a demand made when he bequeathed his fortune to the state; the republic could only receive the money if they allowed his statue to be erected in Piazza San Marco. It was not common practice for Venetians to erect such statues, let alone in their most prominent square. However, the bequest was substantial and, much in need of the money, the Venetians convinced themselves that Colleoni desired his statue to stand in front of the Scuola di San Marco, not in the saint's main square.

The dilemma resolved and the money in hand, Andrea del Verrocchio began work on a grand equestrian statue in 1481, which was completed after his death by Alessandro Leopardi. Colleoni standing erect in his stirrups, a fierce and glorious general marching toward earthly and heavenly glory, is an immortal hero eternalized in a masterful Renaissance work.

The funeral church of the doges since the 15th century, San Zanipolo entombs 25 doges. The doorway of the unfinished facade is framed with Greek marble columns and reliefs of the Virgin and Angel Gabriel. Inside, numerous glorious sepulchres by the hands of the Lombardo family include the monument to *Doge Pietro Mocenigo* (d. 1476) by Pietro Lombardo and his sons (1476–81) which depicts the doge, hero of Venice, born aloft by three warriors supporting his sarcophagus and representing the ages of Man; the monument to *Doge Pasquale Malipiero* (d. 1462) is an early work by Pietro with a delicately carved dead Christ; the monument of *Doge Giovanni Mocenigo* (d. 1485) by Tullio (1500–10); the tomb of *Doge Nicolò Marcello* (d. 1474) by Pietro; and the monument of *Doge Andrea Vendramin* (d.1478) by Tullio and Antonio (1492–95), which depicts the doge accompanied by warriors and allegorical figures. Two other exceptional tombs include the monument to *Doge Marco Corner* (d. 1368), which includes statues of the Virgin and Saints carved and signed by

V

Nino Pisano, and the monument to *Doge Antonio Venrier* (d. 1400) by Paolo dalle Masegne.

San Zanipolo contains many sumptuous paintings. Giovanni Bellini contributed a polyptych of *St. Vincent Ferrer* with a *Pietà and Annunciation* (c. 1465), a *St. Dominic in Glory* (1727) by Giovanni Battista Piazzetta, and Lorenzo Lotto's altarpiece the *Charity of St. Anthony* (1542). The Rosary Chapel, built to commemorate the Battle of Lepanto, includes ceiling paintings by Paolo Veronese moved to the church from the deconsecrated church of the Umiltà in 1867. The canvasses depict *The Annunciation, The Assumption, The Adoration of the Shepherds, The Adoration of the Magi,* and *The Nativity.*

Set on the Island of Giudecca, which refers to a Middle Age settlement of Jews ("giudei") or to the Italian word meaning judgment ("giudicato"), is the church IL REDENTORE, the "redeemer" or "savior." Built in thanksgiving for deliverance from a plague that crippled Venice from 1576 and killed over 45,000 Venetians, the church provides the finale for the Festival of the Redentore, held yearly on the third Sunday in July (observing the day the plague was officially declared over). The doge once led a majestic pageant through the streets and canals of Venice to the church; today the festival is met by throngs of Venetians out on their boats floating under the fireworks and eating "mulberries of the Redeemer," the *mori del Redentore.* One of his greatest churches,

Palladio built the edifice between 1577 and 1592.

The harmonious structure is based on mathematical ratios, the result of which is balance, proportion, and beauty. The decoration emphasizes the role of Christ's suffering in humankind's redemption. Inside the church, above the door upon entering, is a plaque inscribed with the vow made by the doge for his city on September 8, 1576, to erect a church if the plague should pass. Significant works within include Francesco Bassano's *Nativity,* a *Baptism of Christ* by Veronese's followers, a *Flagellation of Christ* by Jacopo Tintoretto's followers, Palma the Younger's *Deposition,* Bassano's *Resurrection,* and Tintoretto's *Deposition.* In the sacristy notice Paolo Veronese's *Baptism of Christ,* which includes the painting's two donors and a *Madonna in Adoration of the Child and Two Angels* by Alvise Vivarini.

The church of SAN GIORGIO MAGGIORE (1566–1610) dominates the Island of San Giorgio Maggiore (St. George Major). Until 982 when the islet was transferred to Benedictine hands, this small island standing across from St. Mark's Square was originally known as the Isle of Cypresses. The island's original church dates 790 and was destroyed to erect the first Benedictine church on the site in the 10th century. Originally dedicated to St. George and St. Stephen, this church crumbled in the earthquake of 1223. The subsequent Benedictine complex was rebuilt in the 15th century.

The church was designed by Palladio and completed after the architect's death. Modeled on a classical temple and the building principles of ancient Rome and Vitruvius, the edifice exudes sacred and structural harmony. Space and light fill the church. Masterpieces adorning the chapels and altars include numerous works by Jacopo Tintoretto: the *Martyrdom of Saints Cosmas and Damian, The Coronation of the Virgin, The Deposition* (1594), *The Last Supper* (1594), and *The Gathering of Manna* (1594). The latter two are complementary pieces seen by parishioners participating in the Eucharist: the Israelites lived in the desert for 40 years nourished only with manna, and its significance parallels communion, "Moses said to them, 'It is the bread the LORD has given you to eat" (Exodus 16:15); the Last Supper is the basis for communion, instituted by Christ. Notice Jacopo Bassano's *Adoration of the Shepherds,* Sebastiano Ricci's *Virgin Enthroned,* and Vittore Carpaccio's *St. George and the Dragon.*

The adjacent monastery once housed Cosimo de' Medici and was the site of the Conclave that elected Pope Pius VII (1799–1800). It now houses the Giorgio Cini Foundation, an organization dedicated to preserving and studying Venetian culture. The Chiostro Palladiano (1579–1646), the Palladian cloister, was designed by Palladio and completed after his death. The Chiostro dei Cipressi (1516–40), the cloister of the Cypresses, is by Giovanni and Andrea Buora. The monumental stairway leads up to the library (1643–44), both designed by Baldassare Longhena, that houses 100,000 art historical texts. Within the refectory, also by Palladio, is Tintoretto's *Marriage of the Virgin.*

For those seeking churches rife with masterful paintings, the following consecrated ground cannot be missed. The Jesuit church I GESUATI (1726–43) or Santa Maria del Rosario, contains ceiling frescoes by Giambattista Tiepolo depicting the *Life of St. Dominic* (1737–39), a painting of the *Three Saints* (1784) by the same artist depicting the *Virgin with Saints Rose, Catherine of Siena, and Agnes of Montepulciano,* a *Crucifixion* by Tintoretto, and Piazzetta's masterpiece depicting *Saints Vincent Ferrer, Hyacinth, and Lodovico Betrando* (1738). The CARMINI (14th–17th centuries) or Santa Maria del Carmelo, was founded by the Carmelite order in the 1300s. Inside, 24 paintings illustrate the history of the order. Notice Cima de Conegliano's *Adoration of the Shepherds with Saints Helena and Catherine, Tobias, and the Guardian Angel* (c. 1509), Francesco di Giorgio Martini's *Deposition* (1474), and Lorenzo Lotto's *Saints Nicholas, John the Baptist, and Lucy* (1529). SAN SEBASTIANO (1505–48) is a shrine to the memory of Paolo Veronese (d. 1588). The artist lived nearby; his celebrated frescoes and canvases adorn the church, and his tomb stands near the presbytery. Veronese's most notable contributions

V

include ceiling frescoes illustrating the *Story of Esther* (1555–56) and the *Madonna and Child with St. Sebastian* (c. 1570). Veronese also designed the church organ and decorated its wood panels. In 639, disguised as a beautiful woman, the Virgin Mary appeared to St. Magnus, who in turn built SANTA MARIA FORMOSA (Latin for both beautiful and buxom) to commemorate his vision and honor the beautiful Virgin. Rebuilt in the 12th and 15th centuries, its prized artworks include a triptych of the *Madonna of Mercy* (1473) by Bartolomeo Vivarini and a vibrant altarpiece by Palma the Elder depicting *St. Barbara with Saints* (1523). Palma's St. Barbara is both beautiful and buxom, a true *formosa*. SANTA MARIA DEI MIRACOLI (1481–89) enshrines a miraculous and much venerated Renaissance image of the Virgin Mary (1408). A precious jewel, the delicately carved and elegantly decorated church contains a beautifully carved choir by Pietro and Tullio Lombardo and a *Virgin and Child* by Palma the Younger. SAN ZACCARIA (1444–1515) houses the relics of St. John the Baptist's father, St. Zacharias. Among its remarkable artworks are Giovanni Bellini's *Madonna and Christ Enthroned with Angels Playing Musical Instruments and Saints* (signed and dated 1505), Tintoretto's *Birth of St. John the Baptist*, Tiepolo's *Flight into Egypt*, Palma the Elder's *Madonna and Saints*, vault frescoes (1442) signed and dated by Andrea del Castagno, and three altar

paintings (1443) by Antonio Vivarini and Giovanni d'Alemagna. SAN FRANCESCO DELLA VIGNA (1534) is built atop a vineyard *(vigna)* bequeathed to the Franciscans in 1253. Inside notice Fra Antonio da Negroponte's *Madonna and Child Enthroned* (1465), a *Holy Family with Saints John the Baptist, Anthony the Abbot, and Catherine* by Paolo Veronese, and the *Virgin and Child* by Giovanni Bellini.

Magnificent artworks embellish the majestic two-story palaces of Venice's numerous SCUOLE. The *scuola* is not a school but a devotional confraternity for laymen usually of similar ancestry and drawn from the same craft or trade. It was the middle-class substitute for political activity. Men gathered to perform and organize charity works and to serve the sick. The *scuola's* religious and humanitarian aims were not subject to Church authority but to state control. By the 15th century the *scuole grande* (major schools) had become wealthy institutions, administering to its members' moral, spiritual, social, and economic needs. The *scuole* mirrored civic government, and their meeting houses did not resemble churches or monasteries, but the doge's palace. The houses followed a standard plan: a large hall on the ground floor, a chapter hall directly above it, and an adjoining *albergo* or boardroom for the officers. Painted narrative cycles often adorned the second floor, and their art patronage was a statement of pride, duty, and devotion to the Venetian state.

A confraternity of flagellants founded the SCUOLA DI SAN GIOVANNI EVANGE-LISTA in 1261. Napoleon suppressed the community; today its meeting house is used for periodic exhibitions. Inside, Mauro Codussi's great double staircase (1498) leads up to the salon and a wealth of significant paintings. Ceiling decoration by Giuseppe Angeli, Gaspare Diziani, Jacopo Marieschi, Jacopo Guarana, and Giandomenico Tiepolo depicts *Scenes from the Apocalypse* (1760). On the walls 16th-century paintings by Domenico Tintoretto, Sante Peranda, Andrea Vicentino, and Cignaroli illustrate the *Life of St. John the Evangelist*. In the Oratory of the Cross a gilt silver reliquary holds a piece of the True Cross brought from Cypress in 1379.

Founded in 1478 during a plague epidemic, the SCUOLA GRANDE DI SAN ROCCO procured the relics of this famed patron saint of plagues in 1485. The Scuola boasts a celebrated cycle of over 50 paintings by Jacopo Tintoretto. According to legend, a devout and fiercely independent Tintoretto gained the commission through bribery. In 1564 artists submitted designs for depicting the *Glorification of St. Roch*. Tintoretto won the competition by completing and hanging a painted panel instead of simply presenting drawings. On the condition he be awarded the commission, he also offered to donate the piece. Working alone, Tintoretto completed the commission 23 years later; his canvases decorated the walls and ceiling of the chapter house.

The cycle relates to the life and teachings of St. Roch; patron saint of the plague, he protected and nursed the sick. Roch died in prison after recounting how he miraculously survived the plague. On the prison cell floor near the saint's dead body was the inscription, "All those who are stricken by the plague and pray for help through the intercession of St. Roch, the servant of God, shall be healed." The canvasses in the Sala Grande depict Old and New Testament stories: the ceiling paintings represent *Moses Bringing Forth Water from the Rock, Manna from Heaven, Adam and Eve, God Appearing to Moses, Pillar of Fire in the Desert, Jonah and the Whale, Ezekiel's Vision, Jacob's Ladder, Sacrifice of Isaac, Elisha Multiplying the Loaves, Elijah Fed by an Angel,* and the *Passover Feast;* the wall paintings illustrate *St. Roch, St. Sebastian, The Adoration of the Shepherds, The Baptism of Christ, The Resurrection, The Agony in the Garden, The Last Supper, The Miracle of the Loaves and Fishes, The Resurrection of Lazarus, The Ascension, The Pool of Bethesda,* and *The Temptation.* The altarpiece depicts the *Vision of St. Roch.*

Tintoretto also decorated the Sala dell'Albergo between 1564 and 1566. His *St. Roch in Glory* hovers in the ceiling. Also notice the dramatic *Crucifixion* opposite his *Christ Before Pilate, Crowning of Thorns,* and *Way to Calvary.*

In the Salone Terreno are eight more Tintoretto canvases (1583–87): *The Annunciation, The Epiphany, The Flight into Egypt, The Slaughter of the Innocents,*

V

217

St. Mary Magdalene, St. Mary Egiziaca, The Circumcision and *The Assumption.*

The SCUOLA GRANDE DI SAN MARCO (1487–95) has an unusual illusionistic facade by Pietro Lombardo, Giovanni Buora, and Mauro Codussi with *trompe d'oeil* panels by Tullio and Antonio Lombardo. The confraternity of St. Mark now houses Venice's civic hospital. Inside notice Tintoretto's *St. Ursula* and Veronese's *Crucifixion with Madonna and St. John.*

In 1451 Venice's Dalmatian community founded the SCUOLA DI SAN GIORGIO DEGLI SCHIAVONI. Vittore Carpaccio's works decorate the interior (1502–8). The first paintings are the three Dalmatian patron saints, *St. George, St. Jerome,* and *St. Trifone.* Following the portraits are *St. George and the Dragon, The Triumph of St. George, St. George Baptizing the Gentiles, The Miracle of St. Trifone, The Lion and St. Jerome, The Funeral of St. Jerome,* and *St. Augustine's Vision of St. Jerome's Death.*

THE DEBATE OVER RELIGIOUS ART

As early as the reign of Pope Gregory the Great (d. 604), religious art was established as the "Bible of the Illiterate." Through the Middle Ages and the Renaissance, the Church affirmed that religious images intensified devotion. The Church believed that the faithful were more easily moved to piety at the sight of religious images than they were by listening to sermons. Subsequently, controversy arose over what the criteria should be for images placed in the house of the Lord.

Protestant Reformers were alarmed at the growth of idolatry in Christian worship and wished to ban images in churches entirely. Calvin believed worship defined Christianity, and only Scripture should determine the nature and content of worship. Because the second commandment forbade humans to make any image, Reformers discouraged art in the church and worship.

However, at the last session of the Council of Trent (1563), in rebuttal to the Protestant position, the Catholic bishops vigorously reaffirmed the use of religious art. Roman Catholics asserted that the Church's use of images was not contrary to God's second commandment because the Ten Commandments only applied to the Old Law (i.e., the law before the birth of Christ). The Council of Trent did stress the need for decorum in images; that the figures, gestures, costume, activities, and surroundings should be suitable to the subject matter. Further, the execution of all works created for the Church was to be supervised and approved by a bishop.

Founded in 1807 and open to the public in 1817, the **GALLERIA DEL'ACCADEMIA** houses important Venetian works from the 14th century to 18th century. Most notable among the endless halls of stunning works are Paolo Veneziano's *Coronation of the Virgin;* Giovanni Bellini's *Sacred Conversation,* his *Pietà,* his *Madonna and Child with Saints Paul and George,* his *Madonna and Child with Saints Catherine and Mary Magdalene,* and his *Madonna and Child Blessing;* Giorgione's *La Tempesta;* Paris Bordone's *Fishermen Presenting St. Mark's Ring to the Doge;* Palma the Elder's *Holy Family and Two Saints;* Veronese's *Christ in the House of Levi;* Tintoretto's *Transport of the Body of St. Mark* and his *St. Mark Liberating a Slave;* Titian's *Pietà;* Vivarini's *Nativity with Saints;* Carpaccio's *Cure of a Lunatic* and his *Legend of St. Ursula;* and finally, Titian's *Presentation of the Virgin.*

The Venice's Golden Palace, the **CA' D'ORO** (1422–40), houses a splendid art collection worth more than the gold that once coated the exterior of the palace. Originally the palace roof, capitals and statues were gilt in gold, and the structure glittered in the sunlit lagoon. While the facade's delicate tracery and ornament remains, its golden face is lost—fortunately, its art collection still sparkles like an untarnished jewel.

The collection includes the gallery bequeathed by Giorgio Franchetti, who donated his paintings to the state in 1916 to be housed in the Golden Palace whose restoration in 1894 was possible only through his generous funding. The collection's exceptional sculptural and painted works include Bartolomeo Bon's figures for a wellhead depicting *Charity, Justice, and Fortitude,* Mantegna's *St. Sebastian,* Antonio Vivarini's *Passion of Christ,* Andrea Briosco's bronze *St. Martin and the Beggar,* Carpaccio's *Annunciation* and *Transit of the Virgin,* Luca Signorelli's *Flagellation,* Biagio d'Antonio and Antoniazzo Romano's *Madonna in Adoration of the Child with Two Angels,* and a series of frescoes by Pordenone taken from the cloister of Santo Stefano depicting the *Expulsion from Paradise, Christ Appearing to Mary Magdalene,* and *Christ and the Samaritan.*

The **MUSEO CIVICO CORRER** offers a glimpse of Venetian history through paintings, sculpture, and important historical documents. Bequeathed to the city by Teodoro Correr (1750–1830), the collection opened to the public in 1836. On display in the historical collection are the doge's regalia and the military's armor alongside other curio that brings to life Venetian history from its founding to present day. Highlights in the chronologically arranged painting gallery are Cosimo Tura's *Pietà;* Antonello da Messina's *Pietà;* Giovanni Bellini's *Transfiguration, Pietà,* and *Madonna and Child;* Jacopo Bellini's *Crucifixion;* and Carpaccio's *Two Venetian Ladies* (known as "The Courtesans").

V

VOLTERRA

Volterra looks down upon the Cecina and Era valleys and marks the spot where two very different landscapes meet. On one side are deep-eroded crevices and on the other is greenery intermingling with local clay hills. Abundant deposits of alabaster, alum, lead, tin, salt, and sulfur in the area have been mined since its settlement in prehistoric times. The famed local industry, working alabaster, has also proved an enduring industry in Volterra. Begun in the 8th century B.C., alabaster carving continues today as the traditional Volterran trade.

The prehistoric Villanovan settlement (9th century B.C.) evolved and reached its peak in the 5th century B.C., as the Etruscan center Velarthi. One of the most powerful of the 12 cities in the Etruscan League, it grew to three times its present size, flourishing on its commercial trade industry. In the 3rd century B.C., Roman Velaterrae suffered a decline in prosperity when trading links were rerouted. After a brief Lombard occupancy in the Middle Ages, Volterra became a free commune with Ghibelline sentiments. In 1361 the Florentines assumed power, and in 1472 Lorenzo de'Medici demanded control of the local alum industry. The "affair of the alum" caused tension between the Medici and the popes and between Florence and

Volterra. Lorenzo wanted to monopolize alum production (used to dye cloth) to compete with the papal monopoly of the mine in Tulfa and to divert the industry's profit from the Volterrans to the Florentines. The resulting Volterran revolt was crushed by Federico da Montefeltro under the orders of Lorenzo. Though Volterra was dominated by Florence until Italian Unification in 1860, its abundant mineral deposits ensured its survival and continue to be a source of prosperity. Among its most famed citizens are the papal successor to Peter, St. Linus (A.D. 67); Pope Leo the Great (440–61); Pope Sabinianus (604–6) and Pope John X (914–28).

PLACES TO VISIT

The 13th-century church of SAN FRANCESCO is famed for its Croce del Giorno Cappella (the Cross of the Day chapel). Built in 1315, the chapel is decorated with scenes from the *Legend of the True Cross* and the *Infancy of Christ* (1410), painted by Cenni di Francesco. The scenes from both cycles include *Seth Planting the Tree of Sin on Adam's Grave, The Queen of Sheba Envisions the Miraculous Wood, The Wood Is Used to Make the Cross, St. Helen Identifies the True Cross, St. Helen Takes the Cross, Chosroes, the King of Persia, Steals the Cross, The Vision of Chosroes, The Battle of the Milvian Bridge, The Idolatry of Chosroes, Chosroes Beheaded, The*

True Cross Is Returned to Jerusalem, The Nativity, The Adoration, The Massacre of the Innocents, The Holy Sepulchre, The Flight into Egypt, The Annunciation, and *The Circumcision.*

The 12th-century DUOMO or BASILICA DI SANTA MARIA ASSUNTA is the result of four centuries of construction. The Pisan-style facade was built in the 13th century, the campanile was erected in 1493, and, finally, the Medici, whose family coat of arms conspicuously adorns the church, transformed the interior in the 1580s.

The vision of heavenly paradise, on the gold and azure ceiling, is populated with local saints including Volterra's native son and Christendom's second pope, St. Linus. This celestial image hovers above a richly adorned church, rife with significant works. The CAPPELLA DEL DEPOSITIONE (south transept) enshrines a life-size *Deposition* (1228), sculpted, gilded, and painted by a Pisan artisan. The Cappella di Sant' Ottaviano entombs another local patron saint. St. Ottaviano, a 6th-century hermit, delivered the citizens from a plague that struck Volterra in 1522. Notice the tabernacle carved by Mino da Fiesole depicting *The Infant Christ Above a Chalice and Adoring Angels* (1471); below it stand *The Theological Virtues and Four Saints.*

The *Madonna dei Chierici,* carved and painted by Francesco di Valdambrino (north transept), stands near the Cappella di San Paolo, commissioned in 1607 by Jacopo Inghirami

after his troops defeated the Turks. Within is Domenichino's altarpiece, *The Conversion of St. Paul.*

A unique 13th-century carved Pisan pulpit (along the north aisle) was reassembled in 1584 and includes sculptural fragments, supporting columns, and stone lions. Among the fragments are reliefs representing *The Sacrifice of Isaac, The Annunciation, The Visitation,* and *The Last Supper.* Fra Bartolomeo's *Annunciation* (1497) and Francesco Cungi's *Martyrdom of St. Sebastian* (1588) decorate altars along the north wall. Frescoed landscapes by Benozzo Gozzoli in the Lady Chapel, set the stage for two terra-cotta *Nativities.*

Standing opposite the cathedral is Volterra's green and white striped BAPTISTERY. Built in 1283, it is decorated with the local *panchina* stone.

Carved heads of Christ, the Virgin, and the twelve apostles look down from the architrave at those who enter. The dome above them is a 16th-century addition.

Within, an Etruscan funerary stone functions as a holy water stoup. The central font and statue of *St. John the Baptist* are 18th century, as is the marble that frames the *Ascension* altarpiece (1591) by Nicolò Circignani. Andrea Sansovino's baptismal font (1502), originally the central font, now stands against the right wall. Its sculpted reliefs depict the *Baptism of Christ* and representations of *Faith, Hope, Charity,* and *Justice.*

The MUSEO DIOCESANO D'ARTE SACRA (Diocesan Museum of Sacred Art)

V

displays liturgical objects and paintings from Volterran churches. A terra-cotta bust of St. Linus by Andrea della Robbia and a silver reliquary bust of *St. Ottaviano* by Antonio del Pollaiolo are among the significant sculptural works. The painted *Madonnas* are numerous; Segna di Bonaventura, Neri di Bicci, and Taddeo di Bartolo beautifully depict the Virgin. Outstanding representations include the *Madonna of Villamagna* (1521) by Rosso Fiorentino and the *Madonna of Ulignano* (1545) by Daniele da Volterra.

The PINACOTECA AND MUSEO CIVICO is located in the Palazzo Minucci Solaini, attributed to the architect Antonio da Sangallo the Elder. The collection includes works from Tuscan artists between the 14th and 17th centuries.

Room 2 holds three anonymous works by 14th-century Sienese artists: a *Madonna and Child*, a *Crucifixion*, and a *Santi Giusto ed Ugo*. Room 4 features a polyptych of the *Madonna and Saints*, signed and dated in 1411 by Taddeo di Bartolo. In Room 6 are a polyptych (1430) by the Portuguese painter Alvaro di Pietro and statues of the *Virgin* and *Angel Gabriel* (1410) by Francesco di Valdambrino, which originally stood in the cathedral. Domenico Ghirlandaio's beautifully landscaped *Apotheosis of Christ with Saints Benedict, Romualdo, Attinia, and Grecinian* (1492) hangs in Room 11. In the next room are Luca Signorelli's *Annunciation* and *Madonna and Child Enthroned with Saints John the Baptist, Francis, Anthony of Padua, Bonaventura,*

and Jerome (1491). They contrast the Mannerist *Deposition* by Rosso Fiorentino; it was signed and dated in 1521 when the artist was 26 years old.

Two significant works by local artists on the second floor include Daniele Volterra's *Justice with the Medici Coat of Arms* (1532) and Baldassare Franceschini's *Madonna and Child in Glory with Saints Francis, Claire, John the Evangelist, Stephen, Mary Magdalene, and Paul* (1639). Do not miss the collection of 17th-century and 18th-century silver, coins, and medals.

SAN MICHELE ARCHANGELO is a Pisan-Romanesque church with a 13th-century medieval tower. A 15th-century statue of the *Madonna and Child* overlooks the doorway and Piazza San Michele. Within the church is a terracotta *Madonna and Child* by Giovanni della Robbia.

Volterra is rich with Etruscan remains. Its MUSEO ETRUSCO GUARNACCI houses one of the most comprehensive collections in Italy, providing an enlightening survey of the life and culture of the area from the prehistoric 8th century B.C. to the Roman period. The collection is the combination of two donations: that of Canon Pietro Franceschini in 1732 and Monsigneur Mario Guarnacci (a local prelate) in 1761. On exhibit are over 600 Etruscan cinerary urns. The Etruscans cremated their dead, and the cinerary urn was part of conventional burial practice.

Evidence of Volterra's ancient culture can be seen outside its museums. The

PORTA ALL'ARCO is a 4th-century B.C. Etruscan gateway surmounted by three weathered heads representing the Etruscan gods Tinia (Jupiter), Uni (Juno), and Menvra (Minerva). The nearby PARCO ARCHEOLOGICO, the site of the Etruscan and Roman acropolis, is now a public garden. Excavations in 1926 revealed two temples (2nd century B.C.) and a cistern known as the piscina.

A marvelously preserved ROMAN THEATRE (1st century B.C.) AND BATH (3rd century B.C.–4th century A.D.) lies outside Volterra's medieval walls. Ancient *Velathri's* impressive ETRUSCAN WALLS can be seen in the distance. At some points the remains are 11 meters tall.

Two churches outside Volterra are worth a visit. SANTI GIUSTO E CLEMENTE, founded in 1627 and completed in 1775, was built to replace an earlier church that was engulfed by the eroding terrain. Volterra's patron saints, Giusto and Clement, are the city's guardians. Originally from Africa, these missionary saints arrived in the 6th century. SAN GIROLAMO (15th century) is both a church and a monastery. Giovanni della Robbia decorated two chapels in the portico in 1501 with reliefs depicting *St. Francis Giving the Tertiary Rule to St. Louis of France* and *The Last Judgment.* Within the church, note two works flanking the high altar, a *Madonna Enthroned with Saints* by Domenico di Michelino and an *Annunciation with Saints Michael and Catherine of Alexandria,* signed and dated by Benvenuto di Giovanni in 1466.

V

GLOSSARY OF RELIGIOUS TERMS

ANGELS: The word *angel* derives from the Greek word *angelos,* meaning messenger. Angels are bringers of tidings and ministers from God. They are often cited in the Scriptures (Isaiah 6:1–2; 1 Samuel 4:4; etc.). In the 5th century A.D., Pseudo-Dionysus the Areopagite, the convert of St. Paul, codified angels in his book *De Hierarchia Celesti* (The Hierarchy of Angels). He ranked the various angels in nine categories (or choirs) which were grouped into three hierarchies. The first hierarchy included seraphim, cherubim, and thrones. The second hierarchy held dominations, virtues, and powers. And the third hierarchy was composed of princedoms, archangels, and angels.

The first hierarchy surrounds God in perpetual love and adoration. Seraphim and cherubim are usually depicted with heads only, and one, two, or three pairs of wings. Seraphim signify divine love and are usually painted red and hold burning candles. Cherubim denote divine wisdom and are usually painted golden yellow or blue. Thrones symbolize divine justice and are usually shown wearing the judiciary robes and holding rods of authority.

The second hierarchy governs the stars and elements. Dominations represent the power of God. They are crowned and carry scepters and occasionally orbs as symbols of their authority. Virtues carry white lilies or, sometimes, red roses as symbols of Christ's Passion. Powers are usually dressed in armor as warriors against the hordes of demons.

The third hierarchy are the executors of God's will. The princedoms are the dispensers of the fate of nations and the protectors of the kingdoms of the earth. The archangels are the warriors of heaven. Angels are the guardians of the innocent and the just. Archangels and angels are the messengers of God to mortals.

ANNUNCIATION: The Annunciation is the announcement by the

Archangel Gabriel to the Virgin Mary, "You will be with child and give birth to a son, and you are to give him the name Jesus" (Luke 1:31). The Feast Day of the Annunciation is March 25.

ARCHANGELS: The four archangels mentioned in the scriptures are Michael, Gabriel, Raphael, and Uriel. Of these four, only the first three are given distinct personalities and hold the title of saint.

ST. MICHAEL, whose name means "like unto God," is the guardian angel of the Hebrew nation (Daniel 10:13, 21) whom Christianity adopted as the protector of the Church militant. He is often seen wearing armor, carrying a sword or spear and shield, wings rising from his shoulders, doing battle with Satan. This refers to a passage in Revelation 12:7–9: "And there was war in heaven. Michael and his angels fought against the dragon, and the dragon and his angels fought back. But he was not strong enough, and they lost their place in heaven. The great dragon was hurled down—that ancient serpent called the devil, or Satan, who leads the whole world astray. He was hurled to the earth, and his angels with him." At depictions of the Last Judgment St. Michael is sometimes depicted holding scales, or balances, weighing the souls of the dead to measure their just rewards.

ST. GABRIEL, whose name means "God is my strength," is the guardian of the celestial treasury, the angel of Redemption, and the principal messenger of God. He is the herald of birth. St. Gabriel is not only venerated by Christians; he is mentioned in the Old Testament and the Koran and is venerated also by Hebrews and Moslems. It is Gabriel who is sent to Daniel to announce the return of the Jews from captivity (Daniel 8:16; 9:21). Gabriel is also the angel of the Annunciation. "In the sixth month, God sent the angel Gabriel to Nazareth, a town in Galilee, to a virgin pledged to be married to a man named Joseph" (Luke 1:26–27).

ST. RAPHAEL, whose name means the "Medicine of God," is the principal guardian angel and the guardian of all humanity. He is usually represented as a friend of those he serves, often the young and the innocent. He watches over the pilgrim. According to tradition it was Raphael who appeared to the shepherds on Christmas night with the message: "Do not be afraid. I bring you good news of great joy that will be for all the people. Today in the town of David a Savior has been born to you; he is Christ the Lord" (Luke 2:10–11).

URIEL, whose name means the "Light of God," is an interpreter of judgments and prophecies.

BENEDICTINE ORDER: One of the great monastic orders which evolved out of the work of Benedict and was based on his monastic rule. The order encouraged both learning and the practice of piety. It played an important role in the development of Western liturgy. Its members are recognized by their black robes.

THE CAMALDOLESE ORDER: Founded in 1012 by St. Romualdo, a Benedictine monk from Ravenna. The order follows a strict rule of silence and solitude and is known for its ecologically minded service. The monks are vegetarians, farmers, and the world's first organized reforesters.

CANONIZATION: The process by which an outstanding Christian is proclaimed a saint by the Roman Catholic Church. The process allows devout Roman Catholics to venerate the dead person, who is said to have entered eternal glory. A long legal procedure, which includes the collection of testimonies to miracles attributed to the saint and his or her relics, precedes the final announcement by the pope. The process allows for the development of the cult of saints.

CARTHUSIAN ORDER: Founded in 1084 as a community of hermits by Bruno of Coloune (1030–1101). A particularly severe monastic order, it claims to be the only Roman Catholic monastic order that never needed to be reformed because its monks always remained faithful to its original rule.

CISTERCIAN ORDER: Founded in 1098 by Robert of Molesme as the White Monks, at Cîteaux in Burgundy. It is a strict religious order based on the Rule of St. Benedict. Historically the Cistercians played an important role in the development of agriculture, especially in England and northern Europe.

CONCLAVE: Meeting of the College of Cardinals to elect a new pope. Locked within the Sistine Chapel, cardinals cast votes twice daily. Ballots are burned after each vote and emit a black smoke until a majority (over two-thirds) is reached and white smoke issues forth.

CULT OF RELICS: During the Middle Ages a cult of relics closely associated with the popularity of pilgrimages developed. The three most sacred pilgrimage places to visit were Jerusalem (regained for Christendom in 1099), Rome (where the relics of Saints Peter and Paul are situated), and Santiago da Compostella in Spain (which housed the body of the apostle St. James the Greater).

The reverence for relics was a result of the belief that the relic was a visible point of contact between the faithful and the saint. It was believed the spirit of the deceased saint still resided in the relic. Thus, relics were thought to have miraculous properties. The most sacred relics would be those associated with Jesus, the Virgin Mary, and so on in order of the individual's importance. Large churches were built to house relics and to accommodate the visiting pilgrims. In 1140 a guide to the pilgrimage route was written detailing the various routes in France which converged in northeast Spain.

Protestants came to regard the veneration of relics and other devotional objects as superstition abetted by the Roman Catholic clergy. In 1563 the Council of Trent gave general approval to relics provided they were genuine. The cult of relics was emphasized by the papacy during the Counter-Reformation. Pope Urban VIII (1623–44) provided the four most significant relics—the *sudarium* (veil) of Veronica, a piece of the True Cross, the lance which pierced the side of Jesus, and the head of St. Andrew—with a grandiose setting in the church of St. Peter's in Rome. The relics are placed in the niches for each of the four great piers supporting the church dome.

CULT OF SAINTS: The cult of saints and martyrs flourished during the Counter-Reformation. The Catholic Church's traditional teaching was that saints were able to intercede with Christ; therefore they could be asked to pray on one's behalf. Protestants denied this because there is no Scriptural authority for it.

CULT OF THE VIRGIN MARY: The cult of the Virgin Mary refers to the veneration and adoration of the Mother of Jesus Christ. It began in 431 with the Council of Ephesus, which declared her Mother of God. The cult developed until it reached its greatest popularity during the 12th and 13th centuries. This Mariolatry (adulation of Mary) was inspired by the medieval theologian St. Bernard of Clairvaux (1090–1153), who interpreted the *Song of Songs* as an elaborate allegory in which the bride of the poem was identified with the Virgin Mary. Since many of the stories of the Virgin Mary lacked Scriptural authority, Protestants dismissed them. John Calvin believed that the veneration accorded to the Virgin, especially in her role as intercessor, was idolatrous.

DOCTORS OF THE CHURCH: There were many saints in the Eastern and Western church. Highest in the rank were the Evangelists and Apostles. Next came the Martyrs and the Fathers. The latter were priests who had left a powerful impression upon church history, usually through their writings to the formation of doctrine. These Fathers were known as Doctors of the Church.

There are four Latin (Western) Doctors—St. Ambrose (c. 340–97), who helped crush Arianism; St. Augustine of Hippo (354–430), the Church's most celebrated theologian; St. Gregory the Great (c. 540–604), who established the reform of the liturgy and its music (Gregorian Chant); and St. Jerome (342–420), who translated the Old and New Testaments into Latin (known as the Vulgate).

There are four Greek (Eastern) Doctors—St. Basil the Great (329–79), founder of the monastic movement; St. Gregory of Nazianius (329–90), identified as the "theologian" for his writings on the Trinity; St. John Chrysostom (c. 347–407), called the "golden mouth" for his eloquent sermons; and St. Athanasius (c. 296–373), the opponent of Arianism.

EXULTET ROLLS: Exultet rolls are large scrolls named after their use in the ceremonies blessing the paschal candle on Holy Saturday in Easter (*Exultet iam engelica turba callorum*—Let the angelic choirs of heaven now rejoice). These large scrolls have pictures painted upside down in the text so that the congregation could follow the deacon as he unwound the roll from the pulpit.

FIFTEEN MYSTERIES OF THE VIRGIN MARY: The 15 mysteries are celebrated events in the life of the Virgin Mary. They are divided into three categories—the Five Joyful Mysteries, the Five Sorrowful Mysteries, and the Five Glorious Mysteries. The Joyful Mysteries are the Annunciation, the Visitation, the Nativity, the Presentation, and the Finding in the Temple. The Sorrowful Mysteries are the Agony in the Garden, the Scourging at the Pillar, the Crowning with Thorns, the Carrying of the Cross, and the Crucifixion. The Glorious Mysteries are the Resurrection, the Ascension, the Descent of the Holy Spirit, the Assumption of the Virgin Mary, and the Crowning of the Virgin Mary.

FRANCISCANS: The monastic order founded by Francis of Assisi in 1209 based on the rule of poverty, preaching, and penance. Two modified versions of the original rule, which relaxed its stricter obligations, followed and opened the order to a wider selection of candidates, but Francis always preferred his original, stricter rule. For four centuries after his death conflict divided the order over which rule ought to be followed. The order is noted for its charity works, hospitals, schools, and missionary endeavors. Five members of the order have become popes, and it has produced such outstanding philosophers as Bonaventure (1217–74), Duns Scotus (1264–1308), and William of Ockham (1285–1349).

THE GOLDEN LEGEND: Jacobus de Voragine (1228/30–98), a Dominican priest and the archbishop of Genoa famed for his learning and piety, is best remembered as the author of *The Golden Legend*. Written about 1290, it was one of the most popular books in the Middle Ages and was translated into every Western European language. *The Golden Legend* chronicles the lives of hundreds of saints, and compiles Scripture and Christian theology organized according to the Church's liturgical year. Late in the 16th century, the Catholic Church pronounced the text as containing more fable than fact. In the next century the Church substituted the *Liber Sanctorium* (Book of Saints) for *The Golden Legend* as a source for the lives of the saints.

HERESY: Heresy is any religious belief opposed to the orthodox doctrines of the church. Heresy was considered the greatest of all sins because it was an affront to God. In the 12th century heretical groups such as the Albigenses around Albi and the Waldenses around Lyons had risen to challenge papal corruption. The papal response was to institute the Holy Office of the Inquisition. In 1233 under Pope Gregory IX, the bishops who had previously investigated heresy were replaced by papal inquisitors.

IMMACULATE CONCEPTION: Roman Catholics believe that the Virgin was conceived without sin in the womb of her mother, Anne. According to the doctrine, Mary alone was chosen to be free from Original Sin, and thus the vessel of Christ's Incarnation. This idea became the subject of heated debate during the 13th century. The Dominicans, including St. Thomas Aquinas, denied the possibility of the Immaculate Conception, while Franciscans upheld it. In 1476, Pope Sixtus IV instituted the feast of the Immaculate Conception, and in 1563 the Council of Trent declared the Virgin exempt from Original Sin. The Immaculate Conception was confirmed in 1854 by Pope Pius IX as an article of faith. The feast day of the Immaculate Conception is December 8.

INDULGENCES: The Roman Catholic Church defines an indulgence as a remission of the temporal punishment for sin after the sin has been forgiven through the sacrament of penance. The treasury of indulgences is limitless; its sources are Christ, the Virgin Mary, and all the saints, whose boundless contribution of merits serves all Christians, living and dead. A plenary indulgence is the total remission of punishment, and a partial indulgence remits only part of one's punishment.

In the early Church, individuals took upon themselves public and sometimes painful acts of penance for serious sins before they gained absolution and were received back into the Church community. If a Christian who had been persecuted for his faith interceded for a sinner, the sinner's penance could be remitted. Later, this remission of public penance (not the remission of sins) became known as an indulgence.

However, means soon developed by which a protracted penance could be commuted; they included substituting periods of fasting, special prayers, or payments of money to be used for religious purposes. Pope Urban II (1088–99) granted an indulgence to those who went to Jerusalem on the First Crusade (1095). By the 12th century, the practice of paying for indulgences had become the equivalent of doing penance and a great source of income for the Church. Crusades, cathedrals, roads, religious centers, universities, and various social and cultural projects were all financed in part, if not in whole, by the monies raised from the indulgences. For example, in order to defray the cost of building the new church of St. Peter's, Pope Julius II (1503–13) allowed the sale of indulgences to guarantee not only the forgiveness of the penalty of sin but of the sin itself. Thus, the indulgence became a substitute for sincere sorrow and confession and could bring one freedom from all guilt and punishment.

In response to the misuse of indulgences and the luxuries afforded the Roman clergy, Martin Luther in his 95 Theses argued against the practice of indulgences and complained about the money being drained from Germany to

Rome. Luther quipped that if the pope had any real power over purgatory, he should empty the place for free. He refused to accept the possibility of a treasury of merits through Christ, the Virgin, and the saints, and he suggested that the faithful should willingly suffer for their sinfulness and not rely on the monetary dispensation of grace. Convinced that indulgences imperiled the souls of parishioners, Luther and subsequent Protestant reformers believed that only Jesus could excuse sin.

Though Luther was excommunicated for his views, the Church did reassess the use of indulgences and eventually condemned and eliminated the abusive practice. Today the Catholic Church asserts a theological approach to indulgences and encourages the faithful, in God's grace, to obtain indulgences.

INQUISITION: This was instituted about 1231 by Pope Gregory IX (1227–41). He published the *Excommunicamus,* which proposed capital punishment for the unrepentant heretic. The judges or inquisitors of the heretics were nearly always either Dominicans or Franciscans.

One of the effects of the Inquisition was the reappearance of torture, previously forbidden under canon law. The Italian inquisitors were probably the first to make use of it after Innocent IV (1243–54) declared a papal bull indicating that torture used to force confessions from heretics was proper. Just as secular courts punished treason with death, the Inquisition proposed the same punishment for heretics, since they were considered guilty of treason towards God. Death by public burning faced heretics convicted of treason.

At the end of the 15th century, Pope Sixtus IV (1471–84) created a new tribunal at the request of the Catholic monarchs Ferdinand and Isabella of Spain. The pope allowed the Spanish Inquisition to act independent of Rome. Ferdinand and Isabella appointed a Dominican, Tomas de Torquemada (d.1498), as Grand Inquisitor to head their Supreme Council of the Inquisition. His zeal to eliminate heretics made previous inquisitors appear angelic by comparison. The Spanish Inquisition was permanently suppressed by a decree on July 15, 1843.

In 1542 Pope Paul III (1534–49) revived the Congregation of the Roman Inquisition (the Holy Office), which was given punitive powers of censorship in order to combat Protestant heresy. It was the central authority in the war against Protestant Reformers. Its victims included theologians, mathematicians, scientists, philosophers, and artists. The only inquisitorial group active into the 20th century, the council was renamed the Congregation for the Doctrine of the Faith in 1965 by Pope Paul VI.

INTERCESSION: According to the Church's traditional teaching, the saints and the Virgin Mary were able to intercede with Christ; therefore they could be invoked to pray on one's behalf.

231

JESUITS: In 1540 Pope Paul III officially recognized the Society of Jesus (Jesuit Order). Founded by Ignatius of Loyola in 1534, the Jesuit zeal is fueled by their motto "for the Greater Glory of God." The Jesuits model their ministries and activities on *The Spiritual Exercises,* a handbook written by their founder emphasizing the tangibility and realism of sacred experience.

The Jesuits were instrumental in spreading the ideas of the Council of Trent (1545–63) and challenging the Protestant reformers of Europe on behalf of the papacy. They helped promote the Inquisition and the Index of Forbidden Works (a list of books that Catholics could not read without special permission). It was, however, their missionary zeal that defined the order; the Jesuits traveled in Europe, to the New World, and to the Orient. By the time of St. Ignatius's death in 1566, there were over 1000 Jesuits working as teachers, confessors, and advisors in Europe, India, China, Japan, West Africa, and Brazil.

To the Jesuits, unquestioning obedience to Rome was the hallmark of true Catholicism. In addition to the usual three monastic vows of poverty, obedience, and chastity, the Jesuits took a fourth, a vow of loyalty to the pope.

Ignatius and the Jesuit Order understood the power of art to intensify religious feeling. Subsequently, the Jesuits encouraged richness and splendor in church services and the prolific use of painting and sculpture to give Roman Catholicism a visual emotional appeal that was missing in Protestant forms of worship. Jesuits believed that religious paintings should reflect decency, decorum, clarity, realism, and drama. A work must also didactically reaffirm all that Luther and Calvin had denied, thus involving the viewer psychologically and emotionally.

MENDICANT ORDERS: A mendicant is a friar who begs for alms and moves from town to town to preach the Word of God. The friars take vows of poverty, supporting themselves through work and charitable contributions, adhering to a life of simplicity and poverty. Unlike monks who live in closed communities far from the populated areas, mendicant monasteries rose within the civic unit. The mendicant mission requires living among and preaching to the populace, not retreating into secluded monasteries.

The Franciscans and the Dominicans, founded by St. Francis (1210) and St. Dominic (1216) respectively, were the first and most influential mendicant orders. Both believed that friars should own nothing individually or communally; all worldly goods were kept in trust by the papacy. As the popularity of the preaching friars rose among the communities, large mendicant churches were built with great attention paid to spaciousness and acoustics.

Other important mendicant orders include the Carmelites, the Servites, the Augustinian Hermits, the Trinitarians, the Mercedarians, the Hospitalers of St. John, and the Teutonic Order.

MONASTICISM: Originated in the Middle East during the late 3rd century. In the 6th century, St. Benedict (c. 480–547) founded the oldest Western monastic order, the Benedictines. He established the monastery at Monte Cassino, where he devised a set of regulations known as the Rule of St. Benedict. The Rule stressed work and prayer. It became the standard model for monastic life in the West. Other important monastic Rules (laws established by the founder of a religious order for observance by its members) were the Rule of St. Basil (c. 330–79), still surviving in the Orthodox church; the Carthusian Rule founded by St. Bruno (c. 1030–1101); the Cistercian Rule (a reformed Benedictine Rule) founded in 1098 by St. Robert of Molesme; and the Clunaic Rule (a reformed Benedictine Rule) founded in 910 by William I the Pious. The monastic way of life in the West was a community of monks living together under the leadership of an abbot. Monastic life was dedicated to prayer and the praise of God. Monks were separated from the rest of society and took vows of chastity, poverty, and obedience. Monasticism also increased the opportunities for women to lead a religious life, either in convents or in "double monasteries" shared by both sexes.

NATIVITY: The Nativity refers to the birth of Christ, which is described only by Matthew and Luke (Matthew 2:1–12; Luke 2:1–20).

PASSION: The Passion is the suffering and death of Christ on the cross. In Christian art the term includes the last events of Christ's earthly life. The Passion scenes usually included the following: the Entry into Jerusalem, Christ Washes the Feet of the Disciples, the Last Supper, the Agony in the Garden, the Betrayal, Christ before Caiaphas, the Denial of Peter, Christ before Pilate, the Flagellation, the Mocking of Christ, *Ecce Homo*, the Road to Calvary, the Stations of the Cross, the Crucifixion, the Descent from the Cross, the *Pietà*, and the Entombment.

POPE: The pope is believed by Roman Catholics to be the vicar of Christ on earth and his temporal leader of the Church. As St. Peter's successor, the pope is the bishop of Rome and the head of the Catholic, Apostolic, and Roman Church.

RELIC: A relic is the material remains of saints, or an object associated with them. Relics are often encased in sumptuous reliquaries of silver or gold and housed in a special chapel, where they are venerated by the faithful.

RULE OF BENEDICT: The monastic rule, based on the Rule of Basil, drawn up by Benedict at Monte Cassino, which became the basis of the Benedictine order.

SACRAMENTS: Sacraments are acts that confer grace. Roman Catholics believe there are seven sacraments—Baptism, Confirmation, Eucharist, Penance (Confession), Holy Orders, Matrimony, and Extreme Unction (Last Rites). Protestants maintain there are only two sacraments—Baptism and the Lord's Supper (Eucharist).

SEVEN GIFTS OF THE HOLY SPIRIT: The gifts include Wisdom, Understanding, Counsel, Might, Knowledge, Piety, and Fear (Isaiah 11:1–2).

SEVEN SORROWS OF THE VIRGIN: The Seven Sorrows of the Virgin are the following events: the Presentation in the Temple ("This child is destined to...be a sign that will be spoken against....And a sword will pierce your own soul too" [Luke 2:34–5]), the Flight into Egypt, Christ Lost by His Mother, Bearing of the Cross, Crucifixion, Descent from the Cross, and the Ascension (when Christ finally parted from his mother).

STATIONS OF THE CROSS: The Stations of the Cross refer to Christ's journey to Calvary. There are 14 stations of the cross: Jesus is condemned to death, Jesus bears his cross, Jesus falls the first time under his cross, Jesus meets his mother, Simon of Cyrene helps Jesus carry his cross, Veronica wipes Jesus' face, Jesus falls a second time, Jesus speaks to the women of Jerusalem, Jesus falls a third time, Jesus is stripped of his garments, Jesus is nailed to the cross, Jesus dies on the cross, Jesus is taken down from the cross, and Jesus is laid in the tomb.

STIGMATA: The stigmata refer to the five wounds suffered by Christ upon the cross or to similar marks supernaturally impressed upon certain persons of high religious character such as St. Catherine of Siena, St. Francis, or, more recently, the Padre Pio, known as "the Blessed."

TRANSUBSTANTIATION: Meaning "to change the substance," is the doctrine in Roman Catholic and Orthodox Eastern Churches that holds that during the Eucharist, the whole substance of the bread and of the wine are changed into the body and blood of Christ.

TRINITY: The Trinity is the doctrine that God is of one nature yet three persons—Father, Son, and Holy Ghost (Matthew 28:19)—and is held by all orthodox Christians based upon the biblical teachings that there is only one God, yet God exists as Father, Son, and Holy Spirit.

VIRGIN BIRTH: Refers to the birth of Jesus, the Son of God, born to the Virgin Mary.

VIRTUES—THEOLOGICAL AND CARDINAL: During the Middle Ages the principal Christian Virtues were made up of three theological virtues—Faith, Hope, and Charity (1 Corinthians 13:13)—and four cardinal virtues—Justice, Prudence, Fortitude, and Temperance. Plato formulated the latter in his *Republic* (4:427ff).

VISITATION: The Visitation is the visit the Virgin Mary (already with child) made to her cousin Elizabeth. Elizabeth was in her sixth month of pregnancy and had been advised by the Archangel Gabriel that she would give birth to St. John the Baptist. It was Elizabeth who first perceived the true character of Jesus, for she said to Mary, "But why am I so favored, that the mother of my Lord should come to me?" (Luke 1:43). The Feast Day of the Visitation is July 2.

The Christian Travelers Guides

"In an era that often overlooks the significance of the past as such, and certainly the Christian past, Professor Hexham's well-crafted guides for heritage tourists truly fill a gap. Don't leave home without one!"

—J. I. Packer, Author of *Knowing God*

By describing and interpreting the religious significance of people, places, and events in various countries, Irving Hexham illustrates the incredible impact Christianity has had on Western Civilization. Each guide is organized alphabetically according to the names of the cities and sites. The Christian Travelers Guides will help you deepen your faith by bringing to life the struggles and triumphs of great Christian leaders and common believers through the living witness of places where the saints once walked.

The Christian Travelers Guide to France
Irving Hexham, General Editor;
Written by Mark Konnert, Peter Barrs, and Carine Barrs

- Relive the experience of the Huguenots and the creators of such masterpieces as Chartes and Notre Dame.

Softcover 0-310-22588-4

The Christian Travelers Guide to Germany
Irving Hexham, General Editor;
Written by Irving Hexham and Lothar Henry Kope

- Experience the church's struggle against Nazi paganism, ponder the sorrow of the Thirty Years' War, and see where the modern missionary movement was born.

Softcover 0-310-22539-6

The Christian Travelers Guide to Great Britain

Irving Hexham, General Editor;
Written by Irving Hexham

- Come into contact with the Venerable Bede, who almost single-handedly preserved European civilization in an age of death and destruction, become a pilgrim with John Bunyan in his beloved Bedford, and see where John Wesley preached against slavery and converted thousands.

Softcover 0-310-22552-3

The Christian Travelers Guide to Italy

Irving Hexham, General Editor;
Written by David Bershad and Carolina Mangone

- Experience a wealth of art and architecture stretching back to the early church and the age of martyrs, travel where Christians died in the arena, and see where great artists such as Michelangelo depicted unforgettable scenes of biblical truth.

Softcover 0-310-22573-6

Pick up a copy today at your favorite bookstore!

We want to hear from you. Please send your comments about this book to us in care of the address below. Thank you.

ZONDERVAN™

GRAND RAPIDS, MICHIGAN 49530 USA

WWW.ZONDERVAN.COM

CPSIA information can be obtained at www.ICGtesting.com
Printed in the USA
LVOW07s1608050114

368135LV00007B/11/P